EXETER HISPANIC TEXTS

Founded by Keith Whinnom and J. M. Alberich
General Editor: W. F. Hunter

LETTERS FROM THE PYRENEES

EXETER HISPANIC TEXTS
General Editor: W.F. Hunter

XLIX   Pedro Manuel Ximénez de Urrea **Penitencia de amor (Burgos, 1514)**
edited by Robert L. Hathaway

L   **'Ensaladas villanescas' associated with the 'Romancero nuevo'**
edited by John Gornall

LI   Emilia Pardo Bazán **Poesías inéditas u olividadas**
edited by Maurice Hemingway

LII   Constanza de Castilla **Book of Devotions Libro de Devociones y oficios**
edited by Constance L. Wilkins

LIII   Salvador Rueda **El ritmo**
edited by Marta Palenque

LIV   Miguel de Unamuno **Political Speeches and Journalism (1923–1929)**
edited by Stephen Roberts

LV   Hernán Chacón **Tractado de la cauallería de la gineta**
edited by Noel Fallows

LVI   **Vida de Segundo: Versión castellana de la *Vita Secundi* de Vicente de Beauvais**
edited by Hugo O. Bizzarri

Volumes prior to to Volume XLIX are available while stocks exist from the Department of Spanish, University of Exeter.

DON LUIS MÉNDEZ DE HARO Y GUZMÁN

LETTERS
FROM THE
PYRENEES

Don Luis Méndez de Haro's
Correspondence to Philip IV of Spain,
July to November 1659

Edited by
Lynn Williams
University of Exeter

UNIVERSITY
of
EXETER
PRESS

For Mabel, Gemma, John and Antony

First published in 2000 by
University of Exeter Press
Reed Hall, Streatham Drive
Exeter, Devon EX4 4QR
UK
www.ex.ac.uk/uep/

© Lynn Williams 2000

The right of Lynn Williams to be identified as author
of this work has been asserted by him in accordance with
the Copyright, Designs & Patents Act 1988.

British Library Cataloguing in Publication Data
A catalogue record of this book is available from the British Library
ISBN 0 85989 692 7

Designed and typeset in 10/12 New Baskerville
by Quince Typesetting, Exeter

Printed and bound in Great Britain
by Short Run Press Ltd, Exeter

Introduction

The letters summarised and transcribed here represent a complete record of the correspondence sent by Don Luis Méndez de Haro y Guzmán to Philip IV of Spain between July and November 1659. Together they constitute a fascinating account of the five months or so that Haro was absent from Madrid for the purpose of negotiating the final points of a peace treaty and marriage agreement with the French representative, Cardinal Jules Mazarin, in the Pyrenees. They include full coverage of events preliminary to the start of the peace conference, as well as detailed reports on the progress of the negotiations themselves. They also shed considerable light on Haro's character and political acumen and on his assessment of Mazarin.

The peace conference was held on the tiny Isle of Pheasants, which divides the waters of the river Bidasoa not far from Fuenterrabía and St Jean de Luz. There Haro and Mazarin met for a series of interviews which culminated, on 7 November, in the signing of the peace treaty and marriage agreement that brought to an end twenty-four years of bitter warfare between Spain and France and signalled, for all the world to see, the demise of Spain as the undisputed master of Europe and its replacement by France.

France had declared war on Spain in 1635 for two main reasons. First, Richelieu feared a possible Spanish–Dutch agreement that would terminate the conflict between Spain and the United Provinces in the Low Countries and therefore strengthen Philip IV's hold on this region. Second, the defeat of the Swedes at Nördlingen in 1634 by Spanish troops under the command of Philip's brother, the Cardinal-Infante Ferdinand, had severely weakened an important ally of France and also enabled Spain, if it wished, to attack the United Provinces from the north and east. The main theatres of the war were Milan, the border area between France and Flanders, Alsace, Luxembourg, Franche-Comté and Germany. In addition to these, there was determined military action both north and south of the Eastern Pyrenees, with the result that France came to control not only the whole of Roussillon but also the strongholds of Roses and Cadaqués located just south of the mountains.[1] Similar successes in Artois and along the Franco-German border meant that when Haro and Mazarin eventually came face to face in order to conclude the peace, France was in a sufficiently strong position to renegotiate its boundaries, thereby changing substantially the geographical shape of the kingdom.[2]

The eventual triumph of France should not, however, be taken to mean either that the progress of the war had been unidirectional or that victory had been easily achieved. The deep internal divisions that had riven both countries significantly influenced the ebb and flow of their military fortunes. For example, whilst the revolts of Portugal and Catalonia in 1640 seriously distracted Castile and brought over to the French side allies ensconced in the east and west of the Iberian Peninsula, France had grave problems of its own.[3] The Frondes (1648–1653) united disaffected French nobles and princes of the blood, prominent churchmen and the Paris Parliament in total opposition to Mazarin's administration. And even after Mazarin had regained control of the country, there were those like the Prince of Condé and the Cardinal of Retz who, in their different ways, gave vital support to Spain right up to the conclusion of the war in a resolute bid to unseat him.

Military might and strategy are clearly the paramount factors in deciding the outcome of all armed conflicts. Nevertheless, the parallel dimension of diplomacy is also of enormous consequence and loomed especially large in the minds of those who waged war in seventeenth-century Europe. Diplomacy embraced not only strenuous efforts to extend one's network of allies but, more importantly for present purposes, the exploration of every opportunity to discuss peace. Richelieu himself underlines, in his *Testament politique*, the importance of bolstering military

---

[1] In 1638, France also attacked Guipúzcoa. However, the French forces were quickly repulsed and the town of Fuenterrabía was brought back under Spanish control.

[2] Although general agreement on boundaries was reached during the peace conference, precise limits in the Pyrenees and in Artois were fixed later in a series of protracted negotiations between commissioners appointed by both crowns specifically for this purpose.

[3] Whereas Portugal persisted in its war with Spain until the latter was forced to recognise it as a separate kingdom in 1668, Catalonia restored its allegiance to Philip in 1652.

action with constant attempts to negotiate with one's enemies.[4] He recognises that war inevitably brings hardship and suffering to all concerned and that therefore a diplomatic solution makes very good sense so long as it can be achieved on favourable terms. Furthermore, Christian monarchs like Philip IV were keen not to be seen to be unwilling to make peace. They were especially sensitive to the fact that they had a duty to secure rest not only for their own kingdoms but also for Christendom, which Rome, no less than Venice, was desperate to see present a united front against the Ottoman Turk.[5] Pragmatic and moral considerations such as these combined to shape the approach to the conflict of 1635–1659 adopted by both sides.

Military campaigns waged during the summer were followed almost invariably by peace initiatives in the winter, some overtures being made by France and others by Spain. The first of these overtures occurred as early as September 1636, when the Count of Salazar, who had been a prisoner in France, was released by Richelieu in order to deliver a message to the Count-Duke of Olivares which intimated a willingness on the part

---

[4] See Elliott 1984: 129.
[5] In Letter 77, which announces the signing of the 1659 peace treaty and marriage agreement, Haro praises his master precisely because of the concessions he has made in the cause of peace. Even though we might be tempted to interpret these remarks as merely an attempt to console Philip for having been forced to accept an unfavourable settlement, we should recognise that the need to safeguard royal honour on the one hand and to secure rest for one's kingdoms and for Christendom on the other generated tensions that necessarily required a willingness on both sides to make concessions of some sort. Both Philip IV and Louis XIV would also have been keenly aware that the need to protect royal honour would generally restrict the nature and number of concessions that could be extracted from their rival. This is why the instructions which were issued to negotiators by their respective masters were normally graduated. If he was unable to secure A, the negotiator was empowered to agree to B or C or D, and so on until he came to the point beyond which royal honour or practical considerations would not permit him to go. Great advantage naturally stood to be gained from discovering the details of the instructions given to negotiators and this explains the many attempts to intercept their mail.

of the cardinal to discuss peace.[6] For the most part, however, such initiatives either never got off the ground or turned out to be simply talks about talks. In fact, prior to 1659, there seem to have been only three sustained attempts to secure a negotiated settlement.[7] The first formed part of the peace conference which ultimately led to the signing of the Treaty of Westphalia in Münster in 1648, ending the Thirty Years' War but not, regrettably, the conflict between France and Spain; the second occurred in 1656, when Mazarin's right-hand man, Secretary of State Hugues de Lionne, visited Madrid for talks with Spain's first minister, Don Luis de Haro; and the third involved Don Antonio Pimentel, an experienced soldier and diplomat sent to Lyons in the winter of 1658 to frustrate the proposed marriage of Louis XIV and Margaret of Savoy and, if this proved possible, to conclude with Mazarin a cessation of hostilities between Spain and France and their respective allies. The second and third of these initiatives are of crucial importance for an understanding of Haro's talks with Mazarin in the Pyrenees during the latter half of 1659 and therefore require some consideration.

Having signed a peace and a commercial treaty with the English Commonwealth at Westminster on 24 October / 3 November 1655, France felt that the time was right to attempt to bring Spain to the negotiating table.[8] Mazarin therefore wrote early in 1656 to the Count of Fuensaldaña, Captain General of Flanders, inviting him to send an envoy to Paris on

---

[6] AGS Estado Flandes 2051: 27, 98, 99, sheds some light on this unfruitful episode in Gallo-Spanish relations. Some peace initiatives were in fact launched in the summer or early autumn. However, the general pattern was to use the winter for diplomatic purposes, including perhaps the negotiation of a cessation of hostilities which would prevent the next summer campaign from getting under-way.

[7] For a comprehensive list of all the emissaries and representatives who were granted powers by Spain to negotiate with France between 1635 and 1659, see Torroja Menéndez and Menéndez Vives 1991: 54–96. In reality, these powers were not used in every case.

[8] There was reason enough on both sides for the diplomatic option to be worth considering. On the one hand, Spain had declared war on the English Commonwealth in 1655 following the capture of Jamaica by Cromwell; the treaty signed by England and France thus represented a most unwelcome development. On the other, also in 1655, one of France's most recent allies, the Duke of Modena, had been decisively defeated at Pavia in a summer campaign directed by the Spanish commander, the Marquis of Caracena.

some false public pretext so as, in reality, to discuss discreetly an important item of business.[9] Fuensaldaña and Archduke Leopold of Austria, Governor General of Flanders, responded by dispatching a seasoned military man, Don Gaspar de Bonifaz, for what turned out to be overtures for peace. Bonifaz, who arrived in Paris on 23 February 1656, discussed with Mazarin various ways forward and then proceeded to Madrid in order to make his report to the king. On 27 March, Philip IV wrote to Leopold informing him that, notwithstanding some misgivings about Mazarin's sincerity, he had decided that Bonifaz should return to Paris and indicate that Spain welcomed this latest peace initiative. So eager does Mazarin appear to have been to engage in peace talks at this time that in April he preferred to stall in response to an English offer of an offensive alliance against Spain, in order to allow time to send Lionne to Madrid to continue negotiations. The French diplomat arrived in the Spanish court on 4 July with orders to complete his mission within eight days. One of the reasons for this restriction was that Mazarin was anxious not to keep the English envoy waiting any longer than was necessary. If agreement with Spain could not be reached quickly, it was Mazarin's intention to accept the English offer. However, Lionne soon became embroiled in the complexity of the negotiations and was persuaded by Haro to send to Paris for further instructions. Reluctantly, Mazarin issued fresh orders and Lionne remained in Madrid until late September. In the end, he came away without having secured agreement.[10]

With hindsight it is easy to see that the Madrid talks were destined to fail. Both crowns had at least one demand which was non-negotiable and

---

[9] AGS Estado Flandes 8334 contains details of Bonifaz's mission.
[10] The Madrid talks of 1656 provide an excellent example of negotiators' being issued with graduated instructions. Both Haro's instructions and those of Lionne included authorisation to give up Roussillon. Lionne was further empowered to abandon Portugal if Spain could be persuaded to desert her principal ally, the Prince of Condé. Valfrey (1881: 37) tells us that Lionne might surrender Roussillon if by so doing he could secure Artois or regain Luxembourg or Franche-Comté. Haro seems either to have been unaware of just how far France was prepared to move on the issue of Roussillon or to have considered the price for its return to be too high. Whichever was the case, the two negotiators finally agreed that the Pyrenees should henceforth mark the boundary between the two kingdoms. For the matter of Portugal and Condé, see Gualdo Priorato 1667: 15–16.

which the other side either could not or would not accept. France, for example, insisted that peace would have to include the marriage of Louis XIV and Philip IV's daughter, María Teresa Bibiana of Austria, but since the infanta was at the time first in line to the Spanish throne, Haro could hardly agree to that. For its part, Spain demanded the restoration of the Prince of Condé's offices and privileges in France, something that Mazarin was unwilling to grant.[11] What is more, news reached Madrid on 31 July that Condé had taken Valenciennes by defeating the Maréchal de la Ferté. This news must have reinforced Spanish optimism stemming from Caracena's successful summer campaign in Italy of the previous year and must have contributed to the inflexible stance thereafter adopted by Haro in his talks with Lionne. Now, although these negotiations in Madrid failed, they are nevertheless historically very important, as much of what was agreed in principle then, provided the framework for Mazarin's talks with Pimentel in Paris in the early months of 1659 and was later adhered to when Haro and Mazarin met in the Pyrenees. An obvious example is the contentious question of sovereignty over the county of Roussillon: what had been agreed in Madrid was accepted, seemingly without debate, in the 1659 peace conference.

A little over two years after the failed Madrid talks, the diplomatic process was resurrected once again. Towards the end of 1658, France was preparing to marry the young Louis XIV to Margaret of Savoy. Philip IV, who learned of the proposed marriage from the Count of Fuensaldaña, now Governor General of Milan, realised immediately that if this marriage went ahead, he would be unlikely ever to achieve a suitable negotiated settlement with France. Fortunately for Philip, the dynastic situation in Spain had improved considerably by this time. Not only had Mariana of Austria borne him a prince in 1657, she was about to give birth to what would be a second son. The birth of a son removed what had hitherto been one of the main obstacles to peace and allowed Spain to enter negotiations with a most valuable bargaining counter, namely the hand of the infanta in marriage. As Haro emphasises in Letter 28 below, 'el casamiento es el que hace la Paz y la prenda que tenemos para ella'. Philip therefore dispatched Pimentel speedily to France in order to spoil

---

[11] Condé, who was a French prince of the blood, had been a bitter enemy of Mazarin since the Frondes. He had also been since the early 1650s Spain's most important ally.

the proposed marriage with Savoy and so enable Madrid to retain the leverage it had unexpectedly acquired. By a happy coincidence, Cromwell's death in September 1658 also permitted France to discuss peace with Spain without prejudicing the offensive alliance it had signed with the Protector in 1657. Had the Englishman lived, it seems likely that he would have strongly opposed any attempt by France to end the war. So, a number of factors came together at this time to make peace a realistic proposition. Pimentel had no difficulty in persuading Mazarin to put the marriage with Savoy on hold and accompanied the French court on its return journey to Paris. There, over several months, he negotiated secretly[12] with Mazarin a cessation of hostilities and, subsequently, a peace treaty.[13]

Even though it was always understood that Haro and Mazarin would meet at the border later in the summer to resolve specific matters, the Spanish version of what had been agreed in Paris was signed in June 1659 by Pimentel and sent to Madrid for ratification by Philip. Unsurprisingly, it was not well received. The clause relating to the Prince of Condé particularly horrified Haro and the Spanish king, not simply because Mazarin had refused to restore to the prince his offices and governments in France but also because any compensation which might

---

[12] There are many reasons for the secrecy surrounding the complicated negotiations for an international treaty. The most obvious has to do with the defence of the interests of one's allies, since their loyalty would continue to be needed if the talks failed. Clearly, it was not always possible to cut a deal that would satisfy all of one's allies. If, by some chance, they were to discover that there was a willingness to sacrifice their interests in the cause of peace when those of others were being stoutly defended, there was a very real risk that they would withdraw their allegiance and, perhaps, even shift it elsewhere.

[13] When Pimentel left for Lyons he carried powers only to negotiate a cessation of hostilities. On Mazarin's request, however, Madrid sent to Pimentel in Paris further powers to agree a peace treaty, and these included authorisation to negotiate with England, if necessary. It was at this same time that Madrid also agreed to Mazarin's demand that the basis for the negotiations should be what had been agreed in principle in Madrid in 1656. The alternative was to pick up what had been agreed between Spain and France at Münster in 1648. Whereas the Madrid talks contemplated peace with marriage, Münster did not, but stipulated that each side would retain the conquests it had made. AGS Estado Francia K1618: 3 reports on a meeting of the *Junta de Estado* in which these matters are discussed.

be offered to him by Spain would require the approval of young Louis XIV.[14] This was something which royal honour found extremely hard to swallow. Even so, the Council of State, which was anxious to sign a treaty with France at almost any price, eventually persuaded Haro and the king that peace should not be sacrificed for the sake of an ally, no matter how important, and that, in any event, Haro would be able to take advantage of the conference scheduled to be held shortly in the Pyrenees in order to secure an honourable settlement for the prince. After lengthy deliberations and much debate, a courier was dispatched to France with the Paris treaty duly ratified. By this time Mazarin was well on his way to meet with Haro at the border. He had left Paris on 24 June, and when the ratified treaty reached him on 6 July he was in Escures, a small town

---

[14] Pimentel had been faced with a terrible dilemma. Although he had strict instructions to defend the interests of the Prince of Condé, he had also been instructed not to permit the talks to break down. In his memoirs, the Count of Brienne (1824: 242) writes as follows about this most difficult aspect of the negotiations: 'Pimentel s'en defendit sur les ordres précis qu'il avoit. Enfin l'on proposa un *mezzo termine* à la manière des Italiens: ce fut que l'Espagnol consentiroit que cet article [the one relating to Condé] se mît dans le contrat tel que le cardinal le proposoit, mais qu'il ne seroit point obligatoire avant qu'il eût été approuvé par le Roi d'Espagne.' Unfortunately for Pimentel, the Paris talks provide a clear instance of how considerable advantage could be gained from intercepting a negotiator's mail. In this regard, BL Add. MS 14000: 46 contains an important dispatch from the Prince of Condé to his minister in Madrid, Pierre Lenet. In it, we learn that Pimentel's mail addressed to the Spanish court was escorted to the border by guards assigned by Mazarin; there it was delivered to Watteville, the military governor of Guipúzcoa, who forwarded it to Madrid. According to Condé, the letters were copied and deciphered during their passage through France, so that Mazarin had detailed knowledge of Pimentel's communications with Haro. Pimentel must therefore have found himself in an impossible situation as he negotiated the Paris treaty.

between Blois and Amboise, not far from Tours. The cardinal evidently was confident that Philip dared not reject the document.[15]

The day the ratified treaty was handed to Mazarin by Pimentel in Escures was the day Haro left Madrid for the border. En route he sent dispatches back to Madrid from Buitrago (10 July), Aranda (12 July), Lerma (13 July), Bribiesca (15 July), Vitoria (17 July), Salinas (18 July) and Villafranca (19 July), before arriving in San Sebastian on the morning of the twentieth of the month. The journey was eventful and arduous. For example, the Marquis of Jódar, a captain of Haro's guards, succumbed to illness in Burgos on 14 July and had to be left behind with 2,000 *reales de a ocho de plata* to cover his expenses.[16] Writing from Vitoria, Haro laments having to travel regularly well into the night in order to cover seven and even eight leagues per day, and he complains of the crowds of people who dog him, preventing him from resting once he has arrived at his lodgings and even from attending to his correspondence. In fact, he says he has been forced to detain for two days a regular courier

---

[15] Gualdo Priorato (1667: 31) records, however, that Mazarin had declared that he would go no further than Poitiers until the ratified treaty arrived, and this is confirmed in Spanish sources and in the memoirs of Gramont (1827: 43), where we learn that it was Pimentel himself who took delivery of the ratified treaty from the courier in Poitiers. The cardinal, then, must also have recognised that ratification would be no easy decision for Madrid. Given that Philip had promised Condé that he would put his interests before those of Spain, and given that Condé controlled a large army and a number of vital strongholds in Flanders, Haro was naturally fearful of how the prince might react when he learned of his fate. He therefore persuaded the Council of State and the king that Lenet should be told that Pimentel had acted without orders and that the king was furious with him. A messenger should also be dispatched immediately to Flanders to enquire what compensation the prince would like Haro to try to agree for him with Mazarin at the peace conference (AGS Estado Francia K1619: 9). Outside the Council of State, on the other hand, there were many who were violently opposed to the Paris treaty. Among these were the ministers and supporters of Condé in Madrid and those, including Mariana of Austria, who favoured marrying María Teresa to the emperor. Both groups also exerted enormous pressure on Haro at this time and continued to do so at the peace conference in the Pyrenees. Particularly vocal among them was Haro's own *secretario de lenguas*, a Carinthian who appears in Spanish sources as Cristóbal Angelati Crasempach.

[16] AGS CMC 3551 (2): 28 refers to this unfortunate incident.

travelling from San Sebastian to Madrid because he has not been able to find the time to write. He reports too that he has been advised that the roughness of the terrain will require him to make the final stages of the journey on horseback. Haro eventually reached San Sebastian thoroughly exhausted and suffering from exposure to the sun as a result of not having been able to complete the journey by coach.[17] Mazarin, however, had still not arrived at the border by this time, despite having left Paris approximately two weeks before Haro set out from Madrid. An attack of gout forced the cardinal to interrupt his journey at Bidache, a magnificent country house owned by the Duke of Gramont about seven leagues from Bayonne, so that it was not until 28 July that the cardinal finally reached his base in St Jean de Luz.

According to one of Contreras's letters, regular prayers for the success of the mission had been said in Madrid from the day when Haro left the court. The king had also asked to be informed as soon as a date had been agreed for the first meeting with Mazarin so that on that crucial occasion prayers might be general throughout the city.[18] This was indeed a tense time for the Spanish court. It was also a time when it would have to exercise great patience, since the first meeting with Mazarin was not to take place until some considerable time after Haro's arrival at the border. As he waited for the peace conference to begin, Haro busied himself by writing letters in which he queried the wording of the powers he had been given and discoursed over matters ranging from the relative strategic

---

[17] By the time he had reached San Sebastian, Haro had already spent a considerable sum of money, as the accounts for the peace conference clearly reveal. AGS CMC 3551 (2): 103 records that during the two weeks or so he was on the road to the border, Haro gave away 21,460 *maravedíes* in alms to a variety of convents and to the many destitute individuals who approached him for assistance. This pattern continued until he arrived back in Madrid in early December. Entry 104, for example, records that between 5 August and 15 October he shared out 715, 428 *maravedíes* among the convents situated close to the border and the widows, heirs and dependants of those who had died defending Fuenterrabía against the French in 1638 (see note 1); and entry 108 registers 2,794,120 *maravedíes* as the amount dispensed by Haro on alms during his return journey to Madrid. This kind of expenditure, which was incidental to the peace conference, goes some way towards explaining why Haro was constantly short of cash.

[18] AGS Estado Francia K1621: 7, 8 and K1622: 10, 16.

value of strongholds in Flanders to the unpredictable state of affairs in England.

During the preliminary period before the negotiations began, both ministers were greatly exercised over the diplomatic niceties of precedence in relation to courtesy visits and the place where they should meet for their interviews. Pimentel and Lionne were used to convey messages back and forth during this time, and Haro at last gained the king's permission to assign Pimentel to make the first courtesy visit (see Letter 4, note 17), with Lionne corresponding on behalf of Mazarin. By the time the visits took place, it was already more than a week into August. The discussion over a suitable venue for the main interviews was no less protracted or complex. In the end, it was agreed that for the purpose of the peace talks the Isle of Pheasants should be declared neutral territory and that on it a conference centre should be constructed and paid for jointly by the two crowns. This solution would permit both plenipotentiaries to enter the conference room, half of which was deemed to be in Spain and half in France, and negotiate without ever having to set foot on foreign soil. By this means the tricky points of honour that would arise over precedence in doorways and permissions to sit to one's right or left were also avoided.[19]

On 8 August Haro moved his court from San Sebastian to the walled town of Fuenterrabía in order to be within easy reach of the island, believing that the conference would soon be underway after the long delay caused by Mazarin's ill health, the resolution of questions of precedence and the construction of a conference centre.[20] As it happened, the delay had suited Haro's purpose, since he was fearful that the negotiations might still fail and therefore hoped to stretch things out just long enough to see the summer campaign period through. This

---

[19] Haro and Mazarin further agreed to dispense with their titles and use only that of *plenipotentiary*. In this way, they removed the difficulty of having to decide whether or not Spanish grandees should yield to cardinals of the Church.

[20] Haro found Fuenterrabía and the neighbouring town of Irún exceedingly cramped in comparison with San Sebastian and saw this as a potential health risk to his *familia*, the servants who attended him at the border (AGS Estado Francia K1618: 30 and K1619: 24). In Letter 9, he says that he intends to move his quarters from San Sebastian to Fuenterrabía as soon as the date of the first courtesy visit has been agreed.

tactic seems to have had the support of the king and *Junta de Estado*[21] at the time Haro left the capital; in the meantime, however, Haro had received a letter from Contreras, instructing him on behalf of the king to conclude negotiations as speedily as possible. Haro's reply was little short of sarcastic. He promised to venture nothing that might jeopardise the peace, even if this meant that he had to allow Mazarin to walk all over him. In response, an anxious king emphasises that it had never been intended that Haro should abandon the attempt to improve the terms of the treaty.[22]

The pace of life quickened enormously for the Spanish plenipotentiary following the start of the conference. In addition to dispatching the business which continued to flow from Madrid, maintaining contact with ministers in Catalonia, Milan and Flanders and entertaining large numbers of Spaniards and Frenchmen curious to see him, Haro now had to review vast amounts of documentation in preparation for his jousts with Mazarin, brief his diplomatic team and liaise with the ministers of Spain's allies in attendance at the conference. The life of the surrounding area, especially the border towns of Fuenterrabía, Irún, Hendaye and St Jean de Luz, was similarly transformed for the duration of the conference.

---

[21] The *Junta de Estado* had been used effectively by *validos* (royal favourites) since the time of Olivares in order to bypass the *Consejo de Estado* (Council of State) or to restrict discussion of a particular item of business to a handful of specialists. It met as required and was composed of men loyal to the *valido*.

[22] AGS Estado Francia K1621: 9, 14, K1622: 35 and K1623: 35. The king had also written to Haro to negotiate speedily (see Letter 9). His change of heart probably had to do with the influence which certain members of the Council of State, especially the Duke of Medina de las Torres, began to exert over him in Haro's absence. It should, however, be noted that the prestige of the Council was very low at this time. For instance, although the Marquis of Balbases had a hand in preparing Pimentel's instructions in 1658, the mission to Lyons seems to have been hidden from the rest of the Council. Contreras's complaint that the Council did not respect confidentiality would explain this precaution and Haro certainly attributed to leaks from the Council the fact that Mazarin appeared to have detailed knowledge of his instructions. Later in the summer, Haro accused the Council of being uninformed and of meddling in things they did not understand, and he insisted that he needed complete freedom in order to be able to negotiate effectively. AGS Estado Francia K1622: 43, 50 and K1623: 50 report the views of Contreras and Haro on the Council of State.

Large numbers of prominent Frenchmen and Spaniards, as well as the representatives of the allies of both crowns, joined those who were directly or indirectly involved in the negotiations coming and going across the border for reasons of business and pleasure. Indeed, so great did the influx of people to the island eventually become on public holidays that Mazarin and Haro decided not to meet on such occasions.

The main items of business transacted by Haro and Mazarin at the border in twenty-five separate interviews were the royal marriage, appropriate settlements for the principal allies of both crowns, sovereignty over the Conflent in the eastern Pyrenees, the fate of the key strongholds of Bergues and La Bassée situated along the border between France and Flanders, and France's alliance with Portugal. Additionally, considerable time was devoted to the problems surrounding the naming and ranking of those who would witness the marriage agreement, the naming and ranking of allies in the peace treaty, the release of prisoners serving at the oars on French and Spanish galleys, and the complex procedure governing the evacuation of those strongholds to be handed over to the other side.[23]

The first interview was set to begin at noon on 13 August. Haro travelled the half league from Fuenterrabía by boat, reaching the island at 11.30 a.m. By this time Mazarin was already there, having covered the two leagues from St Jean de Luz by coach. Both ministers arrived with great pomp and ceremony and an impressive train, although it had been agreed in advance that only sixty persons of quality representing each crown should cross to the island. According to Haro, this first meeting was

---

[23] The inclusion of certain items and the omission of others merit brief comment. The question of Condé's offices and governments in France was discussed even though Mazarin could legitimately have insisted on addressing only the nature of the compensation to be given to him by Spain, the principle having been agreed in Paris and ratified by both crowns. On the other hand, the cardinal failed for some unknown reason to raise the question of the restoration of the monarchy in England, although he had confided to Pimentel in Paris that he keenly wished to discuss it with Haro. As for the inclusion on the agenda of France's alliance with Portugal, it must be remembered that it was not just French successes along the border with Flanders and the formation of the Rhine League (see note 30) that brought Spain to the negotiating table. Madrid longed to be able to devote all of its attention to the recovery of Portugal. Haro's aim was thus to make peace with France conditional upon the latter's willingness to abandon its Portuguese alliance.

devoted entirely to the required compliments and courtesies. French sources, however, report that more substantive issues were aired, particularly satisfaction for Condé.[24]

The negotiating sessions between Haro and Mazarin lasted five, six and even seven hours. Spanish sources record that Haro had often eaten no more than a piece of chocolate beforehand and that this was all that sustained him through the day as he debated with, and frequently struggled to placate, a Mazarin who was all too prone to outbursts of temper. Little wonder that he sometimes simply did not have the energy, following his return to Fuenterrabía, to report to Philip on the progress of the day.

The Madrid talks of 1656 and those between Pimentel and Mazarin held during 1658–1659 share features which we do not find in those celebrated in the Pyrenees. In the first place, Lionne and Pimentel lacked the benefit of a team of advisers they could consult quickly. Instead, they had to rely almost entirely on the written instructions they had been given. Consultation with their respective governments was possible through the postal service but this was a lengthy process and, in some instances, access to the service was restricted and even denied.[25] Secondly, crushing military defeats at the time of the talks weakened the negotiating position of both envoys. Lionne, we may recall, learned of the French disaster at Valenciennes while he was in Madrid in July 1656, and Pimentel had to face an exultant Mazarin as news reached the French court in January 1659 that Haro, who had been campaigning along the border with Portugal since the autumn of the previous year, had been thoroughly trounced by the Portuguese at Elvas.[26] In the summer and autumn of 1659, the circumstances were very different. The cessation of hostilities, though fragile, nevertheless held and both Haro and Mazarin had immediate access to able men with whom they could review strategy,

---

[24] Discrepancies of this kind are not uncommon. Generally, Haro's account suggests that certain key matters were discussed and agreed later than do French sources. See Gualdo Priorato 1667 and Mazarin 1690 and 1693.

[25] Mazarin refused to allow Pimentel to consult Madrid over the article relating to Condé, a tactic which was deemed reprehensible by members of the Spanish Council of State. AGS Estado Francia K1619: 9.

[26] AGS Estado Francia K1624: 16, 18a, 19. Haro had gone to relieve Badajoz and, ironically, carried powers to grant the Portuguese a general pardon and to confirm their ancient *fueros* and privileges (Estado Francia K1686: 16).

although in Haro's case the benefits were limited, because the advisers either tended to advocate a tough approach to the negotiations or were totally opposed to them.

These two advantages for the negotiators do not mean, however, that they had no distractions or difficulties to overcome. Among those facing Haro were problems of communication. Whereas the French court was based in Bordeaux during the conference and could, if necessary, be consulted fairly quickly, a response from Madrid in under a week was virtually impossible. And for this to happen, Philip usually had to convene an extraordinary meeting of the Council of State, irrespective of whether it might fall on a Sunday or some other holiday.[27] Keeping in touch with ministers in Flanders, Catalonia and Milan was a further complication, involving both time and great expense.[28] Then again, Haro constantly had to ensure that Condé's ministers at the border did not communicate directly with Mazarin and, perhaps, divulge to him the kind of compensation which Spain had in mind to try to secure for the prince. Mazarin, for his part, had Sweden, Portugal and England pressing him hard to renew treaties which would otherwise lapse. In addition to these difficulties, which affected Haro and Mazarin separately, there were others which were common to them both. First, neither minister enjoyed good health, and the punishing schedule to which they were forced to submit inevitably took its toll. Mazarin appears to have fared worse, having to take a ten-day break from the negotiations in October. Second, no one could predict what the future held for England and this uncertainty made it difficult for the two plenipotentiaries to decide how to respond to overtures from the English Commonwealth and from the English king-

---

[27] AGS Estado Francia K1619: 63 contains the following instruction issued by Philip to Contreras on 16 November 1659: 'Veranse enel consejo de estado (comvocandose para mañana Domingo ala tarde sin embargo de ser dia feriado) las dos cartas Inclusas de Dn Luis de Haro q̃ han llegado con correo extr^{rio} y sobre el contenido de ellas se me consulte lo q̃ se ofreziere y pareziere.'

[28] AGS CMC 3551(2) provides detailed information on the cost of mail. For example, it usually cost Haro 600 *reales de plata* to send a dispatch from San Sebastian to Madrid, 650 *reales de plata* to send one from Fuenterrabía to Madrid, 3,000 *reales de plata* to send one to Milan and 4,600 *reales de plata* to send one to Brussels. These are substantial sums of money. In fact, what Haro spent on mail during the five months or so that he was absent from Madrid comes to about 7% of the total cost of the peace conference.

in-waiting, both of whom sent representatives to the conference.[29] Third, French troops billeted in Catalonia and Spanish troops billeted in Flanders committed, over the summer, excesses of various kinds in contravention of the terms of the cessation of hostilities agreed in Paris. Furthermore, Spanish troops were subsequently billeted in the Liège in contravention of the terms of the treaty of Tillemont signed by Spain and Cologne on 17 March 1654. Clearly, these matters needed to be addressed urgently if the peace process was not to collapse. Mazarin, at the request of Haro, took immediate action in August by instructing Monsieur de Beauvais, the French commander in Catalonia, to keep to the terms of the truce, but he had to issue two sets of instructions before French troops were brought under control (see Letter 15). The situation in Flanders was more complex. The terms of the cessation of hostilities relating to this area allocated more space to France for the billeting of troops than they did to Spain. The Marquis of Caracena therefore found it extremely difficult to keep within agreed territorial limits and so took several weeks to obey the orders which he received from Madrid and from Haro (see Letters 5 and 12). Most precarious, however, was the situation arising subsequently in the Liège, since it affected parties other than just Spain and France (see Letter 66). Specifically, the Electors of Cologne and of Mainz threatened to invoke the Rhine League if Spain did not call to heel the Marquis of Caracena, who was responsible for Spanish forces in

---

[29] As it happened, Haro and Mazarin responded very differently. Whereas the former was extremely careful not to give offence to either party, the latter appears to have upset Sir Henry Bennett, resident of the English king in Madrid, by refusing to see him even though Haro had just given audience to the Commonwealth's representative, Will Lockhart. This at least is what Gualdo Priorato (1667: 73) seems to say. Haro, on the other hand, suggests in Letter 62 that Mazarin was more subtle than this. According to the Spaniard, Mazarin saw Bennett secretly so as not to arouse the suspicion of the English Commonwealth.

Flanders and for their illegal billeting in the Liège.[30] Fortunately for the peace process, enough concessions were made by Spain at this time to dissuade the electors from resorting to such action. Stresses and strains of the kind outlined here complicated enormously the regular business of the conference.

With regard to the conduct of the talks themselves, Haro and Mazarin seem, for the most part, to have negotiated alone. Mazarin implies that this was at Haro's request and attributes it to the fact that the Spaniard, out of fear that he might be humiliated at the negotiating table, did not wish anyone to witness the proceedings.[31] While the two plenipotentiaries tackled outstanding items of business on the Isle of Pheasants, Lionne and the Spanish Secretary of State, Pedro Coloma, worked together, alternately in Fuenterrabía and in Hendaye, on the drafting of those articles of the treaty already agreed. According to French sources, the whole process was slowed down because Coloma, at sixty-eight years of age, was not able to work at the same pace as his French counterpart and because he was not authorised to decide anything without first consulting with Haro. Each article was drawn up initially in French and then translated into Spanish by Coloma. As soon as they had agreed a form of words, Coloma and Lionne appear to have taken the text of the article to the island and read it to Haro and Mazarin, who either accepted it or referred it for revision. Furthermore, both Spanish and French sources confirm that most of the revisions to the wording of the treaty were demanded by Haro, but whereas Haro declares that the document was

---

[30] In 1657, Gramont and Lionne were sent by the French king to the Diet of Frankfurt in order to try to influence the election of the new emperor and to form the Rhine League. As a result of this diplomatic effort, France struck a defensive alliance with several German princes designed to preserve the peace of the empire. Members of the league were sworn to refuse Spanish troops provisions, winter quarters and passage through their dominions, and France was committed to assisting them if they suffered attack or abuse by Spain. This is what was being invoked by the Electors of Cologne and Mainz in connection with the billeting of Spanish troops in the Liège. Furthermore, in order to secure election the emperor had to agree to the terms of the league and these prevented him from rendering any assistance to Spain. The formation of the league, then, is another of the key factors in persuading Spain of the absolute necessity of striking peace with France. See Gramont 1827: 18–38 and Letter 9.

[31] Mazarin 1693: 118–19.

often so unsuitably worded that it could not be left in its original form, Gualdo Priorato claims that the Spanish favourite merely yielded to pressure from his advisers at the conference to make unnecessary adjustments to the text. Whichever explanation is true, those revisions made towards the end of the negotiations necessitated the re-copying of the whole document and thus prolonged the conference considerably.

The preparation of the marriage agreement seems, on the whole, to have posed fewer problems. The drafting process was handled, on the French side, by Lionne and his team of experts and, on the Spanish side, by Coloma aided by Joseph González and Francisco Ramos, the two advisers Haro had brought with him from Madrid for this purpose. The chief responsibility of these advisers was to ensure that no legal difficulties might accrue to Spain from the clauses relating to the renunciation by the infanta of her claim to the Spanish throne or any of its territories.[32]

During the time he was absent from court (between 6 July and 5 December), Haro prepared and sent out an estimated 109 dispatches (nine to Flanders, four to Milan, eighty-four to Madrid, three to Saragossa, two to St Jean de Luz, two to Tolosa,[33] and one each to Burgos, San Sebastian, Vitoria, Bayonne and Barcelona. The number and destination of the dispatches reflect Haro's determination to consult Madrid on all major issues and to provide the king with regular news from the border.[34] At least fifty-one of the dispatches contained letters to the king and many others were addressed to Contreras, who, as the king's personal secretary, would have shared most, if not all, of them with Philip. Apart from only four brief intermissions (17–23 September, 12–17 and 21–26 October, and 1–7 November), Haro wrote to the king every two or three days. Some of his letters are substantial communications indeed; others are remarkably brief and merely fulfil the requirement to maintain contact

---

[32] Information on the drafting process can be found in AGS Estado Francia K1618: 34, 37, 46 and K1623: 118; Mazarin 1693: 118–19, 199, 249, 261–62; Gualdo Priorato 1667: 44–45, 185–87, 202–05.

[33] The cost of the two dispatches (136 and 100 *reales de plata*) suggests Tolosa in Spain as the destination, not Toulouse in France. CMC 3551 (2), 27.

[34] Contreras had written to Haro on 23 August informing him that the king wished Coloma to send with each courier news of his dealings with Lionne and of Haro's interviews with Mazarin. Haro was unwilling to accept this arrangement and argued that it was easier for him to produce his own reports. Estado Francia K1623: 52.

with the court. So far as we can tell, Haro normally dictated his letters to his secretary, Juan de Escobedo, who then took a rough version to the secretariat, where the final draft and at least one copy were prepared. The clean version was returned to Haro for his signature and then entrusted to a courier for delivery. Because of the demands on his time, there were occasions when Haro did not complete his correspondence until the early hours of the morning. Since Fuenterrabía was a walled town whose gates were locked at night and since the secretariat also remained closed until the morning, the dispatch of these letters could be delayed by up to twelve hours or more. When this happened, Haro would instruct Escobedo to inform Contreras that nothing of note had transpired during the intervening period.[35]

The letter most anxiously awaited by Madrid was naturally the one announcing that the peace treaty and the marriage agreement had been signed. According to French sources, had it not been for the death of the younger of the two Spanish princes, the infant Fernando Tomás, in late October, the formal ceremony for this purpose would probably have been held on 3 November. However, the tragic news from Madrid caused Haro to refuse to proceed until he had received confirmation from the king that he might do so.[36] It was thus not until the morning of Friday, 7 November, that a group of Spanish and French nobles gathered on the

---

[35] Estado Francia K1620: 74 is a note from Escobedo to Contreras containing information on the way dispatches were prepared and referring to delays of the kind mentioned here. Apart from direct evidence of this kind, the letters themselves contain examples of syntax normally associated with the spoken language. For instance, in Letter 29 we read: 'Yo viendo la cossa reduçida â estos terminos [. . .] me pareçio no apretar mas este punto'; and in Letter 33: '[Mazarino] se dejò deçir que si Callet ô Lenet quisiesen verse con el ô tuuiesen algo que informarle y yo tenia gusto dello, que no reusaria el oirlos.' On a related point, we learn from CMC 3551 (2) that it was also Escobedo who received and signed for Haro's mail. Finally, it should be noted that, because of his distrust of the Council of State, Haro did not route all his letters through the secretariat. Sensitive material intended for the king's eyes only was put in a *carta reservada* and seems to have been routed differently. Estado Francia K1622: 16.

[36] See Gualdo Priorato 1667: 212–14. His explanation is entirely consonant with Haro's general determination to consult Madrid on all issues. However, the Spanish version of the impact of this tragic news on the negotiations is somewhat different. See Letter 77 and note 224 below.

Isle of Pheasants to witness the reading and signing of the peace treaty and then the marriage agreement. Although Mazarin and Haro met once more, on 11 November, in order to say farewell, the signing ceremony marked the formal closure of the peace conference.

After the ceremony, Haro returned to Fuenterrabía, where he prepared a short letter in which he conveyed to the king the eagerly awaited news. The letter was collected by a courier on Saturday, 8 November, and delivered to the palace at two o'clock on the following Tuesday afternoon. Given the length of the war and the fact that there had been many tense moments over the preceding months when the talks had been brought almost to the point of collapse, one can only imagine how Philip must have felt as he read Haro's opening sentence: 'Señor: Las Capitulaçiones y la Paz quedan firmadas' (Letter 77).[37] The news was celebrated in Madrid the next day with a public act of thanksgiving at the church of Nuestra Señora de Atocha and a grand display of fireworks.[38] Philip and Spain could at last heave a deep sigh of relief. Even so, there was still much to be done. The treaties had to be ratified by the two monarchs and exchanged; strongholds had to be evacuated; commissioners had to agree precise new borders for France; and the infanta had to be married by procuration and delivered in the spring to her husband. The delivery of the infanta would occasion another journey to the frontier and another set of talks. Haro and Mazarin would once again cross diplomatic swords on the Isle of Pheasants.[39]

---

[37] The most serious hiccough occurred on 30 September. For information on this and the completely divergent explanations for it supplied by Haro and Mazarin, see Letter 52 and note 163.

[38] BNM MS 2387, fols 75–76v, records the events of 12 November, namely Philip's visit to the Church of Santa María de Atocha and the subsequent firework display organised to celebrate the signing of the peace treaty.

[39] A discussion of the personality and character of the two plenipotentiaries, as well as an assessment of the treaty itself, must be left for another occasion. Suffice it to say here that a number of independent observers and even some French sources view Haro and his achievements in a favourable light. See, for example, Robert Southwell's remarks concerning how Mazarin and Haro each treated the English king (BL Add. MS 20722, p. 39), and also the memoirs of the Count of Brienne (1824: 247–51) for a candid evaluation of the performance of the two negotiators on the Isle of Pheasants.

TEXT AND EDITORIAL CRITERIA

The peace of the Pyrenees represents a watershed in the history of Europe and the events surrounding it not unnaturally aroused considerable contemporary interest, which continued virtually undiminished throughout the remainder of the century. Many of the letters which Mazarin sent to the French court from the peace conference were published in Amsterdam in 1690 and 1693 and there are also several other published accounts of the proceedings in French. In contrast, only one of the letters which Haro wrote to the Spanish court from the border has, so far as I know, been published,[1] and I am not aware of any comprehensive published account of the proceedings from a seventeenth-century Spanish perspective. This volume is an attempt to begin to redress the balance by making available enough material to provide some idea of the Spanish version of the progress of the negotiations which culminated in the signing of the peace treaty and marriage agreement.

For reasons of space, it has not been possible to reproduce in full the more than eighty letters which Haro is known to have written to Philip IV during the five months he was absent from court. Instead, the book presents detailed summaries in English of all of the surviving letters, as well as the complete Spanish text of twenty-five of them covering a broad range of issues connected with the peace conference. Both summaries and letters are arranged in a single chronological sequence.

---

[1] Routledge (1953: 125–28) transcribes AGS Estado Francia K1619: 44, a copy of the letter which Haro wrote to the king from Fuenterrabía on 23 September 1659 about English affairs. Although Routledge is generally a first-rate historian, his transcription is seriously defective, exhibiting unnecessary orthographical alterations, important misreadings, and inexplicable additions to, and omissions from, the original manuscript. As a result, several fragments of this letter have been rendered meaningless. For my transcription, see Letter 45 below.

The letters in Spanish have, on the whole, received only the lightest of editorial touches. Original orthography has been scrupulously observed, and this includes attention to written accents, contracted forms and the scribal inconsistencies that characterise the diplomatic documents of the time. Similarly, use of brackets reflects faithfully the practice of the scribe who penned the document. Where possible, original capitalisation has also been respected; however, this has not been achieved with quite the same regularity since, in the case of such graphemes as *c* and *e*, it is often impossible to distinguish between capital and small letters. Word boundaries, which may be affected by the rhythm of penlifts or some other accident of the scribal process, are, in the source, frequently not those of modern Spanish and produce fusions such as *apagar* for *a pagar* and *ya* for the conjunction *y* followed by the preposition *a*, as well as divisions such as *des aprouar* for *desaprouar* and *sua chaque* for *su achaque*. This particular feature, which is not at all restricted to the ends of lines, gives the documents a visual appearance which is quite different from that of handwritten texts which observe current usage. Although from a philological point of view it would, of course, have been highly desirable to have retained the original scribal practice, editorial considerations regrettably recommended adherence to modern norms. Finally, punctuation, which in the originals is used at times sparingly and at other times excessively, has been adjusted where necessary so as to render the subject matter more accessible to those unused to reading documents of this kind. For example, semicolons are added or removed as required, and direct speech is introduced by a colon followed by capitalisation of the first letter of the first word of the utterance.

Despite the sorts of editorial intervention mentioned here, it is nevertheless hoped that this volume will prove of interest not only to the historian of Franco-Spanish relations in the seventeenth century but also to the philologist concerned with the language of the late Golden Age.

To assist those unaccustomed to reading this type of material, there follows a list of the contracted forms which appear in the Spanish texts:

ag^{to} : agosto
$anteçedentem^{te}$: anteçedentemente
$breu^d$: breuedad
$cant^d$: cantidad
$card^l \sim car^{al}$: cardenal
$casam^{to} \sim casami^{to}$: casamiento

$cat^a \sim cat^{ca}$: catolica
$christ^d$: christiandad
$claram^{te}$: claramente
$conformi^d$: conformidad
$conss^{ta}$: conssulta
$conuen^{te}$: conueniente

cumplim^{to} : cumplimiento
dho ∼ *d^{ho}* : dicho
dificult^d : dificultad
Diz^{re} : diziembre
D^n ∼ *D* : don
D^s : Dios
Duq̃: Duque
em^a : eminencia
embax^{or} : embaxador
emp^{or} : emperador
estimaz^n : estimazion
ex^{rio} : extraordinario
ex^{to} : exercito
fran^{co} : francisco
fran^{os} : franciscanos
g^{de} ∼ *gu^e* : guarde
gen^{l}mente : generalmente
gou^{or} : gouernador
hau^r : hauer
Haz^{da} : Hazienda
igualm^{te} : igualmente
juntam^{te} : juntamente
Ju^o : Juan
lejitimam^{te} : lejitimamente
Mag^d ∼ *Mg^d* ∼ *M^d* : Magestad
Marq̃ ∼ *Marq̃^{s}* : Marqués
mat^{ria} : materia
may^r : mayor
M^d : Madrid
men^r ∼ m^r : menester
Monsr : Monsieur
Mre : Maestre
neçess^d : neçessidad
neçess^{rio} : neçessario
noti^a : notiçia
n^{ros} , *n^{ras}* : nuestros, nuestras
num^o : numero

ott^{re} : ottubre
p^a : para
pass^{do} : passado
part^r : particular
porq̃ : porque
preçisam^{te} : preçisamente
Prin^e : Principe
p^{ro} : primero
q̃ : que
q^{al} : qual
q^{ta} : quenta
Repp^{ca} : Republica
Rey^o : Reyno
rez^{do} : reziuido
R^l : Real
s ∼ *s^t* : san
s^a : señora
SA : Su Alteza
s^d : santidad
seb^n : Sebastian
seg^{da} : segunda
sentim^{to} : sentimiento
sep^{re} ∼ *sept^{re}* ∼ *s^{re}* : septiembre
serui^o ∼ *seru^o* : seruiçio
s^r : señor
s^{re} : sobre
sup^{co} ∼ *supp^{co}* : suplico
tpo ∼ *t^{po}* : tiempo
VE : Vuestra Excelencia
VEm^a : Vuestra Eminencia
VM^d ∼ *VMg^d* ∼ *VMag^d* : Vuestra Magestad
verdaderam^{te} : verdaderamente
volunt^d : voluntad
xpt^d ∼ *x^{pnd}* : christiandad
xpt^{mo}, *xpt^{ma}* : christianisimo, christianisima

Acknowledgements

This collection of letters and summaries of letters is the product of extensive archival research in Simancas, Madrid, Paris and London, made possible by the generosity of various institutions and numerous individuals. I am deeply indebted to the staff of the archives I have visited, especially that of the Archivo General de Simancas, all of whom invariably gave unstintingly of their time and expertise in order to help me find my way in the labyrinth of seventeenth-century diplomatic history. Thanks are also due to the British Academy, the Dirección General de Relaciones Culturales del Ministerio de Asuntos Exteriores español, the trustees of the Keith Whinnom Travel Fund of the Department of Spanish of the University of Exeter, and the Research Committee of the University of Exeter for financial support for research trips at home and abroad. My greatest debts, however, are to Professor Luis Ribot of the University of Valladolid, whose intimate knowledge of the period studied in this book has been inspirational; to Mary Furlong, for invaluable help in preparing the index, and to my colleagues in the Department of Spanish at Exeter, who unselfishly covered for me during two periods of research leave. Alex Longhurst, Richard Hitchcock, Willie Hunter, Raymond Calcraft, Elizabeth Matthews, Simon Barton, Claudio Canaparo, Marta Simó and Raquel Fernández have shown themselves to be not merely colleagues but also true friends.

Exeter, April 2000

Letters From The Pyrenees

1

Haro to Philip IV: San Sebastian, 22 July 1659 [K1618: 5][1]

Baron de Watteville[2] had met Haro when he arrived at the frontier and reported that the French gazettes[3] were claiming that Spain had abandoned her two main allies, namely the Prince of Condé[4] and the Duke of Lorraine;[5]

---

[1] Dispatches usually contained numerous letters and normally took three days to reach the capital from San Sebastian. This one arrived on 25 July.

[2] Watteville (spelt *Bateuila/Batiuila/Vateuila* in Spanish sources) was a Burgundian who had negotiated for Spain an alliance with Madame la Princesse de Condé, the Duke of Bouillon and other disaffected French nobles in 1650. At Haro's request, he had just been appointed *Capitán General de la Provincia de Guipúzcoa*. He served Haro so effectively during the peace conference that he was subsequently appointed Spanish ambassador to London but was recalled in disgrace in 1662 because of a skirmish with the French ambassador over the matter of precedence on the occasion of the entry of the Swedish ambassador into London. This skirmish, which resulted in a number of deaths and was something of a *cause célèbre* at the time, is recorded in the diaries of Pepys, Evelyn, the Count of Brienne, Madame de Motteville and many others.

[3] Even prior to the start of the conference France seems to have engaged in a campaign of propaganda designed to alienate Spain's allies and thereby weaken her negotiating position.

[4] Louis Bourbon, known as the *Grand Condé*, was a French prince of the blood. As indicated briefly in the Introduction, he had fallen out with the French queen and with Mazarin and had joined forces with Spain in 1651. One of the most difficult articles of the Treaty of the Pyrenees to agree was an acceptable settlement for Condé. This was largely because Spain's treaty with the victor of Rocroi stipulated that she would only make peace with France on condition that Condé was fully restored to his estates and offices in France.

[5] Charles, Duke of Lorraine, had entered the service of the Spanish king in 1654. However, partly because of the longstanding rivalry between the duke and Condé and partly because the latter was beginning to control more and more of Lorraine, Charles became less than lukewarm in his support of the Spanish cause. He abandoned the siege of Guise, withdrew from the assault on Rocroi and was even thought to have designs on the imperial title. Eventually he was arrested in Brussels and taken to Spain. His period of imprisonment in Toledo ended in the autumn of 1659, thus allowing him to make his way to the border by late October, some two weeks before the treaty was signed. By this time, however, the negotiations relating to Lorraine had been completed.

he had also reported that a Portuguese *capitan de cavallos*[6] and friend of Pimentel[7] had arrived in San Sebastian with the intention of warning the latter that Madrid was furious with his handling of the negotiations leading to the Paris treaty, especially the article relating to Condé and his intcrests. Haro comments on Pimentel's mission and emphasises the enormity of the task which lies before him. Pimentel has so failed the king that Haro doubts whether much can be done to improve the terms of the treaty.[8]

---

[6] Elsewhere we learn the name of this curious individual. In some sources, he is known as Faria; in others, his name is Jorge Farias de Sosa (Sousa?). It seems he had served under Pimentel in Italy and in Flanders. AGS Estado Francia K1619: 9; K1620: 37.

[7] Antonio Pimentel y Prado, who belonged to the House of Benavente, had served for many years as a soldier in Italy and in Flanders. In 1653–1654, he was entrusted with a diplomatic mission to Sweden. There he established a very good relationship with Christina, the Swedish queen, and encouraged her to follow through with her decision to convert to Catholicism. As we have already seen, Pimentel left Italy for Madrid late in 1658 with news that the French court had set out for Lyons in order to agree the marriage of the young Louis with Margaret of Savoy. He was quickly dispatched by the king to Lyons with instructions to stop the marriage by suggesting that Spain was ready to discuss terms for peace which might include a marriage alliance with France. His excellent relations with Mazarin (he had met the cardinal previously on several occasions, notably during the Frondes; AGS Estado Flandes 2078) meant that he was invited to return to Paris with the court so as to continue the negotiations.

[8] By stressing that little can now be done to improve the terms of the Paris treaty, Haro prepares the king for the worst. Furthermore, any victory he subsequently wins at the negotiating table may be claimed to have been won against all the odds.

2

Haro to Philip IV: San Sebastian, 24 July 1659 [K1623: 17][9]

Haro remits to the king copies of letters from Caracena.[10] One of these, dated 28 May, had arrived before Haro left Madrid and concerned the Cardinal of Retz.[11] Haro now requests guidance on how to proceed, noting that Mazarin will be well aware of Retz's very public visits to Brussels and confirming that if the matter is raised at the conference, he will do his best to play the visits down. Caracena's other letter answers Haro's queries about the strategic value of the emplacements of Bergues, La Bassée and Le Quesnoy.[12] Haro reminds the king that under the Paris agreement the fate of the first two was to be decided by himself and by Mazarin at the peace conference and that he had therefore requested additional information from Flanders so as to be in a position to assess properly the worth of these strongholds and agree appropriate levels of compensation for them. Caracena, he says, has ranked Bergues above La Bassée, and St Venant above them both. Since the French are certainly aware of the strategic value of St Venant and since the Paris treaty has already assigned it to France, Caracena doubts that anything can now be done to secure it for Spain. Le Quesnoy, on the other hand, is, in Caracena's view, considerably less important than

---

[9] This letter arrived in Madrid on 27 July.

[10] Late in 1658, Philip decided that his illegitimate son, D. John of Austria, should resign the Governorship General of Flanders in order to assume responsibility for the reconquest of Portugal. On the recommendation of the Count of Peñaranda, it was decided that the Marquis of Caracena should replace D. John in Flanders until such time as another *príncipe* could be appointed in his stead—the position of governor general of Flanders was traditionally reserved for members of the royal House of Austria.

[11] As we have seen, Jean-François-Paul de Gondi, Cardinal of Retz, had been bitterly opposed to Mazarin for a number of years. He held the influential position of Archbishop of Paris at this time and had been in contact with Condé and the Marquis of Caracena in Flanders, inviting them to join the disaffected nobles of the French provinces and the Paris clergy in an attempt to overthrow Mazarin. The latter's best efforts to persuade Retz to give up the Archbishopric of Paris in exchange for a lucrative appointment elsewhere proved unsuccessful.

[12] Bergues and La Bassée are strongholds located in what is today French territory. The former is just south of Dunkirk, the latter a short distance to the southwest of Lille. St Venant is also close to the Franco-Belgian border on the French side, lying between St Omer and Bethune. Le Quesnoy is in the same general area, but in Belgium, specifically the Hainault.

either Bergues or La Bassée. Haro promises to negotiate with this ranking in mind.

3

Haro to Philip IV: San Sebastian, 24 July 1659 [K1623: 18][13]

Pimentel has been escorted to the frontier by the *Commandeur de Gault*. Haro encloses a letter from Gault which says that Mazarin has been forced to break his journey in Bidache because of an attack of gout. He has instructed Pimentel to write to Mazarin, requesting him not to undertake the remainder of the journey to the frontier until he is fully recovered; Haro secretly welcomes the delay caused by Mazarin's gout since it reduces the opportunity for a summer campaign; he has sent Pimentel to enquire after Mazarin's health and expects the cardinal to discuss with Pimentel arrangements for their first meeting; he expresses his satisfaction at having arrived in San Sebastian on the morning of 20 July, believing that in this Philip has been well served.

Señor

En 20 y 22 deste tengo dada quenta a VMg^d de mi llegada a esta plaza y de haber D. Antonio Pimentel despachado un correo a Bayona al Comendador de Goo, que era la persona que le hauia conduçido, para que le auisase luego que huuiese llegado alli el Card^l para voluer a buscarle

---

[13] This letter was dispatched with Letter 2 and also arrived on 27 July.
[14] I have not been able to trace Haro's letter of 20 July mentioned here. Moreover, his letter of 22 July summarised above as Letter 1 coincides only in part with the very brief summary of earlier letters provided by Haro here. It is therefore possible that Haro wrote two letters to the king on 22 July and that one of these is also missing.
[15] The *Maréchal de Gramont* is described in Valfrey (1881: 299–300) as 'souverain de Bidache, ministre d'État et lieutenant-général du Roi en Navarre'. He is Antoine III de Gramont-Toulongeon, second Duke of Gramont. As already noted, he accompanied Hugues de Lionne on a diplomatic mission to Frankfurt in 1657. In French sources he is generally known as the *Maréchal de Gramont*; in Spanish sources, and in the English summaries of Haro's letters contained here, he is given mainly the title of *duke*.

y ajustar el dia, sitio y forma de n^{ro} auocamiento.[14] Lo que ahora se ofreze que añadir es que, ayer a la una, voluio el correo y que con el tubo D. Antonio la carta del Comendador de Goo que remito a VM^d inclusa aqui, por donde VM^d vera lo que le auisa de que al Card^l le hauia sobrevenido la gota en Vidache, que es una casa de campo del Mariscal de Agramont,[15] siete leguas mas alla de Bayona. Visto esto y que el Comendador de Goo diçe a D. Antonio que el Card^l se haria traer aunque fuera con una litera a S. Juan de Luz por no causarme la descomodidad de esperarle mas, hize que D. Antonio le despachara luego un correo, diziendole de quanto sentim^{to} seria para mi que se hiziese mouer por respecto mio hasta tanto que el estado de su salud le permitiese poder hazerlo sin riesgo, pareçiendome que la razon pedia el pasar yo este acto de cortesia con el; considerando tambien yo que siendo lo que mas puede combenir al serui^o de VM^d el ir ganando t^{po} y saliendo de la campaña, assi como no se deuieran buscar ocasiones afectadas para hazerlo que pudiesen dar a conozer el intento, no combendria tanpoco [*MS: tan poco*] desaprouechar las que se fuesen para este fin ofreçiendo tan naturalmente como ha venido esta. Este Correo se despacho ayer tarde, una hora despues de hauer reçiuido la carta del Comendador de Goo, y esta mañana al amanezer, he despachado tambien a D. Antonio para que visite al Card^l de mi parte y le diga el sentim^{to} que he rez^{do} con la nueua de su achaque y la orden que lleua mia para despacharme un correo, auisandome de su mejoria por el cuydado con que quedo; y que juntamente le represente quanto sentiria yo el daño que podria causar para la breuedad del mismo negoçio si aventurase su salud, mouiendose antes de lo que el estado de su achaque le diese lugar para ello, hauiendome parezido este un cumplim^{to} preçiso. Y Juntamente pareçe que se hablara en el sitio y forma de n^{ro} avocamiento porque no hauiendo traydo Don Antonio entendido nada sobre esto, he tenido por mas combeniente el esperar a ver las proposiçiones que el Card^l haze para ello que el antiçiparme a hazerlas yo. A su vuelta, o con los auisos que tuuiere suyos, dare quenta a VM^d de lo demas que se ofreziere. Vueluo a repetir a VM^d que no puedo arrepentirme de haber procurado, aunque fuera con un poco de mas trabajo mio, entrar en esta plaza el dia preçisso de los 20 por la mañana porque tengo muchas razones para juzgar que se ha hecho el serui^o de VM^d en ello. Gu^e Dios la Cat^a y R^l persona de VM^d como la cristiandad ha menester. San Sebastian a 24 de Julio 1659

Dluismendezdeharo

4

Haro to Philip IV: San Sebastian, 26 July 1659 [K1623: 23][16]

Haro reports on Mazarin's progress and notes that the cardinal is considering making his way to St Jean de Luz by water; he discusses some of the difficulties surrounding the choice of a venue for the peace conference, as well as the highly important and potentially controversial matter of precedence as it relates to courtesy visits. One of the possibilities he and Mazarin have explored is that they should each visit the other in their lodgings. Since neither of them enjoys good health, the host in each case might remain in bed to receive his visitor. No discussion has yet been given to which of the two should make the first visit but courtesy and etiquette suggest it should be Haro since the cardinal is suffering from gout.[17]

5

Haro to Philip IV: San Sebastian, 26 July 1659 [K1623: 24][18]

Haro summarises the contents of his second letter of 24 July; he reports briefly on problems with the troops in Flanders and on how he has already sent a dispatch on this matter to Caracena; he writes further on possible venues for the peace conference and refers to his conversation with Pimentel concerning Mazarin's response to Spanish proposals on this question and, more particularly, to the cardinal's determination to secure precedence for himself during the conference; Watteville's constructive contribution to these deliberations; Haro encloses two letters from Flanders concerning affairs of England and news of a rumour that the king (see note 25) may wed Mazarin's niece; he requests instructions on how to proceed.

---

[16] This letter did not leave San Sebastian until 27 July, arriving in Madrid at 8 a.m. on 30 July.

[17] In a letter to Haro dated 26 July, Pimentel reports that Mazarin has mentioned that it is the custom in Rome and in royal courts for the person who arrives first to make the first courtesy visit (AGS Estado Francia K1623: 26). Since Haro arrived at the border before Mazarin, he should make the first visit.

[18] Letter 5 arrived in Madrid on 30 July.

Señor

Antes de ayer, que se contaron 24 deste, di quenta a VM^d [19] de la carta que se hauia reziuido del Comendador de Goo, auisando como al Card^l le hauia sobrevenido en Vidache un poco de gota, el correo que yo le hauia despachado, pidiendole que no hiçiese mouimiento hasta que lo permitiese el estado de su achaque, y como hauia embiado antes de ayer mañana a Don Antonio Pimentel para que repitiese este mismo ofiçio y le vissitase de mi parte, pareziendome que era un acto de cortesia preçisso que se deuia pasar con el. Lo que ahora puedo añadir es que ayer tarde a las quatro tube de D. Antonio la carta cuya copia remito inclusa a VMg^d, Juntam^{te} con la del papel que refiere le hauia dado Monsr de Leone[20] sobre la mala inteligençia que comenzaua a correr entre las tropas de flandes.[21] He respondido a D. Antonio lo que VM^d vera por la copia que tambien va aqui inclusa y despachado el correo que se refiere en ella a flandes, hauiendo Juzgado por muy conforme a la intençion y serui^o de VM^d el antiçipar esta diligençia sin esperar la orden de VM^d para ello, por lo que se deuen procurar escusar en la coyuntura presente, aunque

---

[19] See Letter 3 above.

[20] Hugues de Lionne was born in 1611 in Grenoble into an ancient aristocratic family of the Dauphiné. He held the title of Marquis of Berni and was a member of the French Council of State and right-hand man of the cardinal, whom he had met in Rome sometime between 1636 and 1640. Diplomatic missions to Madrid (1656) and Frankfurt (1657), as well as work on the Paris Treaty with Mazarin and Pimentel, meant he was an experienced negotiator. His main role at the peace conference was to work closely with Pedro Coloma, the Spanish Secretary of State, on the preparation of the text of the treaty, which was drafted in French and in Spanish.

[21] We have seen in the introduction that the problems with the troops in Flanders had to do largely with billeting. Despite French protestations to the contrary, the cessation of hostilities worked out by Mazarin and Pimentel in Paris seems to have favoured France rather more than Spain. In a letter to Haro dated 25 July, Pimentel reports French complaints that Caracena is not observing the terms of the truce. He has apparently allowed his troops to pillage areas protected from such excesses and this has meant that these areas are no longer in a position to pay their dues to France. Furthermore, Caracena is accused of having disregarded a complaint from the French commander, Turenne, and a letter from Gamarra implies that Spain will not observe the terms of the truce or pay compensation for damages. France has warned that the truce will not last unless Caracena is quickly brought under control. AGS Estado Francia K1623: 19.

sea pasando por algunos daños y incombenientes, todas las ocassiones que pudieren turbar el estado desta trataçion hasta ver el fin de ella.

Diçe Don Antonio Pimentel en la carta que me escriuio ayer que hauiendo insinuado al Cardenal quan a proposito seria el puesto de la Ysla para n^{ras} vistas, aunque no le hauia desaprouado, hauia tomado t^{po} para pensar y responder a ello. Y porque VM^d se halle con mayor inteligençia de lo que hasta [a]hora [*MS: hastahora*] ha passado en esto, me pareze que deuo dar a VM^d quenta de ello por menor.[22]

El primer medio que el Card^l propuso para n^{ras} vistas, para poder tener en ellas la preçedençia que desea, fue que vendria a ser mi huesped, que se pondria en mis manos con toda confiança y que, estando en mi casa, yo no podria reusar el hazerle este honor. Y tambien creo que a VMg^d le sera presente como los medios que de n^{ra} parte se propusieron para quitar estas dificultades fueron tres: que reçiuiesemos las vissitas reçiprocamente en n^{ras} casas, estando ambos en la cama, pues ambos teniamos achaques q̃ harian bien prouable esta neçess^d; que nos viesemos en el campo y que, o bien fuese en territorio de españa o de françia, entrando el en mi coche tendria la preferençia; o que se elijiese un lugar neutro como lo seria vna Iglessia. Don Antonio Pimentel respondio que todos tres medios le hauian parezido muy razonables pero que parezia que se hauia inclinado mas al de la Iglessia.

Sobre estos anteçedentes, el dia que Don Antonio llego aqui le pregunte la intençion en q̃ el Card^l venia sobre el sitio y forma de n^{ro} avocamiento. Respondiome que no le hauia d^{ho} nada en esto; y pareziendome a mi combeniente procurar ganar la ventaja de que lo propusiese el Card^l, assi por poder yo elijir lo que tuuiese por mejor sobre sus proposiçiones como por la combeniençia que se sigue al serui^o de VM^d de ir ganando t^{po} y que vaya pasando el termino de la campaña, le respondi que yo holgaria de saber la intençion del Card^l puesto que de n^{ra} parte se hauian ya d^{ho} los tres medios que se Juzgauan por razonables y que el Card^l, segun lo que el me hauia escrito, los hauia aprouado todos. Respondio inmediatamente que si y que parezia se hauia inclinado mas al de la Iglessia. Y hauiendole yo respondido que de mi parte no habria dificultad en venir en qualquiera de los tres que el Card^l elijiese en cumplimiento de lo que yo hauia escrito y viendo que el anteponia el de la Iglessia, pase a preguntarle en qual hauia discurrido el Card^l. Hiço demonstraçion de que discurria en las que podia haber y dixo que entre Yrun y S. Juan

---

[22] Haro's decision to relate these matters to the king in detail underlines the crucial importance of precedence at this time.

de luz no hauia ninguna pero que el Card^l hauia discurrido en un combento de frayles fran^{os} que hauia mas aca de S. Juan de luz y que se podria hazer la conferençia en alguna çelda donde podria hauer bufete y recado de escriuir. Y preguntando y repreguntando yo por el sitio del combento, vine en conozimiento de que era en los mismos Burgos de San Juan de luz, con que le respondi que aunque era verdad que uno de los medios propuestos era el vernos en un lugar neutro, como era vna Iglessia, no podia dejar de causarme mucho reparo el hauer de ir a buscar al Card^l para todas las conferençias al lugar de su misma corte y hauerlas de tener todas en un combento que se podia dezir que era lo mismo que su propia casa; y que hauiendo de hauer en la çelda Puerta y silla, huuiese de tener en uno y otro [sic] siempre la preçedençia porque en esto vendria a quedar muy perjudicado el derecho o, por mejor dezir, la posesion de los grandes de tratarse igualm^{te} con todos los Cardenales; y que este no podia llamarse un lugar neutro sino muy lejitimam^{te} casa propia del Card^l y con una çircunstançia tanto mas agrauante como la de hauerle yo de ir todos los dias de las conferençias a buscar tres leguas dentro de la françia y a su misma residençia. A que Don Antonio, viendo mi dificultad y quiza la fuerça que le deuio de hazer la razon de ella, me respondio que de ninguna manera se lo hauia d^{ho} el Card^l para que me lo propusiese sino que hauia discurrido con el acaso en ello y que le hauia parezido no dejar de referirmelo. Pero yo creo verdaderam^{te} que deuia traer comision positiua de procurar ajustarlo en esta forma y que viendo la resistençia que yo haçia a esto y que no seria façil el persuadirme a consentir en ello, le pareçio ponerlo en cabeza de discurso y no de propossiçion.

Con esta ocasion y hauiendose llegado a discurrir en los demas sitios que pudiesen tener menos desigualdad que este, propuso el Baron de Batiuila [sic], como quien tiene mas particular noti^a de la tierra y de las Riberas, que no podia hauer ninguno mas a proposito como [sic] el de una Ysla que esta en medio del Rio, q̃ fue la misma en que se hiçieron las entregas,[23] porque aunque ambos Reynos pretenden que es de su

---

[23] This is a reference to the exchange of Anne of Austria and Isabella of France, following their respective marriages to the future Louis XIII and Philip IV which, according to Watteville, occurred on the Isle of Pheasants in 1615. Other sources suggest, however, that the exchange of princesses occurred on a temporary floating platform constructed in the middle of the river out of wood and resting on four boats lashed together (BNP Mss Français 11191, fol. 124v). Whatever the case, it is clear that on both occasions the river is regarded as neutral territory so as to avoid difficult questions of precedence.

jurisdiçion, por este mismo caso se podria Juzgar por neutral, aunque en la verdad fuese de la Jurisdiçion de Fuenterrabia. Esto pareçia harto razonable y lo mas combeniente que se podia elijir por muchas consideraçiones porque mirando a lo mas exempçial, siendo la Ysla verdaderam^{te} n^{ra}, haçiendo yo en ella una Barraca y aderezandola de mi casa, no podria haber reparo en dar lugar al Card^l en ella, estando en el territorio de españa y siendo mi huesped, que virtualmente es lo mismo que el propuso en primer lugar de venirse a alojar en mi casa y entrarse con toda confianza en ella y VMg^d se siruio de aprouarlo. Demas desto, consideraua que a la Ysla pudiera yo llegar desde Fuenterrabia en dos o tres Barcos y tener al Card^l preuenidos y aderezados otros tantos arrimados en su Ribera para que llegando hasta ella en los Coches, los puedan tomar para pasar a la Ysla, viniendo los unos y los otros embarcados de cada parte solo con aquel num^o y genero de personas prinçipales del sequito que se ajustare de parte a parte y que se tuuiese por mas a proposito para mantener la conbersaçion mientras durasen las conferençias entre el Card^l y entre mi [sic]. Conque todo lo restante del sequito menor de Cocheros, Lacayos, Palafreneros y las guardias vendrian a quedar diuididos de cada parte de la Ribera, cada uno en su territorio por no ser por aquella parte esguazable, conque se aseguraua que entre tanta gente inferior y entre naçiones tan opuestas no suzediese algun desorden que comenzando por menores prinçipios pudiera pasar a mayores, como es tan façil de suzeder en semejantes ocasiones. Y en acauandose las conferençias, tomando los unos y los otros los barcos en la Ysla, vendriamos a desembarcar cada uno en la Riuera de su pais y nos retirauamos a nros quarteles, cosa que parezia de mucha igualdad y combeniençia por todas consideraçiones.

Don Antonio Juzgo lo mismo quando se le propuso y esperò que el Card^l vendria en ello. Pero despues de hauer llegado alla y hauerselo propuesto por via de discurso, como de aqui se le encargo, pareze que aunque el Card^l no lo desaprouo, dixo que hauia en que reparar y tomo tiempo para pensarlo y responder a ello, como VM^d lo vera por la carta de Don Antonio, el qual pareze que no podra dejar de llegar a esta plaza de aqui a mañana, y se sabra mas a la clara la resoluçion que ha tomado y los demas medios que huuiere propuesto en razon de esto, que es quanto por ahora se ofreze dezir a VM^d sobre esta materia.

Del Marques de Carazena y Don Alonso de Cardenas[24] he reçiuido las cartas inclusas que remito a VMg^d en materias de Ynglaterra, sobre que VMg^d se serbira de mandarnos embiar a mi y a ellos las ordenes de lo que huuieremos de hazer, como ellos lo desean; y a mi mas particularmente sobre el punto que tocan del casamiento del Rey con la sobrina del Card^l,[25] porque, aunque si yo me hallara sin esta preuençion confieso que me causara mucha nouedad y escandalo que me introduxeran una proposiçion semejante, particularmente siendo una cosa tan distinta de la paz de corona a corona, que es de lo que se trata, como quiera que en el mundo suelen a vezes suçeder algunas cosas que por razon nunca se pudieran esperar y el Rey se halla, demas de su dignidad, con la calidad de sobrino de VMg^d, holgaria yo harto que VMg^d se siruiese de mandarme dezir lo que deuo hazer si se mouiese un punto desta calidad; porque querria usar poco de mi arbitrio propio en todas aquellas cosas que el tiempo me permitiese el poder tener entendido la Real intençion de VMg^d, pues gouernandome conforme a ella se asegurara el açierto en el

---

[24] Alonso de Cárdenas, formerly Spanish ambassador to London, had enjoyed a stormy relationship with Cromwell and was known for his antipathy towards the English. His role in Flanders included advising Caracena on English affairs.

[25] It is not easy to determine whether this reference to a possible royal wedding involves the French king or Charles, the English king in exile. On the one hand, Marie Mancini, one of Mazarin's seven nieces, had been romantically involved with Louis XIV since 1656. Their torrid love affair continued even as the French were making their way to the peace conference in the Pyrenees and ended only late in July as a result of continued and determined intervention by Anne of Austria and Mazarin in favour of marriage with Spain. In a letter dated 22 July, Mazarin (1690: 32) complains bitterly to Louis that Madrid has already received news of the affair from persons in Paris and Flanders wishing to halt the peace process. It is therefore not impossible to conclude that these persons may have started a rumour that Marie and Louis intended to marry. In this letter, Haro identifies the king in question as a nephew of Philip IV, something that suggests a reference to Louis rather than to Charles. On the other hand, Letters 11, 62 and 74 make explicit mention of a rumour that Mazarin is scheming to marry a niece to the English king and a nephew to the English king's sister. Either of the two marriages would naturally have given Haro serious cause for concern. A marriage between Louis and Marie Mancini would have threatened the conference about to start in the Pyrenees since the whole of the peace process rested on a Spanish–French marriage alliance; a marriage between Charles and one of the cardinal's nieces would have been worrying because at this time Charles was an ally of Spain, not of France.

seruiº de VMgᵈ, que es el unico fin de mi deseo en esta y en todas ocasiones. Guᵉ Dios la Catolica y Rˡ persona de VMᵈ como la cristiandad ha menester. San Sebⁿ A 26 de Julio 1659

Dluismendezdeharo

6

Haro to Philip IV: San Sebastian, 28 July 1659 [K1623: 28][26]

Haro explains that as he has time on his hands, he has decided to query the wording of the two sets of powers he has been given by the king for the peace conference. He questions, firstly, the accuracy of the reference, in the powers given to him to negotiate the peace treaty, to Pimentel's intention to continue to Flanders after completing negotiations with Mazarin;[27] secondly, he questions in the powers granted to him for the purpose of negotiating the marriage agreement the appropriateness of the title given to Mazarin and also expresses his wish to be addressed in them as *primo* (cousin).[28] On this last question, he refers to the precedent of the Duke of Lerma, who represented Louis XIII on the occasion of his marriage to Anne of Austria,

---

[26] Dispatches written on 28 July left for Madrid the following day.

[27] In response to this query, the king's secretary, Fernando de Fonseca Ruiz de Contreras, wrote to explain that Spain was at the time negotiating the treaty of Turin and it was therefore felt desirable that Mazarin should not think that Pimentel intended to leave Paris for Italy, even though it had been agreed that he would. Consequently, it was decided that the powers should state that Pimentel was bound for Flanders to attend to some personal business. Haro did not know this because he was not in Madrid at the time Pimentel's powers and instructions were drafted by the Marquis of Balbases. Further information can be found in AGS Estado Francia K1623: 36.

[28] Haro questions the decision taken in Madrid to use in the powers simply the title *el Cardenal Julio Mazarini* and argues, initially at least, that a more appropriate form of address would be *Muy reuerendo en Christo Padre el Cardenal Julio Mazarini* (Very Reverend Father in Christ). Contreras, in the same document referred to in note 27, explains the reasons behind this decision and also why Haro is not addressed as *primo*. Nevertheless, he forwards to Haro two slightly different sets of powers, both of which meet Haro's objections. Haro may choose which to use after he has seen how the French have drafted the powers which Mazarin brings with him. Further details can be found in the same document.

and to that of the Duke of Guise, who represented Philip IV in his marriage to Isabella of France, and he also recommends that the form of address used to refer to Mazarin in the Spanish powers should follow the pattern used to refer to him in the French powers.

7

Haro to Philip IV: San Sebastian, 28 July 1659 [K1623: 29]

Haro reports on Hugues de Lionne's visit to San Sebastian. He says that he dispatched D. Cristóbal Idiáquez, a local gentleman who had served in Flanders and thus spoke excellent French, to meet Lionne. The latter had stopped off at Pimentel's house and from there requested an appointment with Haro; subsequently Lionne was accommodated in San Telmo in lodgings with a spectacular view reserved by Haro for such visits. He himself intended to move there if the English king arrived at the peace conference. San Telmo, Haro says, is also where Watteville resides. During his visit to San Sebastian, Lionne had questioned Haro about Pimentel and was particularly keen to discover whether or not Madrid was pleased with the way Pimentel had handled the negotiations in Paris. Haro claims not to have given anything away. Lionne had returned that evening to take his leave of Haro so that he might have an early start the following morning, and had lamented that Haro had already been kept waiting by Mazarin for nine days. Finally, Haro requests instructions on how to proceed in the event that Mazarin proposes marriage between the emperor and the daughter of the Duke of Orleans.[29]

8

Haro to Philip IV: San Sebastian, 1 August 1659 [K1623: 31]

Mazarin has at last arrived in St Jean de Luz and is reported to be not at all well; more news on the conference venue; Mazarin is apparently still exercised by the refusal of Spanish grandees to give precedence to cardinals of the Church; Haro continues to support the island as the most suitable venue for the peace conference and says that Mazarin will agree to this on condition

---

[29] Gaston de France, Duke of Orleans, was the uncle of Louis XIV. His daughter, Anne Marie Louise of Orleans, was Duchess of Monpensier and reputed to be ugly. She was known as *Mademoiselle*.

that Haro makes the first courtesy visit; Haro asks for a representative of the Duke of Lorraine to be sent to the border to advise him on the duke's interests; more news from Flanders about the English king.

Señor

A los 28 deste[30] di quenta a VM^d de la venida de Lione, de la sustançia de su comision y de la forma en que hauia hablado conmigo sin pasar de los cumplimientos a ninguna materia de negoçios, y que se boluia el dia siguiente por la mañana, como lo hizo. Yo bolui â embiar a Don Antonio Pimentel al cardenal, assi para mostrarle la estimaçion que hauia hecho de todo lo que Lione me hauia significado de su parte como para sauer como hauia llegado a s^t Juan de Luz, y le escriui quatro renglones de cumplimiento en esta razon, a que me ha respondido la carta de que remito a VMg^d la copia inclusa.

Llegó a s^t Juan de Luz hechado en vna Litera, y, al apearse, diçen algunos Mercaderes desta Plaza, q̃ se hallaron presentes, que lo hizo con muchas demostraçiones de venir mui agrauado porque le suuieron entre seis hombres. Pero juntamente refieren que sus mismos Françeses no querian consentir en que todo el achaque fuese verdadero. D^n Antonio Pimentel boluio anoche, hauiendole yo esperado para despachar este correo para poder añadir algo a lo que hauia dicho a VMg^d en mi vltima carta de los 28 del pasado. Diçe que ha padeçido muchos dolores y que tiene todavia muy inchadas las rodillas pero que muy breuemente pareçe que se hallara en estado de comenzar a tratar.

Hauiendose escluido el combento de s^t Juan de Luz para nuestro abocamiento, de que tengo dado [sic] quenta a VM^d, y hauiendose despues acà conferido sobre el sitio de la Isla, que se ha juzgado por el mas a proposito, de mayor combeniençia para nosotros y de mayor seguridad para que no sobrevenga algun acçidente entre ambas Naçiones, como tengo representado a VM^d, avnque hauian dado â entender que, yendo yo primero a visitar al cardenal, como lo pedia la razon y era costumbre en todas partes hauiendo el llegado el vltimo y hallandose enfermo, y buelto el a pagarme la visita a fuente[r]rauia [MS: fuente rauia] estando yo tambien en la cama, vendria en que la trataçion se tuuiese en la Isla, como de acà se proponia. Despues Lione, al tiempo de su partida, dixo

---

[30] 'A los 28 deste' suggests that Haro began this letter before the end of July. Note, however, the reference later to 'mi vltima carta de los 28 del pasado'. The letter referred to is Letter 7 above.

que el Car^al hallaua grandes reparos en esto por que demas de que el habria de venir siempre dos leguas y media de san Juan de Luz a buscarme y yo salir solo media legua por agua desde fuenterrauia, la Isla verdaderamente era en territorio de españa y n^ra.[31] Y que hauiendo yo de haçer la barraca y adrezarla [sic] de mi cassa, yo diera mi lugar de la misma manera en ella a qualquiera otro Plenipotençiario del Rey christianisimo en quien no concurriera la dignidad de Cardenal. Yo hize responder a Lione que esto era verdad assi pero que tambien lo era que si la barraca se huuiese de haçer en territorio de françia, fuera menester que qualquiera Plenipotençiario de su M^d xpt^ma me le diera a mi sin que obstase para esto la çircunstançia de ser cardenal por quanto los grandes no podian pasar por otra cosa, y que avnque yo, por lo que tocaua a mi, reparaua muy poco en semejantes cosas, No podia ser dueño de perjudicarles su derecho y posesion. Conque a mi no se me ofreçia que pudiese hauer medio mexor que el que estaua propuesto ni de mayor combeniençia y seguridad reçiproca de ambas partes para euitar las desordenes que podian sobrevenir entre las dos naçiones, hauiendo de concurrir tanta gente inferior de ambas todos los dias que se tuuiesen las conferençias, pues pasando solo a la Isla en barcas las Personas prinçipales que el car^al y yo llebasemos con nosotros y quedando todo el demas sequito y las guardas â ambas orillas, se resguardaria este punto enteramente, como el mismo Car^al hauia dado â entender a Don Antonio que lo juzgaua por muy combeniente y que holgaria que yo concurriese en aprouar esta diuision en qualquiera sitio y forma que se acordase p^a la trataçion.

La respuesta que D^n Antonio me ha traydo es que viendo el Cardenal que yo no vengo en darle mi lugar si no es formandose y adrezandose por mi la barraca en territorio de españa, ni en que siendo en el de françia ô bien hecha la barraca por el, ora sea en el de françia ô en el de españa, deje el de darme el mexor lugar, en lo q^al no puede consentir porque assi como yo quiero defender el derecho de los grandes el no puede dejar de satisfaçer ni perjudicar al Colejio de los Cardenales, tiene por preçiso hauer de conformarse en el medio propuesto de la Isla, avnque sea de tanta ventaxa para nosotros como hauer de venir el todos los dias que se huuiere de tener la conferençia a buscarme tres leguas a vn sitio

---

[31] In his diary entry for 31 July, Priorato (1667: 132–34) records that in order to remove any ambiguity arising out of the judgement of 1510, Haro had agreed to make a declaration to the effect that the island belonged equally to both crowns. For more on this, see also Letter 13 below.

dentro de españa y para donde yo no tengo q̃ haçer mas viaxe que media legua por agua desde vna Plaza fuerte adonde tengo mi residençia. Pero que esto se entiende combiniendo yo en irle a ver primero a s^t Juan de Luz, como lo tiene propuesto y como lo pide el ser el vltimo que ha llegado y hallarse enfermo, y boluiendo el a pagarme la visita en la misma forma antes de que se comienze la trataçion. Y avnque despues acà Lione (cuyo natural es muy aplicado a mouer sutilezas y poner dificultades avn en cosas que por razon no las pudiera hauer) ha buelto a deçir que para llegar a la Isla han de formar ellos la puente que toca a la parte de françia, como se hizo reçiprocamente en la ocasion de las entreguas [sic],[32] le he hecho responder luego q̃ como la barraca se haga en la Isla y en la parte que esta destinada y sea hecha y adrezada por mi cassa, que es la forma en que yo puedo dar el mexor lugar al Cardenal como se le diera a qualquiera otro Plenipotençiario del Rey xpt^{mo}, vengo en que hagan el Puente que proponen y todos los demas que se quisieren puesto que la proposiçion de llegar en barcos y que no huuiese de vna ni de otra parte Puente solo se hauia hecho a fin de tener el concurso de las dos Naçiones mas diuidido, como el Cardenal lo hauia juzgado y propuesto por tan combeniente; con que juzgo este punto por enteramente ajustado si VM^d se huuiere seruido de aprouar que yo vaya a visitarle primero, como lo propone, porque, avnque por lo que toca a mi entender, siendo fuerza que el vno visite primero que el otro y juntandose a esto hauer llegado el vltimo y hallarse enfermo, no se me ofreçe mucho reparo en ello, particularmente quedando ajustado [sic] al mismo tiempo el lugar y forma para la trataçion a satisfaçion nuestra, con todo, hauiendo dado quenta a VM^d dello en carta de los 26 del pasado[33] y dando tiempo para esperar la respuesta la dilaçion que forzosamente se ha introduçido por el achaque del cardenal, holgaria yo harto reçiuir la resoluçion de VM^d de aqui a mañana, como lo [sic] espero, para poder responder y gouernarme conforme â ella.

Acabo de reçiuir el despacho de VM^d de 27 del pasado en respuesta del mio de los 22 del mismo[34] y por no detener este correo con deseo de que a VM^d no le falten frequentes nueuas de aqui, remito el satisfaçer a los puntos que contiene con el primero.

---

[32] A reference to the delivery of Anne of Austria and Isabella of France to their respective royal husbands in November 1615. See also notes 23 and 86, and Letter 6 above.
[33] Letter 5 above.
[34] Letter 1 above.

Juzgaria que combiene que el Duque de Lorena nos embiase luego aqui alguna Persona por su parte que nos pudiese informar de la diuision de sus dominios y de lo que se compreende en cada vno dellos por ser notiçias neçesarias y que a Pimentel le han hecho tanta falta como el mismo negoçio ha mostrado.

Del Marques de Carazena he tenido la carta inclusa que remito a VMg^d con vn correo que me han despachado de Burdeos; y por el contenido della y por los auisos que vienen entrando en esta frontera, se puede probablem^{te} creer que el Rey de Inglaterra deue de hauer entrado ya en aquel Reyno; y no puedo dejar de representar a VM^d quanto combiniera el procurar haçerle en esta ocasion alguna Asistençia de dinero, assi por lo bien que se empleará y lo que se le obligaria con ello, como por ser de tan comun interes a todas las Monarquias el buen suçeso de su expediçion.[35] G^{de} D^s la Catolica y R^l Persona de VM^d como la christiandad ha menester. De s^t Sebastian 1° de Ag^{to} 1659

Dluismendezdeharo

9

Haro to Philip IV: San Sebastian, 2 August 1659 [K1623: 33]

Haro refers to dispatches from the king dated 27 and 30 July. In the former, the king had ordered that Faria must not be allowed to assist Pimentel but be sent to Madrid. Haro points outs that it has already been agreed that Pimentel should not be disciplined until after the conference and that the execution of this order would not merely discredit Pimentel but grieve him far more than a dressing-down from himself. Since Faria cannot do much harm in the six or so days it will take to get a reply from the king, Haro proposes to delay executing it. The king also instructed Haro in the same letter to conclude the treaty as soon as possible. Haro replies that the *Junta de Estado*[36] which met in his house before he left Madrid was clear that priority should be given to discreetly prolonging the proceedings so as to see the campaign season out. Something of which he is ignorant must have happened

---

[35] See note 42 for details relating to the treaty between Spain and the English king.

[36] For the distinction between the *Junta de Estado* and the *Consejo de Estado*, see the Introduction, note 21.

in the meantime to cause the king to alter policy on this matter. However, he confirms that he will obey in so far as it lies within his power to do so, but there are problems: Mazarin has gout and has already kept him waiting at the border for eight or nine days; courtesy visits are being delayed due to matters of precedence and Mazarin has said that the conference cannot start until such preliminaries are out of the way; it has been agreed that the island is a suitable venue for the conference but Mazarin is insisting that a conference centre fit for his court must be built before negotiations commence. With regard to Lorraine, Haro understands his instructions and will discuss the issue with Mazarin. The king has also instructed Haro to attempt to renegotiate with Mazarin the terms of the limits within which troops must be contained in Flanders, Italy and Catalonia. If he is unable to do so, he should write to the troops, ordering them to remain within the limits already agreed. Pimentel has expressed doubt that the terms can be improved, especially as regards Flanders. Haro is aware of the view in Flanders but confesses that he does not have sufficient information himself to assess the situation. He then reports on the powers which Mazarin brings to the negotiating table and encloses a copy of them, as well as a summary of Pimentel's letter on this matter. With regard to the English king, it seems likely that he is now in England. Haro recognises that the absence of news in respect of his reception there makes it difficult to know how to respond to any overtures from Will Lockhart,[37] who is apparently intending to visit Haro on behalf of the English Commonwealth. He therefore requests instructions on how to proceed. Finally, he reports that he has sent Pimentel again to enquire after Mazarin's health and, perhaps, to make arrangements for the first courtesy visit. Once Pimentel returns with this information, he will move his quarters to Fuenterrabía.

---

[37] Sir William Lockhart, formerly governor of Dunkirk and now ambassador of the English Commonwealth to France. He had been judge itinerant in Scotland and had married the daughter of Cromwell's sister.

10

Haro to Philip IV: San Sebastian, 2 August 1659 [K1623: 34]

Haro announces the arrival at the border of Monsieur Caillet.[38] Caillet had left Madrid some days before Haro in order to inform the Prince of Condé of the treaty signed by Pimentel in Paris and which Philip had felt obliged to ratify. He had travelled through France and had visited Mazarin on his way back from Flanders at the latter's request; Haro rehearses to the king the oral report which Caillet has given him and lists those territories which Condé is prepared to accept as compensation. Condé will not accept estates in Naples, Sicily, Sardinia, the Vicariate General of Italy or Flanders. He would, however, accept either Cambrai with the territory indicated to him, or whatever remains to Spain in Luxembourg.[39] He appears to prefer the latter. Since Caillet has made an oral report, Haro has no papers which he can forward to Madrid.

11

Haro to Philip IV: San Sebastian, 6 August 1659 [K1623: 37][40]

In response to the king's letter of 1 August, Haro discourses over the English question and the difficulty, in view of the instability of the English Commonwealth, of knowing how much support to give the English king

---

[38] Caillet (spelt *Callet* in Spanish sources) was one of Condé's ministers in Madrid. According to Mazarin (1690: 122–23), Caillet had begged the cardinal, on his way back from Flanders, not to oppose the Spanish proposal to cede to Condé estates in Flanders since it was merely the intention of the prince to hand them over to the French king. He seemingly also told Mazarin that Condé had refused the government of Flanders because he was not prepared to swear an oath of allegiance to the Spanish king which would naturally prevent him from regaining Louis's favour. In Letter 29 below, we find Haro saying the same thing. However, other Spanish sources suggest (1) that estates in Flanders would merely be leased to Condé until such time as his offices and governments in France were restored to him, and (2) that Condé was considered for, but never actually offered, the position of Governor General of Flanders. AGS Estado Francia K1686: 106 and K1623: 14.

[39] Cambrai was, perhaps, the most valued Spanish possession in the border area between France and Flanders.

[40] Letter 11 reached Madrid on the morning of 9 August.

should he arrive at the peace conference. He refers to the proposal made to Pimentel by Mazarin in Paris that France and Spain might join forces in order to restore the monarchy in England and to the implications of Spanish policy on England for the war with Portugal. The English question, he maintains, is the most difficult of the conference.

Señor

En carta de primero deste se sirue VMg^d de mandarme decir sobre las materias de Inglaterra las palabras siguientes:

En quanto a lo de Inglaterra tambien he visto lo que Don Alonso de Cardenas os escriue en la carta que remitis, y el estado que tenia la platica de las negociaciones que por alla se han intentado por parte del Parlamento, de que os da noticia para que os gouerneis con ella en lo que ahi se ofreciere; en que he querido responderos que parece conueniente ir con tal tiento en esto que no se desconfie al Parlamento (pues como allá estan presumiendo) de los tratados que se hicieren en n^{ro} beneficio se puede seguir daño a franceses de quien se fiaran menos.[41] Y assi auisareis al Marques de Carazena y a Don Alonso vayan continuando la platica y dandoos quenta a vos de lo que se ofreciere; y pues han intentado por vna y otra parte (como saueis), os gouernareis sin empeño grande; y en asistir a aquel Rey, pues Don Alonso no dice que el lo haya pedido, no saldreis a ello.

Señor, esta materia toda es la mas dificultosa que se puede ofrecer en este congreso y en que será menester mayor asistencia de Dios y mas distintas y especiales ordenes de VMg^d para poder gouernarla con el accierto [sic] que conuiene; porque hallandose tan dudoso el estado de las cosas de aquel Reyno y no sabiendose el Gouierno que al cabo vendrá á prebalecer, no se puede hacer Juicio cierto de presente sobre ello. Y aunque por esta causa fuera sin duda lo mas conueniente el irse gouernando (como VMg^d me lo manda), procurando entretener y no desconfiar al Parlamento y no hacer empeño grande en las Asistencias del Rey, deuo representar a VMg^d que aunque procuraré lo primero, tengo por totalmente imposible lo segundo y que en el estado en que se hallan las cosas del Rey y poca satisfacion con que salió de flandes, viene a ser precisamente necesario ô el asistirle ô el perderle. Y para que VMg^d se halle con mayor inteligencia dello, me parece que debo dar quenta a

---

[41] This is how the manuscript, which is virtually illegible at this point, seems to read.

VMg^d muy distintamente desta materia y de lo que entiendo sobre ella. Segun los auisos que se tienen de flandes de Don Alonso de Cardenas y del Marques de Carazena, otras noticias que me han llegado despues que llegué a esta frontera y lo que Gen^lmente estan entendiendo en francia, parece que hauiendo muerto el Protector pasado y viendo el Rey de Inglaterra que por esta causa quedaua la francia fuera del empeño de la coligacion que tenia hecha con el y Juntandose a esto la poca satisfacion con que se hallaua de que VMg^d y los Ministros de flandes no huuiesen asistido a que executase su expedicion en Inglaterra como tantas veces lo hauia solicitado y se le ofrecia por el tratado hecho con el, persuadido de la Reyna su Madre que se halla en Paris y de los ministros Ingleses que asisten cerca de su persona, se hauia hechado enteramente en manos de la francia, procurando su restablecimiento por aquel medio. Y para facilitarlo y dar mayor apoyo â ello, no solo se tiene por cierto que se trataua del Casamiento del Rey con la sobrina del Card^l sino tambien el de su sobrino con la hermana del Rey que está en Paris, declarandole por Principe de la sangre de Inglaterra y dandole el Virreynato de Irlanda por su vida y la renta de aquel Reyno hasta la extincion entera del gasto hecho por la francia para su restablezimiento. Y aunque estas no son cosas a que se puede dar vn absoluto credito hasta sauerlas con entera certitud, segun lo que escriuen de flandes y todo quanto se puede reconocer por las noticias particulares que se han tenido despues que llegue a esta frontera, parece harto probable que deuia de ser cierto como se refiere.

La Venida del Rey de Inglaterra â este confin (la qual tubo determinada como aqui lo decia su residente y como VMg^d lo verá mas particularmente por la carta inclusa del Marques de Caracena que he reciuido retardada por duplicado estos dias) no solo se hacia con noticia del Cardenal sino aconsejada y persuadida por el, en que yo Juzgo que deuia de tener dos fines muy perjudiciales: el vno que si, haciendo el la proposicion que tantas veces hauia dado á entender a Pimentel de vnirse ambas coronas para el restablecimiento del Rey, nosotros concurriesemos en ella, diuertirnos por este camino de la Conquista de Portugal y dejar al mismo tiempo sus sobrinos casados, si no como la razon lo pidiera, como su ambicion y sus conueniencias particulares se lo deuian de persuadir; y si nosotros no concurriamos al restablecimiento del Rey por no diuertirnos de la conquista de Portugal (que es lo que mas nos puede conuenir), dejarnos autores de todo su daño y, por consequencia, de todo el odio que le resultaria contra nosotros, y, dandole despues la francia sola asistencias para su restablecimiento y estrechandose la vnion con los casamientos del Car^{al}, dar motiuo para que quedase con vna Guerra contra nosotros, como hasta ahora lo hauiamos tenido con el Protector; a que no seria fuera de proposito creer que, viendole desobligado y ofendido, le procurasen persuadir para impedirnos por este camino la Conquista de Portugal. Y assi tengo por vna gran merced que Dios nos haya hecho que el Rey se haya resuelto pasar a aquel Reyno en esta coyuntura porque Juzgo que su asistencia en este congreso nos fuera muy dañosa por estas consideraciones.

Sobre este presupuesto y este discurso, deuo decir a VMg^d que Locart tengo auiso que ha llegado ya a s^t Juan de luz y que trae poder de aquel Parlamento para proponerme la pacificacion con el, en que me gouernare conforme VMg^d me manda y como yo Juzgare por mas conuen^{te} sobre el mismo hecho en orden a entretenerle y no desconfiarle, ni tampoco entrar en empeño. Pero en quanto a la forma en que me he de gouernar con el Rey, es menester que VMg^d se sirua de embiarme mas especiales ordenes porque por horas se pueden esperar nueuas del suceso que ha tenido su expedicion. Si se huuiese perdido, tendré poco que preguntar ni que sauer porque el mismo suceso nos dira el camino que hemos de lleuar. Pero si huuiese tomado pie dentro del Reyno, en cuyo caso es cierto que sauiendo que me hallo en esta frontera me solicitará luego con sus cartas, como ya lo ha empezado â hacer su Residente aqui, para que yo le embie algunas Asistencias y Armas, suplico a VMg^d se sirua de mandarme decir lo que le he de responder y executar porque en este caso es cierto que será menester asistirle o perderle. Porque si sobre todas las quejas pasadas y poca satisfacion con que ha salido de flandes se le diese el Vltimo desengaño en esta precisa coyuntura de que depende toda su fortuna y restablecimiento, tengo por cierto que quedara por declarado enemigo y nos seria muy peligroso que con su propia espada, las inteligencias que tiene dentro del Reyno y la Asistencia de francia fuese restituido, reciuiendo al mismo tiempo este desengaño y ofensa de nosotros.[42] G^{de}

---

[42] According to the treaty of Westminster (24 October/3 November 1655), Cromwell agreed, among other things, to expel Condé's agents from England and Mazarin to exclude the English king and certain of his supporters from France. Spain, for her part, signed a treaty with Charles II in Brussels on 2/12 April 1656 which included a promise of Spanish assistance to recover the English throne in exchange for the services of Charles's English and Irish troops against France and help against Portugal after the English king's restoration. By this treaty, Charles also received an irregularly paid pension and was allowed to reside in the Low Countries.

Dios la Catolica y R^l persona de VMg^d como la christ^d ha menester. San Sebastian 6 de Agosto de 1659

12

Haro to Philip IV: San Sebastian, 6 August 1659 [K1623: 38][43]

Following the king's instructions, Haro has written to Caracena in Flanders and to Fuensaldaña in Milan about the cessation of hostilities agreed by Pimentel and Mazarin in Paris, emphasising that the king wants the agreement observed to the letter even though it may not favour Spain. He has received no complaints from Mortara in Catalonia on this matter and assumes that the king will have instructed him along the same lines that he (Haro) has instructed Caracena and Fuensaldaña.[44] He promises to contact Caracena about the Cardinal of Retz and about England, as instructed. However, he expresses concern over Caracena's proposal that Spain should attempt to retake Dunkirk and advises the king to give the matter earnest thought. He further promises to keep Caracena abreast of peace negotiations with England but reminds the king that the cessation of hostilities includes the English Commonwealth and that it would therefore be imprudent to undertake any military operations in Flanders until the situation in England is clearer.[45] The English dimension is the most difficult aspect of the negotiations because of the uncertainty of English internal affairs.

---

[43] Letter 12 arrived in Madrid on the morning of 9 August.

[44] The Count of Fuensaldaña and the Marquis of Mortara are the military governors of Milan and Catalonia respectively. In French sources, Fuensaldaña is identified as one of the few Spaniards of the time who believed that Mazarin was sincere in his desire to end the war with Spain. It was he who sent Pimentel to Madrid in 1658 in order to warn the king of the proposed marriage between France and Savoy and to encourage him to try to frustrate it with an offer of a dynastic alliance with Spain. Along with Anne of Austria, he is therefore held up as one of the architects of the peace. See note 75 and Gualdo Priorato 1667: 22.

[45] It is quite clear from Caracena's dispatches to Haro that the cessation of hostilities came at something of a bad time since it prevented him and Condé from rendering assistance to the Cardinal of Retz and a significant number of disaffected Frenchmen inside France who were opposed to Mazarin and Anne of Austria. AGS Estado Francia K1623: 4.

13

Haro to Philip IV: San Sebastian, 6 August 1659 [K1623: 39][46]

Pimentel has reported that Mazarin is now claiming that the debate over sovereignty of the Isle of Pheasants has a long history and that the island must therefore be considered neutral territory; accordingly, the French proposal, which Haro accepts, is that construction of the conference centre on the island should be undertaken jointly by both crowns; Mazarin and Haro have agreed to dispense with all titles except that of *plenipotentiary* of their respective masters; Lionne, Pimentel and Watteville met on the island on the afternoon of 5 August to plan the construction of the centre and of the bridges; Haro hopes to hold the first interview with Mazarin on about 10 August.

Señor

En Despacho de p^{ro} deste,[47] di quenta a VM^d de que pareçia que quedauamos combenidos en que se hiçiere la trataçion en el puesto de la Isla porque, hauiendome vltimamente embiado a proponer q̃ querian haçer vn puente para llegar allà sin pasar en nuestros barcos, yo me hauia conformado en ello. El dia siguiente reçiui vna carta de VMg^d su fecha de los 30 del pasado, en que VMg^d se sirue de deçirme hauia resuelto que fuese yo ha haçer la primera visita al Cardenal, en cuya conformi^d embie luego a Don Antonio Pimentel para q̃ viese el estado en que se hallaua su achaque y se ajustase el dia y forma del abocamiento. Boluio a deçirme que avnque el Car^{al} hauia propuesto q̃ vendria ha haçer su residençia a Ortunia, vna casa fuerte que es media legua del rio, para reçiuir alli mi visita, le hauia dicho aora al tiempo de su buelta que, hauiendola reconoçido, no pareçe tenia tanta comodidad como el hauia pensado quando la propuso y que asi le pareçia que no deuia haçer nouedad de s^t Juan de luz ni perder las comodidades que alli tenia en el estado de salud en que se hallaua; conque virtualmente pareçe que queria ver si podia llebar con esta ocasion mi visita allà, avnque deuia de estar dudoso de si lo podria conseguir por la resistençia que yo hauia hecho en ir a la trataçion al combento de s^t Ju^o de luz que se me propuso al prinçipio, de que entonçes di q^{ta} a VMg^d. Dijome juntamente Don Antonio

---

[46] Letter 13 also arrived in Madrid on the morning of 9 August.
[47] Letter 8 above.

que avnque el Carᵃˡ hauia combenido en que la trataçion se hiçiese en la Isla, haçiendo y adrezando yo la barraca y dandole mi lugar en ella, no se hallaua muy satisfecho de hauerlo combenido assi porque, teniendo ambos Reynos pretension de que el Rio y lugar de aquella Isla era de cada vno y hauiendose hecho sobre esto muchas protestas en diferentes tiempos de parte aparte [sic] y pudiendo por lo menos por esta causa juzgarse aquel sitio por neutral entre ambas coronas, El consentir en que yo hiçiese la barraca en el pareçe que virtualmente seria demostraçion de reconoçerle por territorio nuestro; y q̃ el darle yo el mejor lugar en ella no lo tenia por de gran ventaxa, pues en nuestro Pays y en mi propia cassa siempre se le diera yo a qualquiera otro Plenipotençiario del Rey xptᵐᵒ en quien no concurriera la çircunstançia de ser Carᵃˡ; y que, considerando esto y que quiza yo tambien hallaria reparo en irle ha haçer la primera visita a sᵗ Juan de Luz, no permitiendole la poca comodidad de Ortunia el poder venir à haçer alli su residençia como lo hauia ofreçido, se podria pensar en algun medio en que yo escusase el ir â haçerle la primera visita y el escusase tambien el venir a buscarme cada dia dentro de nuestra casa y en mi misma barraca para la trataçion; y que para que se escusase lo vno y lo otro y que quedasemos ambos en la representaçion solo de Plenipotençiarios de dos Reyes iguales y con igualdad en todo, como yo hauia dado â entender siempre que lo pedia la razon y declarado que, como grande, no podia permitirle ninguna preçedençia avnque fuese Carᵃˡ, se le ofreçia proponerme vn medio que era que, siendo la Isla confin de ambos Reynos y estando contrabertido el derecho de a qual de los dos tocaua el Dominio del Territorio, se podria haçer la barraca a medias, formando ellos la mitad con su puente y nosotros la otra mitad con otro puente para llegar por ellos cada vno a la parte que le perteneçiese; y que en la pieza en que huuiese de ser nuestro abocamiento, podia assi mismo adrezar el Carᵃˡ la mitad della y yo la otra mitad y, poniendo vn bufete en medio y vna silla de cada parte, llegar cada vno por la de su Pays a tomar su silla sin dependençia ni preçedençia el vno del otro. Esta fue su proposiçion y avnque en ella alteraua de aquello en que estaua combenido, considerando yo que en todos los demas medios en que VMᵈ me hauia permitido consentir, como era el de la Iglesia, el de mi cassa, y el del coche en el campo, venia el a quedar siempre con la preçedençia y mexor lugar y que el ir yo â hacerle la primera visita era virtualmente darsela tambien, avnque en lo aparente se quisiese honestar con hauer llegado el vltimo y hallarse enfermo, y pareçiendome por estas causas que este vltimo medio que se hauia visto obligado a proponerme para salir del empeño en que hauia entrado de venir cada dia a buscarme a mi casa y a mi barraca para la trataçion era de mucha mayor deçençia y ygualdad para nosotros que ninguno de aquellos en que VMg^d me hauia permitido venir, pues sin que le quede ninguna representaçion de Cardenal ni ganar vn paso por esta dignidad, como lo ha pretendido, Veniamos solo a quedar en la representaçion y ygualdad de Plenipotençiarios, me pareçio combenir luego en ello (como lo hiçe), respondiendo q̃ en todo deseaua lo que huuiese de ser mayor satisfaçion del car^{al}, en cuya conformidad se juntaron ayer tarde en la Isla Lione, Pimentel y el Baron de Vateuila, con los maestros de vna y otra parte, para formar de acuerdo la barraca y los puentes a medias; y Juzgo que nuestras primeras vistas podran ser el sabado ô el Domingo que se contaran diez deste a mas tardar. Este es el estado en que esta materia queda, juzgando yo que se ha dispuesto este punto conforme al seruiçio de VM^d y con mayor ventaxa de lo que se hauia pensado. Y de todo lo demas que se fuere ofreçiendo yrè dando quenta a VM^d cuya catholica y R^l Persona g^{de} Dios como la christiandad ha m^r. De San Sebastian a 6 de Ag^{to} 1659

Dluismendezdeharo

14

Haro to Philip IV: Fuenterrabía, 9 August 1659 [K1619: 24]

Haro has finally moved his base to the walled town of Fuenterrabía; he comments on the construction of the conference centre and the number of people who will be allowed to cross to the island while negotiations are in progress; he describes some of the more humorous things that have occurred during the building of the centre; complaints that Fuenterrabía and Irún are far too cramped to house his party comfortably.

Señor

A los seis deste[48] di quenta a VMg^d de lo que hasta entonçes se ofreçia desde St Sebastian y aora lo hago desde Fuenterrauia a donde mude todo el quartel ayer tarde assi para ponerme tan çercano al lugar destinado para la conferençia como por poder disponer de mas çerca que se abreuiara la fabrica de la Barraca, creyendo que huuieran podido ser las primeras vistas mañana Domingo. Pero D^n Antonio Pimentel que vino

---

[48] Haro appears to be referring to Letter 13 above.

anoche de s.^t Juan de Luz y hizo su pasaxe por la Isla en compania del comendador de Goo me dice que duda pueda executarse y que el mismo comendador lo reconoçio assi por hallarse la parte que toca al cardenal mucho mas atrasada que la mia no obstante la gran furia con que dixeron antes de ayer que hauia de estar todo acabado para oy y con palabras que podian pareçer mas amenaza que prisa, por hauer dicho Lione (segun se refiere) en la misma Isla q̃ era menester darse gran priesa porque se pasaua el termino de la Campaña, queriendo virtualmente dar â entender por las palabras y por la forma de deçirlas que si no nos combeniamos luego, seria menester procurar, antes que espirase el termino della, sacar las ventaxas que pudieren por el medio de las Armas. Yo, sin darme por entendido desto (comoquiera que no me lo dixo a mi ni me lo embio a deçir tampoco), he procurado solo dar tan gran priesa a la parte de barraca que me toca a mi que se acaue primero que la suya a fin de que, avnque se dilaten nuestras vistas vn solo dia mas, avn esta pequeña dilaçion proçeda dellos y no de mi, como ha proçedido tambien dellos la que se ha tenido hasta aora. Esta tarde han quedado combenidos Don Antonio y Lione de estar en la Isla a las çinco con deseo de ver si pudiese ser el abocamiento mañana. Pero Don Antonio (que es el vltimo que vio ayer tarde al anocheçer el estado que tenia la obra que està a cargo del Injeniero y superintendente embiado por el cardenal para este efecto) duda, como tambien diçe que lo reconoçio el comendador, que se pueda executar por lo menos hasta el Lunes, q̃ se contaran onçe deste.

A la Isla proponen que hayan de pasar solo çinquenta Personas, de cada parte las mas particulares, y que todo el demas sequito de criados, avnque sean de escalera arriba, y todo lo inferior de Lacayos, cocheros, palafreneros y las guardas hayan de quedar de vna y otra parte de la Riuera y ponerse vna compania de guarda en cada cabeza de puente para que no pase ninguna otra Persona, dando por motibo el cardenal que conoçe el humor y lijereza de los françeses y que el Mariscal de Villarroy[49] (a quien estiman por hombre de cabeza) le hauia d^{ho} que juzgaua por de neçesidad preçisa toda esta limitaçion ô diuision porque sinô temia que, no por hecho nuestro sino por el de los mismos françeses, se pudiesen mouer algunas platicas menos a proposito y pasarse quiza dellas â algunas questiones que pudiesen ser de embarazo y de disgusto â ambas partes. Y assi por combenir en su proposiçion como por juzgar yo esto por lo mejor y por lo mas seguro, me he conformado con ello,

---

[49] Nicolas de Neufville, Duke and Marshal of Villeroy, governor of Louis XIV and head of the royal council.

que es quanto por aora se me ofreçe que deçir a VM^d sobre esta materia.[50]

En quanto al modo de aderezar cada vno el pedazo de barraca que le toca han pasado cosas bien graçiosas y algunas anteçedentes del mismo genero sobre algunas çircunstançias del sequito y de los traxes porque han alterado todo quanto hauian dado â entender de la obserbançia de la Prematica, hauiendola lebantado aora el Rey x^{ptmo} por tres Meses.[51] Pero como cosas poco sustançiales para la suma del negoçio, es menester menospreçiarlas y por la misma causa dexo de embarazar a VM^d refiriendolas.

El cardenal deue de hauer salido deste vltimo achaque muy temeroso de su conçiençia porque con ocasion de la priesa que ambos damos a que se acabe la barraca y el gusto que reçiprocamente nos mostramos de poder vernos con mayor antiçipaçion, me embio a deçir esta mañana que para que se pudiese trabajar mañana, q̃ era Domingo, hauia embiado a pedir liçençia al obispo de Bayona y que seria bien que yo la embiase a pedir al de Pamplona para lo mismo. (No puedo negar que me cayo vn poco en graçia el escrupulo.) Respondile que yo venia a reçiuir sus ordenes en todo pero que en esto reçiuiria tambien el buen exemplo y que assi ejecutaria lo que me mandaua.

Este quartel y el de Irun son tan estrechos que no tienen capaçidad ni avn para la quinta parte de la gente que viene con no ser mucha. Con que temo que serà menester ô quedarnos sin familias [sic] ô exponerla a que toda enferme, que podria ser otro incombeniente mayor. G^{de} Dios la Catholica y Real Persona de VM^d como la christiandad ha menester. Fuenterrauia 9 de Ag^{to} 1659.

Dluismendezdeharo

---

[50] For a very different report on the construction of the *barraca* and the numbers permitted to cross to the island during the negotiations, see Gualdo Priorato 1667: 135–37 and Mazarin 1690: 42–47. Both claim that it is Haro who is dragging his feet and who is concerned about limiting the number of those permitted to be on the island while the prime ministers are in conference. Mazarin also claims that Haro is obsessed with *bagatelles* such as the quality of the wall hangings which should adorn the conference room.

[51] I have been unable to trace this ordinance affecting the livery of the guards accompanying Mazarin to the border. Clearly, Haro was surprised that the French should have temporarily suspended the ordinance so as to be able to alter what had been agreed with Pimentel in respect of their dress. Hume (1907: 476), however, records that Spain too suspended an ordinance relating to dress at this time.

15

Haro to Philip IV: Fuenterrabía, 10 August 1659 [K1619: 28][52]

Haro refers to the king's dispatch of 3 August, which includes a letter from the Marquis of Mortara concerning French abuses in Catalonia in breach of the cessation of hostilities. The king had instructed Haro to raise the matter with Mazarin and Haro reports that Pimentel has returned from St Jean de Luz with news that the cardinal has agreed to instruct French officials in the area to observe the terms of the truce.

Señor

En carta de los tres deste, se sirue VMg^d de mandar remitirme la que hauia reçiuido del Marq͂ de Mortara de los 27 del pasado en que representa a VMg^d las estorsiones que en cataluña se haçian contra lo capitulado en la çesaçion de Armas y lo que el Comisario frances hauia respondido en razon de las ordenes que tenia para ello. Y me manda VM^d que recombenga con ella al Car^{al}, disponiendo que embie orden a los Ministros de françia para que se contengan en los limites de la suspension, advirtiendome tambien VMg^d que en los capitulos della se preuiene que lo que se obrare contra lo ajustado se haya de restituir de parte a parte.

    En conformidad desta orden de VMg^d imbie luego a Don Antonio Pimentel â hablar al cardenal de mi parte sobre esta mat^{ria}, a que ha respondido lo que VM^d se seruira de mandar ver por la copia inclusa del papel que Don Antonio me ha escrito en razon dello, del qual he embiado otra copia con correo expreso al Marq͂ de Mortara para que se halle entendido de las ordenes que el Cardenal diçe embiaria luego a los ofiçiales de aquellas tropas para que se contengan dentro de los Limites que se deuen, que es quanto sobre esta materia se ofreçe de que dar quenta a VM^d, Cuya Catolica y R^l Persona g^{de} Dios como la christiandad ha menester. De fuenterrauia a 10 de Agosto 1659

Dluismendezdeharo

---

[52] Letter 15 arrived in Madrid on 15 August.

16

Haro to Philip IV: Fuenterrabía, 11 August 1659 [K1619: 27][53]

Heavy rain on Sunday, 10 August, interrupted work on the conference centre (see Letter 14 for special dispensation requested to undertake building work on this particular Sunday); Haro is keen to get the negotiations underway as soon as the conference room is completed but the French prefer to wait until the apartments are also finished; the French have raised the height of the roof on their side of the building and Haro has instructed his craftsmen to do the same.

Señor

En conformidad de lo que dixe a VMg^d antes de ayer, que se contaron 9 deste,[54] se ha ydo dando toda prisa por ambas partes a la Barraca a que asisten todo el dia con sus mismas personas el Baron de Bateuile [*sic*], Pimentel y leone, pero ayer fue tan grande y tan continua el agua que llouio todo el dia que no se pudo trauajar. Y siendo demas del aposento comun de la conferencia otros tres o quatro los que se fabrican de cada parte para que esté deuaxo de cubierto el sequito de la vna y de la otra y algunos otros apartamientos para el seruicio menor, no se han adelantado franceses tanto como hauian pensado, como ellos mismos lo reconocen. Entretanto se van pasando entre el Car^{al} y entre mi [*sic*] continuos oficios de cumplimiento, mostrandose reciprocamente de ambas partes lo que sentimos qualquiera hora de dilacion por lo que deseamos poder vernos con mayor breuedad. Pero con todo, aunque, por desear yo hacer mas clara la demostracion desto de mi parte, embie oy á proponer a Leone que, acauandose el lugar comun donde hauiamos de tener la conferencia, podriamos anticipar n^{ras} vistas, pues importaria poco que lo demas se fuese acauando despues, No ha salido â ello, diciendo que me asegure que el deseo del Car^{al} de verse conmigo no es inferior al que yo muestro de hacerlo pero que por vn dia de diferencia mas a menos no se puede ni deue, en tiempo de tanto calor, tener al descubierto a tantas personas principales como han de asistir de vna parte y otra. Pero aunque es esta la causa que ha dado, dicen algunos que la verdadera se funda en querer que se acauen todos los aposentos para tenerlos colgados con algunas de aquellas alajas grandes que tiene en Paris que ha traydo para este efecto,

---

[53] Letter 16 also reached Madrid on 15 August.
[54] Letter 14 above.

porq̃ dicen que gusta mucho de que las vean y destas apariencias exteriores y ello se hace harto probable porque, estando ya hechado todo el techo al aposento de la conferencia, el Ingeniero y los criados suyos que tienen por su quenta la obra me refieren que le volbieron a desarmar para darle dos tercias mas de altura y que preguntando los mios para que se hacia aquella mudanza, les respondieron que tenian orden del Car^{al} para ello para dar capacidad con esta may^r altura a que se pudiese colgar la tapiceria de las Sauinas que, segun lo que Pimentel me dice, deue de ser la de mayor estimaz^n que tiene. Y esta mudanza se hizo sin dar noticia al Baron de Vateuile ni a los Maestros que asisten por n^{ra} parte sino de hecho sin participacion de ninguno. Y quando me vinieron a dar quenta dello, ordenê que no le resistiesen ni disputasen sino que dijesen que tenian orden mia para executar todo lo que el Car^{al} ordenase. Y en esto, y en otras cosas deste genero que dexo de referir, se padece mas de lo que se puede encarecer, pero vase procurando tolerar todo por llegar a lo sustancial. La primera conferencia dicen que será pasado mañana Miercoles, que se contaran 13 deste, y que lo tendran acauado todo para entonces. Podrá ser que reciuamos mucho gusto en ver la tapiceria pero bien me parece que estaremos abrigados.

Hauiendo reconocido los poderes que se me han remitido, Juzgo que son vastantes para qualquiera cosa que se huuiere de tratar. G^{de} Dios la Catolica y R^l persona de VMg^d como la x^{pnd} ha menester. fuenterrauia a 11 de Agosto de 1659

Dluismendezdeharo

17

Haro to Philip IV: Fuenterrabía, 11 August 1659 [K1619: 29][55]

Haro acknowledges receipt of letters from the king in response to some of his own; he promises to follow the recommendations of the Council of State to the king on the matters on which he had sought guidance so long as the advice can be judged to be in the best interests of the king.

---

[55] Letters 15, 16 and 17 were dispatched on 12 August, arriving in Madrid on the fifteenth of the month. Haro's letter of 10 August which contains the important news that Mazarin has agreed to look into French abuses in Catalonia was thus held back for two days and sent with the two unimportant letters of 11 August.

Señor

He reçiuido las cartas de VM^d de los 7 deste en que se sirue VMg^d mandar responderme a las que yo hauia escrito a VM^d en 27 y 30 del pass^do sobre diferentes puntos.[56] Y siruiendose VMag^d de remitirme juntamente copia de la consulta que hauia hecho a VMg^d el consexo de estado de lo que se le ofreçia en razon dellos, se sirue VMag^d de ordenarme que me gouierne en todos segun lo que al pie del hecho juzgare por mas combeniente. Lo qual executarè assi con mucho deseo de açertar en todo con quanto fuere mas encaminado al mayor seruiçio de VMg^d Cuya Catholica y R^l Persona Guarde Dios como la christiandad ha menester. De fuenterrauia a 11 de Ag^to de 1659.

Dluismendezdeharo

18

Haro to Philip IV: Fuenterrabía, 11 August 1659 [K1623: 42][57]

More on England: Haro has heard that General Monk and the army under his command in Scotland have declared themselves for the king and that most of the country has reacted favourably to this move. He is suspicious of a report that the English king has already landed in England because Mazarin has informed Pimentel that the latest news from Flanders is that Charles received an urgent dispatch just as he was about to set sail for home, urging him to delay until he received a letter already on its way to him. Mazarin has at last confessed to Pimentel that he is discouraging the expedition and advising the king to make his way instead to the peace conference. This had always been Haro's suspicion, as he had intimated to Philip in his letter of 6 August (Letter 11 above). He would prefer the English king to go to England but recognises that this lies outside his control.

---

[56] I have been unable to locate the two letters dated 27 and 30 July referred to here.

[57] Letter 18 is yet another dispatched on 11 August and arriving in Madrid on the fifteenth of the month.

19

Haro to Philip IV: Fuenterrabía, 13 August 1659 [K1623: 43]

First interview between Haro and Mazarin. A French messenger had arrived late in the evening of 12 August with a request that the first interview be brought forward from 14 to 13 August. Haro had agreed. He arrived at the island at 11.30 a.m. only to find Mazarin waiting for him. Although the conference room had been completed in time for the interview, the apartments were still not ready. The interview lasted five hours and was almost entirely devoted to courtesies and questions about the two royal families. Whilst the carriages and lower orders remained on their respective river banks, the nobles crossed to the island and, contrary to what had been agreed, mingled freely. The heat of the day has been intense and Haro is too exhausted to write at length.[58]

20

Haro to Philip IV: Fuenterrabía, 14 August 1659 [K1623: 44]

Haro reports in detail on the proceedings of the conference of the previous day: he describes the conference room and the ceremony governing the entry of the two plenipotentiaries; Mazarin had enquired whether Haro had any news of the English king and also referred to Will Lockhart's embassy, reminding Haro that Pimentel had powers to listen to proposals from the Commonwealth; Haro had agreed to an audience with Lockhart; Mazarin had expressed approval of the decision of the Spanish king to release the Duke of Lorraine and, recognising that there was pressure to allow the duke to attend the conference, indicated that he would not oppose such a decision;

---

[58] In his letter of 15 August to the French king, Mazarin (1693: 40–41) reports that his first interview with Haro has been enough to convince him that Haro will find it very difficult to persuade him to agree to anything that is detrimental to France. Gualdo Priorato (1667: 140–43) describes the spectacular arrival of both parties at the island and the decor of the conference room. His account suggests that the French apartments at least were ready and he records that they were visited by some three hundred Spaniards in contravention of what had been agreed. He also records that the matter of Condé was raised in this meeting and that tempers flared, although all ended very civilly. Mazarin seemingly spoke Italian and Haro Spanish on this occasion (compare note 95).

all sorts of ministers and foreign envoys are following Mazarin to the border; Mazarin has excluded papal and Venetian representatives because he does not want *medianeros* (third parties) taking credit for the peace; after the conference, high-ranking subjects of both crowns met with Haro and Mazarin.

Señor

Anoche di quenta a VM^d con vnos breues renglones[59] de hauer tenido ayer el primer abocamiento con el Cardenal, que hauia durado la conferençia çinco horas pero que la mayor parte della se hauia pasado en cumplimientos y en otras materias q̃ no perteneçen a la sustançia del tratado. Y no hauiendo podido alargarme mas entonçes, assi por no retardar a VMg^d esta notiçia como por hauer buelto muy fatigado del calor que fue grande, me ha pareçido despachar aora este segundo correo para informar a VM^d con vn poco de mas particularidad assi de algunas çircunstançias en quanto a la forma de las vistas como de algunas otras cosas que se tocaron al fin de la conferençia sobre particulares de Inglaterra y del Duque de Lorena.

El Aposento de la conferençia era quadrado y estaua colgado a medias; y la misma diuision hauia en el suelo porque el medio Aposento que tocaua al cardenal estaua con alombras y la otra mitad que me perteneçia a mi con esteras conforme a n^{ra} costumbre en estos t^{pos} de Verano. A nuestra primera vista no estubo en el Aposento ninguna Persona porque nos detuuimos (tanto el como yo) en vn callexon a modo de Galeria que ay antes de entrar en el y, hauiendose puesto en las dos Puertas Lione en la vna y Pimentel en la otra y auisadose el vno al otro de como ya estauamos alli, entramos ambos en el Aposento, cada vno por su puerta que estauan la vna enfrente de la otra, sin que huuiese ninguna otra Persona en el; y nos venimos buscando cada vno al confin de su medio aposento que estaua diuidido con la linea de las alombras y las esteras y, en hauiendonos hablado, nos sentamos en las sillas que estauan en el mismo sitio y despues de la conferençia nos combenimos en que entrasen las Personas mas particulares q̃ venian con ambos para que reçiprocamente nos llegasen a ver y nos las diesemos a conoçer el vno al otro.

La conferençia (como tengo dicho a VMag^d) durò çinco horas. La primera parte fue toda de cumplimientos en que tube bien a que satisfaçer porque se alargo tanto en faboreçerme y con palabras de tanto encareçimiento que, avnque es lenguaxe que yo debo debo [*sic*] de sauer menos bien, procurè en esta parte no quedar inferior. De aqui se passò â

---

[59] Letter 19 above.

hablar de VMag^d, de la Reyna n^{ra} señora y de todas Sus Altezas y, por consequençia, del Rey y Rey^a xpt.^{ma} y Duque de Anxù,[60] en sus naturales y condiçiones, en las enfermedades de la Reyna n^{ra} señora, en sus sobrepartos, y en la que hauia tenido el Rey xp.^{mo} en cales el año pasado.[61] Y de aqui desçendio a preguntarme por mis hijos y por mis hijas y yo, por consequençia, por sus sobrinas y sus maridos y à hablar en otras cosas deste genero y de las costumbres y estilos de ambos Reynos sin que se introduxese cossa que fuese de mas consideraçion. Pero a lo vltimo por resumen de todo el discurso y hauiendose hablado de ambas partes en terminos de querer despedirnos, hauiendo ya asentado que la seg^{da} conferençia se tuuiese el sabado por dexar desembarazado el dia de Nuestra Señora, Me pregunto si hauia tenido algunas nueuas del Rey de Inglaterra. Respondile que del Marq̄ de Caraçena hauia reçiuido la noche anteçedente vna carta en que me deçia que, estando ya para ejecutar su jornada, le hauia llegado vna Persona embiada de sus confidentes, estimandole la resoluçion que hauia tomado en ir à asistirlos pero que se detuuiese hasta reçiuir segundo aviso dellos y que se hallase prompto para ejecutarlo entonçes, cuya carta remito a VMg^d inclusa aqui. Respondiome el cardenal que el hauia tenido las mismas nueuas porque de parte del Rey se lo hauian avisado assi. Y sin hablar mas palabra en el particular del Rey, pasò a deçir que Locart hauia llegado embiado por embaxador ex.^{rio} por la nueua Republica de Inglaterra çerca de la Persona del Rey xpt.^{mo} para que asistiese en este congreso, que traia poder para tratar conmigo, mostrando deseo de paçificarse con VMg^d y que le hauia pedido que me propusiese que deseaua que le diese avdiençia. Y sin esperar mi respuesta, continuò en deçir q̄ si huuiera reconoçido alguna dificultad en ello, no se huuiera encargado de deçirmelo pero que, viendo que no la podia hauer y que esta nueba Republica introduçida en Inglaterra no hauia roto la Guerra a VM^d ni despues de buelto a restableçer este Gouierno hauia hecho ningun acto de hostilidad contra VM^d y que D. Antonio Pimentel tenia poder para oir lo que se le propusiese de parte del Protector,[62] lo hauia admitido. Yo le respondi que todo era Verdad y

---

[60] An almost phonetic representation of *Anjou*. The Duke of Anjou at this time was Louis's younger brother, Philip of France.

[61] This is a reference to the serious illness which threatened Louis's life in June 1658 while on campaign in Calais and which persuaded Mazarin and the French queen of the need to arrange a marriage speedily in order to secure an heir to the French throne.

[62] Richard Cromwell served as Protector of England from the time of his father's death in 1658 until he was deposed by the army in 1659.

que VMg^d tampoco hauia declarado la Guerra ni tenidola con la Republica sino con el Protector pasado, obligado de la neçesidad y de la reputaçion y probocado con vn atentado tan injusto como el de hauer (debaxo de buena fee) acometido los dominios de VMag^d en las Indias y con vna Armada tan poderosa como lo hizo.[63] Interrumpiome aqui y me dixo que pues hauia llegado accidentalmente la ocasion de hablar en esto, no queria remitir para otra el deçirme que la accion que VM^d hauia hecho en declarar la Guerra al Protector en aquella coyuntura hauia sido digna de vn tan gran Rey y de tener vn gran aplauso en todo el mundo por todas las razones que yo en pocas palabras hauia dado â entender. Finalmente, Señor, por no alargar discursos ni cartas con cosas que no haçen preçisamente a la suma de los negoçios, viendo yo que el consexo de estado en consulta de los 7 deste, de que VMag^d se siruio de mandarme remitir copia y ordenarme que sobre este punto y los demas que se contienen en ella tome sobre el hecho las resoluçiones que juzgare por mas combenientes, propone a VM^d que sera bien que yo oyga â este embaxador la primera vez, y no ofreçiendoseme a mi tampoco razon para escusarlo, porq̃ el no querer oirle seria ponerle en vna gran desconfianza, y considerando tambien que esta nueua Republica ni estubo en Guerra con VM^d en el prinçipio ni ha hecho ningun acto de hostilidad contra los dominios de VM^d despues que se ha comenzado a boluer a estableçer y no pudiendo sauerse tampoco a lo que al cabo podrà obligarnos la neçesidad, Respondi al Cardenal que le daria la avdiençia. Y quando la tenga, procurarè gouernarme en tal forma que, sin entrar en ningun empeño con el ni desconfiarle, se vaya ganando tiempo para que el mismo estado que fueren tomando las cosas de aquel Reyno nos pueda mostrar mas a la clara la resoluçion que se deue tomar. Bien reconozco la dificultad que tiene el no poner en desconfianza a la republica con la protecçion que VM^d hiçiere a los intereses del Rey y, por consequençia, el no dar çelos al Rey en lo aparente con oir â este embaxador. Pero en medio destas dificultades, comoquiera que la materia se halla todavia tan confussa, no veo que se pueda tomar otro partido que el procurar ir caminando por vn termino medio hasta que el tiempo nos diga lo demas y hasta ver lo que el cardenal me propone en razon desta materia, con el qual procurarè irme tambien gouernando con esta misma reserba.

---

[63] The English Commonwealth conducted a vigorous naval campaign in the Spanish main in the mid 1650s. In 1655, Admirals Penn and Venables captured Jamaica. However, British sovereignty over the island was not recognised until the treaty of Madrid in 1670.

De aqui pasò â hablar en la libertad del Duque de Lorena, aprobando la resoluçion que VMg^d hauia tomado de darsela en esta coyuntura. Preguntome si se me haçia instançia de parte de la Duquesa de orleans[64] y del mismo Duque para poder venir â asistir personalmente en este congreso. Dijele que si y que la misma instançia haçian a VM^d allà, hauiendo pasado â esa corte â esforzarla el Baron de la Sose[65] y vnos frayles capuchinos que me hauian traydo carta de la Duquesa, pero que VM^d no hauia tomado todavia resoluçion sobre este punto, hauiendome pareçido deçirselo assi por ver si podia tomar alguna señal de si esto le seria desagradable. Pero luego al punto se declarò aviertamente, diçiendo que a el le apretauan sobre esto mismo de parte del Duque fran^{co}[66] y de la Duquesa de orleans y que si VMag^d juzgase por combeniente el dar al Duque y a sus parientes esta satisfaçion, por lo que tocaua â el no se le ofreçia ninguna dificultad. De que me ha pareçido dar quenta a VMag^d para que VMg^d se halle con notiçia dello.

En la consulta çitada del consexo de los 7 deste con ocasion de hablar del embax^{or} Locart, repara el consexo en que el Rey x^{ptmo} le haya permitido la concurrençia en este congreso, hauiendo negado esta permision, taçita ô expresamente, a los Ministros del Papa, a los del emp^{or} y a los de todos los demas Reyes, Republicas y Prinçipes Catholicos; por cuya causa debo representar a VM^d y poner en su real notiçia que la intençion del cardenal en esto creo que haya sido el negarla solo a los medianeros, como son el Papa y Veneçianos, para que ni el mundo ni ellos puedan atribuirse el hauer tenido ninguna parte en esta gran obra;[67] pero que esta proiuiçion no pareçe que ha alcanzado a los demas porque a vna sola jornada detras del car^{al} han venido los Ministros de Saboya, de Florençia, de Genoua,

---

[64] The Duchess of Orleans is Marguerite of Lorraine, known as *Madame*.
[65] The *Baron de la Sose* is the Sieur de la Chaussée. He had been sent to Madrid by the Duchess of Orleans to request the release of the Duke of Lorraine from prison in Toledo.
[66] The duke's brother, François, also mentioned in Letter 70.
[67] In his letter of 19 August to Le Tellier, Mazarin (1690: 65) reports that it is Haro who does not wish to credit the Pope (Alexander VII) with any part in the peace. The suggestion that only the French king and the Spanish king should be included in the preamble to the treaty, he says, is entirely Haro's. Although it is difficult to determine where the truth lies in this instance, it is probably worth noting that Mazarin's relationship with the Pope was less than cordial and had been so since the latter had acted as nuncio at the peace conference in Münster (see Priorato 1667: 123–24).

de Parma, y de Mantua; y el Nunçio[68] he entendido aora que viene con la Persona del Rey y de la Reyna que (segun lo que el cardenal me dixo ayer) habran entrado hoy en Burdeos.

Hauiendome pareçido embiar esta mañana a pasar vn cumplimiento con el Cardenal para sauer como hauia llegado ayer, ordene â Don Antonio Pimentel que despachase vn correo a Lione en esta conformidad, el qual le responde la carta inclusa que remito a VM^d aqui. Y en todos los demas actos de cortesia, procurarè ir cultibando la buena inteligençia con el en quanto fuere de mi parte, deseando açertar en todo con lo que puede ser mas encaminado al seruiçio de VMg^d Cuya Catholica y R^l Persona g^{de} Dios como la christiandad ha menester. De fuenterrauia a 14 de Ag^{to} de 1659

Dluismendezdeharo

21

Haro to Philip IV: Fuenterrabía, 17 August 1659 [K1623: 47][69]

Haro summarises his second interview with Mazarin held on Saturday, 16 August, and lasting five and a half hours:[70] Mazarin arrived with the Archbishops of Toulouse and Lyons and two bishops; the clergy were introduced to Haro, exchanged pleasanteries and then left. Mazarin did all of the talking, focusing mainly on himself and his reputation. He particularly lamented that he had been the object of calumny and emphasised the sincerity of his desire for peace. He talked about the royal families, Rome

---

[68] The Nuncio referred to here is Celio Piccolomini, Archbishop of Caesarea. Appointed on 27 October 1656, Piccolomini served as papal legate to France until 12 January 1662. He became a cardinal on 14 January 1664 and died in 1681. For detailed information on papal legates to France during this period, see Bluche *et al.* 1990: 843–44.

[69] This letter was dispatched on 18 August. The dispatch cost 734, rather than 650, *reales de plata* because the courier was allowed to change horses more frequently than was usual ('por hauersele mandado dar medio cauallo de ventaxa'). AGS CMC 3551 (2), 15. Although, this particular letter seems to contain nothing that needed to be communicated urgently to Madrid, other letters in the same dispatch may have required haste.

[70] Gualdo Priorato (1667: 45–46) records that the interview lasted five hours.

and the Pope and, in so doing, gave Haro grounds to believe that he did not enjoy good relations with the latter. During their first interview, he had proposed that Lionne and one of Haro's secretaries should do much of the negotiating; he now suggested that they should be allowed to begin to prepare the preamble to the treaty. Haro pointed out that he had already consented to let Coloma and Lionne deal with some of the more general points of the treaty, as well as with what had been agreed at Münster. He further argued that he preferred to debate the *puntos reservados* (reserved matters) personally with Mazarin, on the grounds that he enjoyed his company and believed that together they would be able to reach agreement more quickly. Mazarin also raised during the interview the question of Spanish use of the *exclusiva* (their right of veto) to prevent Cardinal Sacchetti from becoming pope.[71] Haro concludes from all of this that the cardinal does not yet wish to discuss directly those matters specifically remitted to the peace conference. The next interview has been arranged for Tuesday, 19 August.

22

Haro to Philip IV: Fuenterrabía, 20 August 1659 [K1623: 49][72]

Haro repeats to the king what he has already said to Contreras[73] about pressure of time. He then gives his views on French intentions, together with a report on his third interview with Mazarin held on Tuesday, 19 August, and lasting six hours:[74] he believes that the French king and queen regent favour a marriage alliance with Spain and that, for this reason, they have sent a reluctant Mazarin to the frontier to negotiate. Mazarin, he suspects, would prefer a match with the House of Savoy and this may explain why he

---

[71] The cardinal referred to is Giulio Sacchetti (1587–1663), who belonged to a noble family originally from Florence. The right of veto was naturally of crucial importance, for by determining the result of a papal election, as Levin (1999: 12) reminds us, one could influence the course of history.

[72] Letter 22 arrived in Madrid on 24 August.

[73] For information on Contreras, see note 27 above.

[74] Gualdo Priorato (1667: 46ff) says of the third interview that 'le Cardinal y parla tousiours Espagnol'. On the command of languages of the two principals, see also notes 58 and 95.

seems unwilling to get down to business.⁷⁵ French general opinion at the conference is that peace is unlikely to be achieved, and Haro therefore warns that, notwithstanding Spain's earnest desire to end the war, the terms of the marriage agreement set by France may be impossible to accept. In this respect, he is not at all encouraged by Mazarin's insistence on evading discussion of the marriage despite the many openings that have been given to him to discuss it. The cardinal seems content merely to refer to the number of strongholds which France will return to Spain in exchange for the infanta. During this interview, Mazarin also introduced the question of compensation for the demolition of La Bassée and restoration of Bergues. Although neither of the plenipotentiaries had wanted to venture an amount, Mazarin had finally agreed to give the matter some thought before the next interview. Haro closes by reminding the king that Caracena has urged him to make every effort to retain Bergues. He fears, however, that the price fixed by Mazarin may well be too high.

23

*Haro to Philip IV: Fuenterrabía, 21 August 1659 [K1623: 51]*⁷⁶

Haro records that towards the end of the interview of 19 August Mazarin had expressed great dismay over the letter which Haro had written to

---

[75] Gualdo Priorato (1667: 22) indicates that Mazarin was delighted to receive Pimentel when the latter arrived in Lyons with news that Spain was finally willing to discuss peace with marriage, and Valfrey (1881: 57–60, 199) insists that the cardinal had been seeking a marriage alliance with Spain since 1646. The standard view among historians has thus been that the much publicised proposed marriage with Margaret of Savoy was merely a stratagem devised by Mazarin in order to put pressure on Spain to rethink its position on peace talks culminating in a marriage alliance. As is well known, the Madrid talks of 1656 had foundered not only on the rock of Condé but also on that of a dynastic alliance with France. Since then, however, a son had been born to Philip IV, and Mazarin may have seen his chance to exploit a proposed marriage with Savoy in order to achieve his original objective. On the other hand, Pimentel (AGS Estado Francia K1624: 6b) suggests that Mazarin favoured marriage with Savoy in order to prolong war with Spain, and Madame de Motteville (1824: 437–59) is equally clear that, whereas the French queen favoured marriage with Spain, the cardinal, out of personal interest, preferred Savoy. It seems, then, that Haro's assessment of Mazarin could well have merit.

[76] Letter 23 arrived in Madrid on 27 August.

Pimentel to inform him that the Count of Soissons was not thought to be a suitable candidate to request the hand of the infanta.[77] By way of explanation, Haro had acknowledged that as the son of a *primo hermano* (first cousin) of the Spanish king and the husband of one of Mazarin's nieces, there could be no more acceptable candidate; however, there remained the very real difficulty of the Spanish grandees, whose custom and practice in the matter of *tratamiento* (forms of address) were clear.[78] The problem was thus an insoluble one, especially since the importance of the embassy was such that it would be wholly inappropriate for the grandees not to pay the count a courtesy visit. Mazarin's response to this explanation had been at best rather tactless. According to him, the Princess of Carignano was convinced that the difficulty lay not with the grandees but with Haro, who, following the example of his uncle, the Count Duke of Olivares, did not wish to favour her by accepting her son.[79] Haro confesses that he was, of course, offended that the cardinal should have disclosed such sensitive information but assures the king that he managed to reply diplomatically. Mazarin had then proceeded to run through the list of potential candidates, only to discount them all for one reason or another and eventually propose the following: given that the Princess of Carignano would be displeased if her son were refused this honour and another were assigned in his stead, it had occurred to Mazarin that the French king should appoint him and that he should write to Philip expressing his delight in having been selected and should very publicly make the necessary preparations for the journey. Philip should then write saying that the cardinal was far too valuable to the French king to

---

[77] The Count of Soissons was Eugène of Savoy, son of the Princess of Carignano and Prince Thomas of Savoy. He was a great-great-grandson of Charles V and related to the French royal family through his mother. In his letter of 26 August to Turenne, Mazarin (1693: 72) notes that Haro has recommended that the person assigned to this embassy should bear at least the title of duke.

[78] Gualdo Priorato (1667: 157–61) notes that Soissons could not undertake this embassy because the Spanish nobility would not agree to address him as *alteza* (Highness).

[79] The Princess of Carignano visited Madrid in 1637. A number of things happened to upset her while she was there. The Count of Pozo, who was Milanese, a Spanish subject and gentleman-in-waiting of the princess, was involved in a quarrel with the Count of Salazar over appropriate forms of address and was even arrested; the English ambassador, Sir Walter Aston, refused to meet the princess for reasons of precedence, thereby giving the nobility of Madrid much to talk about; and the Duchess of Chevreuse, who arrived from London during this time, was apparently treated much more royally by the court than was the princess. It is likely that Olivares was seen to be behind the last of these. See Hume 1907: 311, 316–19, 329.

undertake such a mission and that it should therefore be abandoned. Haro's immediate assessment of the proposal was that it was a stratagem devised by Mazarin to dispense with the embassy and break with custom and practice, as well as with decorum. Accordingly, he had assured the cardinal that there could be no more suitable ambassador than he but that, since his appointment was not possible, anyone appointed by the French king would be acceptable. Mazarin had nevertheless insisted that the proposal be referred to Madrid and Haro now awaited the king's response.

24

Haro to Philip IV: Fuenterrabía, 24 August 1659 [K1623: 53]

About the naming of allies in the treaty: the Genoese want to be named before the Grand Duke of Florence even though precedent would seem to dictate otherwise. Mazarin has suggested a solution put forward by the Count of Brienne, Secretary of State for France, to the effect that a general clause should be inserted in the treaty stating that 'seran tenidos por Aliados de cada corona aquellos que presentaren despacho de VMag^d, ô del Rey christianisimo, declarandolos por tales' (all those shall be held to be allies of the respective crowns who present a warrant from Philip or from Louis declaring them to be such). Haro supports the proposal but would prefer it not to apply to the Pope, the emperor (Leopold I), the archdukes, the crowned princes and electors of the empire, who should all be named in the treaty. Those not named would request a certificate from the Spanish king which they would present to the French king and which would have the same force as if they had been named in the treaty. He requests guidance on this matter.

25

Haro to Philip IV: Fuenterrabía, 26 August 1659 [K1623: 55]

The fourth interview held on 22 August had lasted five hours and included a very vigorous debate about the renunciation by the Infanta María Teresa of all her rights as a potential successor to the Spanish throne.[80] The fifth

---

[80] Haro's main account of this interview is included in his letter of 23 August to the king. Unfortunately, I have been unable to trace this letter.

interview held on 24 August had again dealt with the renunciation, Mazarin finally agreeing to refer the matter to the French king and queen regent. The question of Juliers and the Duke of Neuburg had also been discussed.[81] Haro had refused to hand the stronghold over to the duke and this had provoked another protracted and heated exchange. In the end, Mazarin had agreed to refer this matter also to the French king and queen. Lionne had visited Haro earlier that day and had rather irritatingly gone over the same ground as if it had never been debated before. Because Juliers is considered to be a very important stronghold, Haro underlines the need to show Mazarin that Spain will not simply cave in to all French demands. Such a policy, however, means that the negotiations may last longer than expected. The French king has reached Bordeaux and the people take this to mean that he desperately wishes to marry the infanta. The practicalities of the marriage arrangements have still not been discussed and this seems likely to push back the *entrega* until the spring. Haro asks how he should proceed in the likely event that the French press for an early marriage. He proposes a possible strategy. Some discussion of Condé has already taken place and Haro has deduced from it that Mazarin bears the prince great ill will.

26

Haro to Philip IV: Fuenterrabía, 28 August 1659 [K1623: 56]

Haro summarises the content of his letters to the king of 23 and 26 August (see Letter 25 above and note 80) and reports on the sixth interview held on 27 August and lasting between six and seven hours. Mazarin had reported that France was prepared to give way on the matter of the renunciation so long as the infanta did not renounce her claim to the Low Countries. Haro had insisted that France would have to back down on this if the marriage was to go ahead and Mazarin had responded by moving on very quickly to the question of the dowry. In view of inflation and of the strongholds to be restored to Spain, he had demanded a dowry of two million *escudos*. Haro had referred to the agreement reached by the cardinal and Pimentel in Lyons that the dowry should consist of the strongholds which Spain gave to France. All that now remained was for the two plenipotentiaries to decide which these should be. Mazarin had accepted that this had been the

---

[81] Juliers is Jülich, a fortress situated about twenty-five miles west of Cologne. The Duke of Neuburg at this time was Philip William, one of France's staunchest allies in the Rhenish League.

agreement but stressed that it rested on the assumption that France would retain all the strongholds it had captured from Spain. Haro has to confess to the king that Mazarin is right in what he says but hopes to report soon that he has managed to reduce the dowry to 500,000 *escudos*. The matter of Juliers had been raised again, with Mazarin declaring that the French king and queen regent could not budge on this because they had already promised the stronghold to the Duke of Neuburg. As a way forward, he had offered to exchange it for something else but Haro refused, arguing that Juliers controlled the only pass from Germany to Flanders and was therefore too important. Haro shares his suspicion that the French have not really promised Juliers to the duke but that they intend to keep it for themselves, rewarding the duke in some other way.[82] By retaining it for themselves, they would cut Spain's only line of communication with Germany and Holland. Condé had once more been discussed at length and Haro promises that he will report on this discussion in a later dispatch (see Letter 29 below). During this interview, 'se disputaron todos los puntos mas esenciales deste tratado' (all the most essential points of this treaty were debated). It had rained heavily during the conference.

27

Haro to Philip IV: Fuenterrabía, 30 August 1659 [K1623: 61][83]

Haro summarises his letter to the king of 28 August (Letter 26 above) and gives an account of his seventh interview with Mazarin which has just concluded. It has been raining all day long. The marriage agreement has been finalised following the pattern of that of Anne of Austria and Louis XIII and that of Philip IV and Isabella of France. The dowry has been fixed at 500,000 *escudos* and the text of the document will be drafted by Coloma, Joseph González and Francisco Ramos on behalf of Spain and by Lionne

---

[82] Spanish opinion on the strategic importance of Juliers does not appear to be wholly consistent. See, for example, Letter 27, which suggests that the French may well intend to give it to the duke. See also the letter which Mazarin (1690: 167) sent to Lionne on 26 August, in which he instructs the latter to suggest to Coloma that the French king is prepared to give way on Juliers but that, in the matter of Lorraine, he will countenance no change to what has been agreed in Paris.

[83] Letter 27 reached Madrid on 3 September.

and his team of experts on behalf of France.[84] Haro summarises the progress of the negotiations and encloses a paper prepared by Coloma which lists precisely what has been agreed so far. Juliers continues to be a sticking point; Haro is convinced that the French are determined to get a better deal for their allies than Spain gets for hers. Philip must be no less staunch in his defence of Condé than is Louis in defence of the Duke of Neuburg's interests. Discussion of the article relating to the Duke of Lorraine awaits the arrival at the border of the duke's representative, who is reported to have reached Bayonne the previous evening. Condé has been discussed positively in the last two interviews and Haro will report on the discussions in a subsequent letter.

28

Haro to Philip IV: Fuenterrabía, 30 August 1659 [K1623: 62][85]

The French want the marriage to take place as soon as possible, preferably by early October. Haro has pointed out the difficulties, which include the need to secure dispensation from Rome and for an ambassador to travel to Madrid to request formally the infanta's hand. Mazarin is of the view that an ambassador travelling 'por la posta' (post haste) could get to Madrid and back in less than the twenty days or so that it would take to secure papal dispensation from Rome but Haro has maintained that the preparations for the wedding mean that the infanta could not possibly embark on her twenty-five- to thirty-day journey to the border until November, by which time the

---

[84] In his letter of 30 August to Le Tellier, Mazarin (1690: 218–29) reports in detail on his talks with Haro concerning the marriage. He mentions how he cleverly secured the dowry, discusses those who will witness the public reading of the agreement and explains that there will be two copies of the agreement, one in which the Spanish witnesses will sign first and another in which the French will sign first. Haro and Pimentel have seemingly indicated that the delay in the marriage is largely due to the difficulty in getting livery for the three companies of guards (Burgundians, Spaniards and Germans) who will attend the ceremony. Furthermore, many of the Spanish higher nobility have been compelled to order their attire from Naples and Milan. None of this is recorded in the Spanish sources I have been able to consult. Finally, we learn from Mazarin that the Duke of Gramont, who has been appointed to undertake the embassy to Madrid to request the infanta's hand, speaks good Spanish.

[85] Letter 28 arrived in Madrid on 3 September.

mountain passes will be blocked with snow. He has therefore suggested March as a more realistic date. Unfortunately, Mazarin refuses to move on this and is pressing for an arrival at the border somewhere between 25 and 30 November.[86] Haro reminds the king that the treaty is not yet fully agreed and that the marriage cannot go ahead until all of the articles are finalised and the treaty has been signed. He cannot in all conscience advise the king to accept Mazarin's proposal because 'el casamiento es el que hace la Paz y la prenda que tenemos para ella' (it is the marriage that makes the Peace and is the gage we hold for it). Once the infanta is in St Jean de Luz, there is nothing to prevent the French from going back on their word.

Señor

Hauiendo quedado combenidos en la conferencia desta tarde todos los puntos pertenecientes al casam^{to} de que doy quenta a VMg^d mas distintamente en despacho aparte,[87] ha llegado el caso que yo temia de que ajustandose primero esto que todos los demas Articulos de la Paz, me hiciesen vna grande instancia para que el casamiento se executase luego, sobre que me ha apretado mucho el Cardenal esta tarde, pretendiendo que se puede abreuiar de manera que la s^a Infante[88] se halle aqui en todo el mes de octubre. Yo combine con el en que VMg^d tenia este mismo deseo de la breu^d pero representandole Juntamente todas las dificultades o, por mejor decir, imposibilidades que en esto podia hauer. Comenzé por las primeras de no hauerse embiado todavia a pedir la dispensacion ni hauer ydo el embaxador del Rey xptianisimo a esa corte a pedir â la s^a Infanta con aquellas solemnidades que se acostumbran. A esto satisfizo luego, diciendo que, despachando de aqui vn correo yente y viniente, podia estar de buelta en veinte dias con la dispensacion y que en quanto â la embaxada, no hauiendo tiempo para hacer todas las preuenciones que fueran necesarias mas de proposito, ya que yo dificultaua la yda del

---

[86] One of the arguments Haro employs to resist Mazarin's demand that the Infanta should be delivered to the border by late November is that snow will by then have blocked the mountain passes. As a point of comparison, it may be of interest to note that when Anne of Austria and Isabella of France married the future Louis XIII and Philip IV respectively in 1615, they crossed the Bidasoa on 9 November. See BNP Mss Français 11191, fol. 71r.

[87] Letter 27 above.

[88] The masculine or neutral *infante* is used interchangeably in the documents with the feminine *infanta*. Subsequent irregularities in the transcriptions are as found in the manuscripts.

conde de Suason[89] embiarian vn sugeto de grados y en quien concurriese la calidad de ser Duque y Par de francia por la Posta para que pudiese llegar á hacer la demanda y, con la respuesta de VMg^d, boluer tambien por la Posta sin detenerse en Madrid vna hora mas de lo que VMg^d tardase en responder por la impaciencia con que el Rey Christianisimo esperaria la nueba de que VMg^d le hubiese hecho fauor de darle por muger a la s^a Infanta. Y que presupuesto que este embaxador no hauia de ajustar alla las condiciones y capitulaciones del casamiento como lo hicieron los Duques de Vmena y de Pastrana[90] reciprocamente en ambas cortes, porque este ajustamiento corria ahora entre el Cardenal y entre mi en esta frontera, le parecia que este modo de embaxada de yr y venir por la Posta, sin detenerse en Madrid mas que tres dias en todo, seria mucho mas a proposito para el caso presente y de menos embarazo para ellos y para VMg^d y que esto tambien Juzgaua que podria executarse dentro de los Veinte dias en que hauia de venir la dispensacion.

Visto que hauia salido a satisfacer â estas primeras dificultades en esta forma, pasé á representarle las del tiempo, diciendole que por muy aprisa que el correo que yo despachase llegase á Madrid, serian los quatro ó cinco de sep^{re}; que las preuenciones que (sin quererlas estender á ostentacion) serian precisamente necesarias para satisfacer muy limitadamente al decoro (aunque se quisiesen dispensar mucho) no seria facil ni quiza posible hacerlas en dos meses y que quando bien se pudiesen hau^r hecho en este termino, comenzaria a caminar la s^a Infanta por Nouiembre y que precisamente habria menester gastar en el camino de veinte y cinco á treinta dias; que le suplicaua considerase como seria tratable ni

---

[89] *Suason*: i.e. Soissons.

[90] This is another reference to the negotiations preceding the marriages of the future Philip IV to Isabella of France and of the future Louis XIII to Anne of Austria. Although the negotiations were conducted in 1612, the marriages did not take place until 1615 because of the ages of the participants. The Duke of Pastrana signed the marriage contract on behalf of Spain and the Duke of Mayenne on behalf of France. This being so, how then might one explain what is clearly recorded in the Spanish text as *Vmena*? One possible answer is that *Vmena* is simply a corruption of the French *Duc du Maine*. However, although the *Contes du Maine* go back a long way in history and, on one occasion, even add to this title that of *Baron de Mayenne*, the first *Duc du Maine* appears to be the second son of Louis XIV, Louis Auguste (1670–1736). It is possible that Haro confused *Maine* and *Mayenne* (sometimes spelt *Maienne*). Alternatively, the error in the name could simply be a false recollection or result from a misreading of a written record.

conueniente que S.A. viniese caminando por tierras tan asperas y frias por Diziembre quando quiza seria posible que se le cerrasen los Puertos de Niebe, como sucedia de ordinario en aquel tiempo por muchos dias, demas de lo que se podia aventurar su salud en ello; y que presupuesto que esto no podria executarse por la misma imposibilidad del tiempo hasta Diz^{re} o henero, la diferencia que hauia hasta el mes de Marzo era de dos meses y que entonces comenzaua á entrar ya la Primavera y se podria executar con mayor comodidad y seguridad de la salud de la s^{ra} Infanta. No quiso combenir con ninguna destas representaciones mias sino persistir y porfiar en que si se daua prisa y se procuraba escusar de muchas cosas que se podian dispensar (porque la s^{ra} Infanta trahia la grandeza consigo misma) podia salir de Madrid a principio [sic] de Octubre y hallarse a los 25 ó treinta de Nouiembre en esta frontera.[91] Y como si el andar por semejante tiempo por estos caminos y montañas de Guipuzcoa fuera muy facil y muy posible, persistio en ello, pidiendome que yo despachase luego correo a VMg^d en esta conformidad, procurando facilitarlo de mi parte porque no podia hacer al Rey y a la Reyna xptianisima gusto mayor. Con que hauiendole yo representado todas las dificultades ó, por mejor decir, imposibilidades que en esto se me ofrecian, no pude dejar de encargarme de escriuirlo a VMg^d, como ahora lo hago.

Señor: las dificultades que por razon del tiempo y de las preuenciones que seran necesarias se ofreceran en esto, demas de la imposibilidad y riesgo de andar la s^{ra} Infanta por Nou^{re} y Diz^{re} por estos caminos, las conozco yo. Pero aunq todas ellas sean tan grandes, cumpliendo con la obligacion que tengo al seru^o de VMg^d como deuo, no puedo dejar de decir a VMg^d que considero yo sobre esta materia avn otras mucho mayores, porque no estando todavia ajustados todos los Articulos de la Paz y estandose persistiendo de su parte en que dejemos a Juliers tan obstinadamente, como refiero a VMg^d en otro despacho,[92] y temiendo yo que por la recompensa de Bergas (sin la qual dice el Marques de Carazena que de ninguna manera podemos quedar y todos lo entienden de la misma manera) me ayan de pedir alguna de las Plazas mas capitales del Pays vajo y siendo tan necesario resistir estos puntos como tan perjudiciales, yo no sé, aunque todos los del casam^{to} esten ajustados, como se podria pasar a la total execucion del sin estar combenidos en todos los de la Paz. Y quando bien estos vltimos lo estubiesen y nosotros

---

[91] It is worth noting, by way of comparison, that Haro and his train took just two weeks to get from Madrid to the border.

[92] Letter 27 above.

de acuerdo en todos y firmada la Paz, yo no me atreuiera á aconsejar a VMg^d que hasta que este executada en todo y entregadas con efecto las Plazas que se restituyen a VMg^d por este tratado, permita VMg^d que la s^{ra} Infanta salga de españa. Porque el casam^{to} es el que hace la Paz y la prenda que tenemos para ella y si se ven con S.A. en San Juan de Luz, yo no me atreuiera á asegurar a VMg^d, segun todo quanto he podido reconocer deste Gouierno, que haya de tener cumplimiento lo demas ni creo que prudentemente pueda nadie aconsejarlo a VMg^d, lo qual he Juzgado por de obligacion mia representar a VMg^d como lo entiendo, Juntamente con lo demas que el Car^{al} me ha pedido para que, teniendolo VMg^d todo presente, pueda VMg^d seruirse de ordenarme la forma en que le deuo responder y gouernarme sobre este punto. G^{de} Dios la Catolica y R^l persona de VMg^d como la xpt^d ha men^r. fuenterrabia a 30 de Agosto de 1659

Dluismendezdeharo

29

Haro to Philip IV: Fuenterrabía, 31 August 1659 [K1623: 65][93]

Haro continues the account of his interview with Mazarin on Wednesday, 27 August, and, as promised in his letter of 28 August (Letter 26 above), reports on the debate over Condé. Mazarin had delighted in reading aloud to Haro extracts from letters which he had supposedly received from the French king and queen regent. Haro expresses some doubt over the authenticity of these letters, arguing that the language used in them could not possibly be that of the young French king. The letters make abundantly clear the antipathy which Anne of Austria and Louis feel towards Condé and are intended to make Haro think that Mazarin has very little room for manoeuvre on this issue. Haro summarises the discussion which he and the cardinal had over a suitable settlement for the prince and explains how he had read aloud a portion of one of Pimentel's letters relating to Condé and the powerful effect which this had on Mazarin.

---

[93] Letter 29 was dispatched on 1 September.

Señor

Avnque en las conferençias anteçedentes destos dias con el cardenal se hauia ydo hablando algo sobre el particular del Prinçipe de condé, y Leone hauia hecho lo mismo algunas de las vezes que ha venido embiado por el a mi possada, No hauia hablado a VMg^d sobre esta materia hasta poder formar juiçio con vn poco de mas fundamento sobre ella. Pero hauiendo en la vltima que se tubo el Miercoles habladose mas de dos horas positiuamente en este punto, me pareçe que ya deuo dar quenta a VM^d de lo que hasta aora se ofreçe sobre el.[94]

Antes de llegar â haçerlo, me pareçe que deuo deçir a VMag^d que lo primero que el Car^{al} ha hecho cassi en todas las conferençias que hemos tenido ha sido sacar dos o tres cartas del Rey y otras tantas de la Reyna, todas de su mano y algunas muy largas, y, diçiendome que reçiue cada dia dos correos de Burdeos, se ha puesto a leermelas muy de proposito con pretexto de la gran confianza que haçe de mi y de la amistad que desea profesar conmigo, en que se ha gastado algunas veçes vna hora sin que esta perdida de tiempo inutilmente la haya podido yo remediar.[95] Los fines que ha tenido y tiene en mostrarme estas cartas juzgo que han sido dos: El vno que yo reconozca los grandes fabores que el Rey y la Reyna le haçen, que todas vienen muy llenas dellos; y El segundo para que yo vea lo que le escriben sobre el particular del Prinçipe, porque en todas le diçen que mire lo que haçe porque yo es çierto que tengo de defender este punto con vna gran fuerça, anteponiendole a todos los demas, y que de ninguna manera se dexe vençer de mi, pues ha traydo entendida la intençion de ambos sobre el, y que no se fie de lo que yo le asegurare de la amistad del Prinçipe con su Persona ni se dexe engañar

---

[94] There had been another interview since the one referred to, namely that of Saturday, 30 August. Perhaps Haro had started drafting this letter before the Saturday conference. If so, he would naturally have referred to the Wednesday conference as the last one.

[95] It is well known that, in addition to Latin, Italian and French, Mazarin had a good working knowledge of Spanish. He even appears to have used them all, with the exception of Latin, at different times in his discussions with Haro (compare notes 58 and 74). What is less clear is the kind of linguistic expertise possessed by the Spanish plenipotentiary. This letter suggests that he at least understood French when it was read aloud to him, while information recorded in note 58 implies that he also understood Italian.

de mi sobre ello porque de la amistad del Prinçipe no puede esperar mas de lo que ha experimentado hasta aqui.⁹⁶

Todas estas cartas se reconoçe manifiestamente que son dispuestas por el cardenal y embiadas en minuta para que vengan en esta conformidad porque demas de que lo da a conoçer assi todo el contenido dellas, en las del Rey hay muchas clausulas que, por la sustançia dellas y por los terminos por donde se explica y algunas otras çircunstançias, se haçe mucho mas manifiesto que en sus años no pueden ser suyas. Y para haçerme creer el cardenal todo lo contrario, acostumbra, quando las va leyendo, pasar quatro ô çinco renglones mal pronunçiados y, en otras partes, capitulos enteros sin leerlos, como queriendo dar â entender que son sobre materias mas reserbadas que no se me pueden partiçipar, pretendiendo con esto darme mejor â entender que son aquellas cartas las intrinsicas [sic] de la confidençia, vsando para ello de estas y de otras muchas aparienças semejantes en las quales no es el mayor trabaxo el oirlas sino el hauer de dar â entender que todas se creen (como yo lo hago), ponderandole mucho el gran fauor que el Rey y la Reyna le haçen y quan justamente le mereçe; Añadiendo en esta razon otras cosas contra lo mismo que se entiende, lenguaxe que yo no sauia hasta aora pero que creo le tengo de llebar bien aprendido de aqui. Y en quanto al particular del Prinçipe (que viene a ser el fin prinçipal por que se representa toda esta comedia) le he respondido siempre en la misma consequençia, mostrando conoçer por aquellas cartas el disgusto que el Rey y Reyna christianisima [sic] deuen de tener con su Persona, conque serà mas lo que se le venga a deuer a el solo en procurar mitigar su disgusto y interponer sus ofiçios con las veras que lo dava â entender para que, por medio de la interçesion de VM^d, pudiesen quedar sus intereses y su Persona en aquella forma que fuese bastante para que, sin seguirse perjuiçio al Rey christianisimo ni a la seguridad de su estado, VMag^d pudiese cumplir con su real obligaçion, que es solo lo que yo pretendia sin estenderme a otro ningun fin.

Hauiendo de llegar ha hablar en lo que ha passado formalmente en el negoçio me seria muy dificultoso el poderlo referir a VMag^d por menor sin gastar mucho tiempo y mucho papel, y assi habrè de reduçirme solo a lo mas sustançial. Segun todo quanto he podido reconoçer, juzgo que

---

[96] Haro's assessement of Mazarin's strategy is perfectly sound. In a letter to Le Tellier dated 28 August, a rather undiscerning Mazarin (1690: 175) reports that the strategy has been a great success and allowed him to put a great deal of pressure on Haro.

el Cardenal tiene muy mala volunt^d al Prinçipe y entiendo juntamente que no es menor que la mala volunt^d el miedo que le tiene (avnque pone gran esfuerzo en dar â entender lo contrario en lo vno y en lo otro). Juzgo que deue de estar harto dudoso en si, para la quietud posterior de la Françia y seguridad propia suya, quedarà mexor el Prin^e dentro ô fuera del Reyno. Pero entre estas dos cosas, segun todo quanto yo puedo alcanzar, creo que holgaria mas que quedase dentro de françia, ajustandose â admitir solo aquella pequeña satisfaçion que le quieren dar, engañandole con las esperanzas de que a pocos dias que haya procurado mereçer la graçia del Rey le restableçeran en lo demas y que, debaxo desta seguridad, se ponga en sus manos sin mas resguardo que el destas buenas palabras. Lo qual entienden todos estos françeses de primera condiçion que han venido aqui que el Prinçipe no lo puede haçer sin gran riesgo suyo si no es dandole algun Gouierno ô Plazas para su seguridad y escusando por aora el meter su Persona en Paris hasta que el tiempo le baya mostrando lo que deue haçer. Y yo, por muchas razones (que por no alargar este despacho dexo de referir), entiendo lo mismo que ellos.

En el primer ingreso del negoçio, pretendio el car^al impedirme el entrar â hablar en el, diçiendome (como siempre se presupuso) que sobre vna cosa ratificada ya por VMag^d no se deuia boluer ha hablar puesto que, si a VMag^d le hauia pareçido que no se deuia consentir en lo que D^n Antonio hauia firmado sobre este punto, pudiera VMag^d hauer dexado de haçer la ratificaçion sin faltar a la fee de la Plenipotençia que D^n Antonio hauia tenido porque mientras no se haçian las ratificaçiones en semejantes tratados, nada estaua hecho. Y hauiendo podido yo luego reconoçer por estas palabras que se encaminaua a disculpar a Don Antonio, me serui despues deste indiçio en todo el discurso del negoçio en la forma que juzgue que podia combenir. Respondile que yo no trataua de disputar sobre lo que ya estaua ratificado sino solo de que viesemos quales eran aquellas recompensas que podian ser sospechosas para la françia puesto que, en todas aquellas que no tuuiesen esta calidad, VMag^d estaua en libertad de poder dar al Prinçipe todas las que fuesen de su real Volunt^d. Respondiome que le dixese yo quales eran las que se le pretendian dar para que el pudiese deçirme lo que se le ofreçia sobre ello. No me pareçio combeniente el explicallas (por las razones que dirè adelante) y assi le dixe que pareçia que no era menester que yo perdiese t^po en esto sino que el me dixese de que calidad eran aquellas que el juzgaua que podian ser sospechosas para que yo no entrase a proponerselas. Boluio a pretender que yo declarase quales eran las que le queriamos dar pero, escusandome absolutamente de haçerlo con las razones que dejo referidas, dixo que las recompensas que serian sospechosas eran todo genero de Gouiernos Y Plazas en souerania. Respondile que VM^d hauia ofreçido al Prinçipe el Gouierno de flandes ô el Vicariato de Italia, segun lo que entre estas dos cosas elijiese; que con Callet me hauia embiado a deçir quando yo llegué a s^t Sebastian que el no podia admitir ninguno de ambos Gouiernos, avnque fuesen tan grandes, ni ninguno otro puesto para que huuiese menester prestar juramento de fidelidad a VMag^d por no poderlo haçer sin liçençia de su soberano, conque, por hecho del mismo Prinçipe, quedaua excluida esta primera parte de Gouiernos, hauiendome pareçido deçirselo assi por juzgar que podia ser combeniente que supiese que el Prinçipe hauia tenido esta consideraçion y atençion. Y que en quanto a las Plazas en soberania, creyera yo q̃ pudieran hallarse algunas de tal calidad y puestas en tal situaçion que se podria bien disputar si podian ser sospechosas ô no a la françia. Aqui me interrumpio con gran furia, diçiendo que ninguna cosa que fuese Plazas con soberania ô sin ella, situadas en esta parte ni en la otra, se hauia de consentir ni el Prinçipe hauia de quedar medio español y medio françes; que era menester que admitiese lo que estaua hecho ô lo dexase de admitir. Y de aqui fue prosiguiendo con todo aquel cartapaçio que Pimentel ha escrito tantas veçes. Yo le dexé hablar todo quanto quiso en esta razon, que fue mucho y dicho con gran veemençia, y, en hauiendo acauado, le dixe: Pues, en fin, señor Cardenal, todo este discurso pareçe que se viene â encaminar a pretender que el Rey mi s^r no pueda dar al Prinçipe mas recompensa que pagarle lo que le deue (lo qual no puede mereçer este nombre) y en tierras que sean aviertas. Porque me pareçio no dar â entender que yo proponia esto sino que lo tenia por vna cosa supuesta y llana, para descubrir su intençion. Respondiome que el darle alguna çierta suma de dinero que no exçediese mucho, al cabo se podia consentir pero que tierras (avnque fuesen aviertas) de ninguna manera. Yo le respondi que no lo proponia ni podia contentarme con esto pero que estrañaua que lo dificultase hauiendo dicho el mismo a Pimentel en Paris que Gouiernos ni Soberanias de Plazas no se hauia de consentir que se diesen al Prinçipe pero que en dinero y territorios aviertos podria VMag^d darle las recompensas que fuese seruido sin que en esto se pretendiese poner limite a la grandeza de VMag^d. Respondiome aviertamente que no hauia dicho tal; dixele que yo lo crehia assi pero que me daria liçençia que le leyese lo que Pimentel hauia escrito sobre este punto en 25 de Mayo. Y sacando la carta (que la lleuaba conmigo para este efecto), le ley todas aquellas mismas palabras que le hauia referido en voz y, sin dejarle que se boluiese â empeñar en deçir que no lo hauia dicho, prosegui consecutiuamente diçiendo: Sr Car^{al}, esto es lo que D^n Antonio me escriuio. Si VEm^a lo dixo en esta conformidad, serà menester no apartarse dello y si VEm^a no lo dixo (como yo lo creo pues me lo asegura assi) es menester que el Rey mi s^r en cabeza de Don Antonio dè satisfaçion a VEm^a y a todo el mundo de que no puede permitir ni dejar sin exemplo que Don Antonio se haya atreuido a lebantar vn testimonio desta calidad a vn Ministro tan grande como VEm^a en vna materia semejante. Yo puedo asegurar a VM^d que mostró mas que mediana turbaçion y, con palabras confusas y mal declaradas, se comenzó â enrredar en si hauia dicho ô no hauia dicho pero sin boluer a negar afirmatiuamente como hasta entonçes lo hauia hecho. Yo, viendo la cossa reduçida â estos terminos y hauiendo tomado ya el indiçio q̃ hauia menester y mostradole bastantemente la intençion en que yo me hallaua, me pareçio no apretar mas este punto por entonçes y assi le dixe (con palabras mas blandas) que no hauia para que apurar mas esto porque estas eran vnas cosas que, avnque no se huuiesen dicho, no se podian dexar de permitir, siendo este vn genero de recompensas que con razon no se podian ni deuian estorbar; pero que, comoquiera que yo no podia contentarme con ellas ni con esto podia VM^d satisfacer a su decoro y obligaçion en la satisfaçion del Prinçipe, seria menester pasar a ver que seguridades se le hauian de dar para que pudiese quedar dentro de françia a los pies del Rey x^{ptmo} y con mucha amistad con el Car^{al}, que era lo que el Prinçipe deseaua y VM^d tambien y yo por consequençia, por sauer que era esto lo que mas combenia al seruiçio del Rey x^{ptmo}, a la quietud de su estado y a la mayor combeniençia del Prinçipe. Negò esto absolutamente y boluio a deçir que no permitiria que se le diesen territorios, avnque fuesen aviertos, y todo lo demas como lo hauia hecho hasta entonçes. Y de vna y otra parte se boluio a disputar con gran fuerza y con esto se acabò la conferençia de ayer, que es la segunda que se ha tenido positiuamente sobre esta mat^{ria}, quedando el muy alto en que se hauia de mantener lo hecho como estaua y yo mucho mas alto en que no podia pasar por ello ni combenir en que de la fuerza q̃ se hauia hecho a Don Antonio en Paris, dejandole sin liuertad avn para despachar vn correo, se me dejase de dar satisfaçion. Que es quanto puedo deçir a VMg^d sobre esta materia por aora y que tengo muy presente que la Volunt^d y la orden de VMg^d es que no se rompa la Paz por nada. Pero nunca se podria intentar sacar ninguna ventaxa de los negoçios (particularmente de los que se hallan reduçidos a los terminos en que ha venido este) si no se llegase, en orden a defenderlos y enmendarlos, a la vltima extremidad. Guarde D^s la catholica y real Persona de VM^d como la christiandad ha menester. De fuenterrauia a 31 de Agosto 1659

Dluismendezdeharo

30

Haro to Philip IV: Fuenterrabía, 31 August 1659 [K1623: 66][97]

One of the items of business held over for when Haro and Mazarin could meet was the compensation due to France in exchange for the demolition of La Bassée and restitution of Bergues. Haro encloses a letter from Caracena on this matter and asks the king to instruct him accordingly. Caracena has identified Avesnes and Marienbourg as the only strongholds in Flanders which could be surrendered.[98] Haro fears that Mazarin will demand one of the most important strongholds in the area in exchange for Bergues.

31

Haro to Philip IV: Fuenterrabía, 1 September 1659 [K1623: 67][99]

On Mazarin's insistence, Haro has drafted the letter from Philip to the Pope requesting special dispensation for the marriage. This has been done at the conference in order for the letters from the Spanish and French kings to have exactly the same format. Haro encloses the letter for the king to sign and notes that the French have suggested that it should be returned to the border for forwarding to Rome. The letter from the French king will not be sent direct to the Pope but will be presented to him by Cardinals Antonio and D'Este.[100] Although Haro is unhappy about proceeding with the marriage arrangements until all the articles of the peace treaty have been agreed and the treaty has been signed, he accepts Mazarin's view that there is no harm

---

[97] Letter 30 was also dispatched on 1 September.
[98] In his letter of 28 August to Le Tellier, Mazarin (1690: 172) states that Haro has asked for this item of business to be postponed until after the arrival of the adviser dispatched from Brussels by Caracena. Avesnes is located in what is today the south-eastern tip of the French department of Nord; Marienbourg is in the Belgian province of Namur.
[99] Letter 31 arrived in Madrid on 5 September.
[100] Cardinal Antonio is Cardinal Antoine Barberini (1607–1671). He was appointed cardinal by his uncle, Urban VIII, when a very young man. Cardinal D'Este is Rinaldo D'Este (1618–1672), a relative of the Duke of Modena.

in having the papal dispensation ready. He observes that it seems unlikely that D. Luis Ponce will have reached the papal court by the time the request for dispensation is made and that the Spanish minister in Rome will therefore probably still be D. Gaspar de Sobremonte. Accordingly, he remits to Madrid for the king's signature a letter to D. Gaspar which contains instructions on how to discharge this mission.[101]

32

Haro to Philip IV: Fuenterrabía, 1 September 1659 [K1623: 70][102]

A report on the discussion over point six of the reserved matters, which has to do with whether or not the Conflent should be ceded to France along with Roussillon: Haro sends the king a summary of the arguments against the proposal which have been put together largely by the Council of Aragon and observes that the French are well prepared to debate this question. Mazarin has with him papers and documents produced by foreigners, Catalans and Frenchmen which support the French claim. Most of these documents emanate from Perpignan. The French position is that the Conflent is a dependency of Roussillon and that, since the Spanish king has already renounced his claim to Roussillon in the Paris treaty, the Conflent should be ceded to France along with it. Haro requests further instructions, stressing that Mazarin will not be moved on this point. The negotiations between Haro and Lionne held in Madrid in 1656 had concluded that the Pyrenees should constitute the boundary between Spain and France, and Mazarin is arguing that the Conflent is on the French side of the mountains.[103]

---

[101] Papal dispensation for the marriage was necessary because María Teresa and Louis were first cousins through their fathers and their mothers. Anne of Austria, Louis's mother, was Philip's sister and Louis XIII, the Sun King's father, was the brother of Isabella of France, María Teresa's mother. Unless it was translated in Madrid, the letter destined for Rome seems to have been drafted in Spanish, not Latin as one might expect. AGS Estado Francia K1623: 68 is a copy of this letter to the Pope and is dated simply September 1659.

[102] Letter 32 arrived in Madrid on 5 September.

[103] In his letter of 25 August to Le Tellier, Mazarin (1690: 145) explains how, in the fifth interview held on 24 August, he adroitly introduced into the negotiations the matter of the Conflent, which, he says, is a substantial territory and includes more than two hundred and fifty *villages*. For detailed treatment of this subject, see Peter Sahlins 1989.

33

Haro to Philip IV: Fuenterrabía, 3 September 1659 [K1623: 72a]

Haro summarises his eighth interview with Mazarin held on 2 September and lasting five and a half hours. They discussed Juliers, compensation for the demolition of La Bassé and return of Bergues, and the question of Condé. With regard to the first of these issues, Haro reiterates his belief that there is a connection between Juliers and the determination of the French king to be seen to have defended his allies more stoutly at the conference table than the Spanish king has defended his. On La Bassée and Bergues, Haro muses over what might be suitable exchanges for these emplacements and encloses a letter from Caracena which provides information on the strategic importance of these and other emplacements in Flanders. On the question of Condé, Haro explains how he has thus far thwarted Mazarin's attempts to secure an interview with either Lenet[104] or Caillet. He is convinced that Mazarin is desperate to discover exactly how Spain intends to compensate Condé for the loss of his estates and offices in France and fears that, if they were to meet, Lenet would tell Mazarin all that he wanted to know about the proposed settlement. If the Cardinal were to become aware that part of the settlement included Cambrai, he would surely agree to restore the prince in all things and demand Cambrai for France.

Señor

Antes de ayer que se contaron primero deste,[105] di quenta a VMg^d del estado en que se hallauan estas materias y aora añadiré lo que se ofreçe. Ayer tube otra conferençia con el cardenal que duró çinco horas y media. Los puntos que en ella se trataron fueron tres: El Presidio de Juliers, las recompensas de la demoliçion de la Basé y restituçion de Bergas, y el part^r del Prinçipe.

En quanto al primero, perseueró en que se hauia de quitar el Presidio de Juliers porque el Rey christianisimo lo tenia capitulado expresamente

---

[104] Pierre Lenet (sometimes spelt *Lainet/Laisnet* in French sources), one of Condé's ministers in Spain, had accompanied Haro to the border and, if we are to believe Mazarin (1690: 84–85, 100), was strongly instrumental, along with others who were agents of Condé at the conference, in persuading Haro that he should not take no for an answer on the Condé question. Mazarin makes the point that Haro is easily swayed; first he had been swayed by Mazarin himself away from pursuing the matter any further, and later by Lenet, who insists that the cardinal will eventually improve the offer on the table.

[105] See Letter 32 above.

assi con el Duque. Boluio â ofreçerme por ello a Tiumbila ô a Grauelingas y avn creo que se estendiera a dexar tambien a Quenoy, que es vna gran prueua del apreçio que haçen de aventaxar mucho a todos sus Aliados.[106] Yo quedè siempre constante en lo que hauia dicho de ser este vn punto en que jamas podria venir por todas las razones que tengo representadas a VMg^d en mis Despachos anteçedentes q̃ dexo de boluer a repetir aora por no alargarme en aquello q̃ se puede escusar. En quanto a las recompensas que se le han de dar de la demoliçion de la Base y restituçion de Bergas, Lo que puedo deçir a VMg^d es que en vna carta que tube el otro dia del Marques de Carazena, me diçe que es tan importante el procurar quedar como quiera con Bergas que quando a mi me quedase elecçion de escojer entre ella y Grauelingas, deuiera elejir a Bergas porque con ella y con acabar vnos fuertes que estan comenzados quedarà bien cubierta por aquella parte la Prouinçia de flandes, y que Grauelingas se puede juzgar por de menos consideraçion y de cuya falta no podremos reçiuir perjuiçio. El cardenal ponderò mucho la calidad de la Plaza, lo que ellos hauian adelantado sus fortificaçiones. Dijome que era vna villa muy grande, dos veçes mayor que Dunquerque, con muchos combentos de frailes y de Monjas y vna gran jatelania.[107] Mostrome vna carta que hauia tenido del Gou^{or} della en que le ponderaua las grandes combenienças de conserbarla y le persuadia a que por ningun caso la restituyese. A esto se junta el conoçer tambien el car^{al} la gran neçesidad que nosotros tenemos della y todo le deue de persuadir a que al cabo (no pudiendo mas) la hemos de comprar a qualquiera preçio que sea. Y la proposiçion que se me ha hecho ha sido a esta proporçion porque me han pedido por recompensa della á s. Tomer, ô, â Duay.[108] Yo huue menester reirme vn poco dello, como me pareçio neçesario haçerlo en vna cosa tan imposible de conçeder, â que solo me respondia que si me pareçia mucho, que el estaua contento con quedarse con Bergas, pues por el tratado firmado por D^n Antonio y ratificado por VMag^d, les quedaua esta Plaza entre las demas y que el no trataua de permutarla porque le estaua mucho mejor el tenerla y solo hauia venido remitido aqui el punto de la recompensa

---

[106] *Tiumbila*, or Thionville, is found along the French border with Luxembourg, just north of Metz; *Grauelingas*, or Gravelines, lies on the coast about 15 miles southwest of Dunkirk.

[107] *Jatelania*: French *châtellenie*, the land belonging to a castle (English *castellany*).

[108] *St Tomer* is St Omer and lies to the southeast of Calais in Pas-de-Calais; *Duay* is Douai, on the banks of the river Scarpe along the border between the French departments of Pas-de-Calais and Nord.

por si a mi me pareçiese de combeniençia del seruiçio de VMag^d el dar por ella cosa que pudiese corresponder a su importançia. Y este punto quedò por esta causa sin conclusion, no pudiendo yo venir en proposiçiones de tanto perjuiçio. Mantendreme en esta conformidad para que se vayan reduçiendo vn poco mas a la razon y entre tanto espero que me llegarà respuesta de VM^d a lo que tengo escrito[109] sobre Avenas y Marienburg con vista de vn capitulo de carta del Marq^s de carazena que remiti a VM^d, en que juzga q̃ estos dos Puestos son los que con menos daño se pueden trocar y los que nos pueden haçer menos falta.[110] Y en caso que a VMag^d le haya pareçido lo mismo, restarà solo el procurar que se contenten con ellos y el intentar (si es posible conseguir) que, en lugar de La Base, nos dejasen a s^n Venant por el gran seruiçio que el Marques representa en todas sus cartas que se haria a VMg^d en ello, por quanto quedaria en este caso la Prouinçia de flandes enteramente cubierta por todas partes.

En el particular del Prinçipe se gastaron las tres horas vltimas y el se descompuso de tal manera y con tales bozes que los que estauan tres Aposentos mas afuera, las oyeron y repararon mucho. Seriame imposible dar quenta a VMag^d por menor de todo lo que pasò y assi habrè de reduçirme solo a referir algunas çircunstançias particulares y el estado en que vltimamente quedò este punto, a cuyo fin, para mejor inteligençia de lo que boy a deçir, me serà neçesario boluer a tomar algo de las conferençias anteçedentes.

En la segunda ô Terçera que tuuimos, depues de hauer pasado vnos lijeros cumplimientos, entrò diçiendo que el dia de la conferençia anteçedente hauia estado en los Apartamientos [*sic*] de mi Barraca Lenet y que, avnque el no tenia ningun disgusto con el ni mala volunt^d al Prinçipe, temia que aquellos françeses que venian con el, sin sauiduria suya ni poderlo el remediar, llegasen â alguna [*sic*] desorden con el y que assi le hauia pareçido deçirmelo. Yo le respondi que hauia entendido

---

[109] Letter 30 above.

[110] It is interesting to compare what Haro says here about the strategic importance of Avesnes, a stronghold situated along the border between France and Flanders due west of Marienbourg, with what Mazarin (1693: 69) says in his letter of 5 September to Le Tellier. The cardinal claims that Haro had offered Avesnes to France as part of a proposal aimed at restoring Condé and subsequently regretted bitterly his rashness in so doing. He apparently feared that neither the king nor the Council of State would approve what he had done, and this thought had given him many sleepless nights.

que Lenet hauia estado en aquella parte de Barraca que me tocaua a mi sin hauer pasado a la suya, avnque lo hauian hecho otros muchos, y que no con menos razon pudiera el cardenal hauer temido que los de mi sequito hiçiesen el mismo desorden con el Residente de Portugal[111] que hauia venido con el; pero que sauiendo que Lenet podia causarle disgusto, y no deseando yo darsele en nada, le ordenaria que de alli adelante se quedase en fuenterrauia. Y con esto pasè â hablar en otras cosas.

La conferençia siguiente, llegandose â hablar (avnque no muy de proposito) en el Prinçipe y en sus intereses, se dejò deçir que si Callet ô Lenet quisiesen verse con el ô tuuiesen algo que informarle y yo tenia gusto dello, que no reusaria el oirlos. Y avnque luego me causò vn poco de reparo que en la diferençia de solos dos dias q̃ hauian pasado de vna conferençia â otra huuiese estado con tanta braueza contra Lenet y, en la segunda, con tanta blandura, confieso que por entonçes no hiçe gran reflexion sobre ello y crey que solo lo hauia hecho por satisfaçerme a la destemplanza con que me hauia hablado el dia anteçedente en razon desto. Y assi solo le respondi que estimaua mucho lo que se seruia de deçirme pero que, hauiendo ya podido entender que su em^a reçiuia disgusto con la Persona de Lenet, no queria de ninguna manera que se le boluiese a dar y que antes bien, hauiendole ordenado que no saliese de fuenterrauia, lo hauia executado assi. Y avnque el boluio â referir que no le causaria disgusto, yo siempre le respondi en la misma conformidad.

La conferençia siguiente, voluiendo â hablarse accidentalmente en la Persona del Prinçipe y estando mui firme en que no se hauia de mudar vna letra de lo que estaua capitulado y ratificado por VMag^d, Voluio a

---

[111] The Portuguese Resident was Dr Feliciano Dourado. He had been sent to Paris from The Hague in order to defend Portuguese interests in France until such time as the Portuguese ambassador, Don João da Costa (Conde de Soure), arrived from Lisbon. Dourado failed to persuade Mazarin to send infantry and horse to Portugal at France's expense and was also refused permission to raise troops himself for Portugal in France. Da Costa, who entered Paris on 9 June, was similarly unsuccessful in his negotiations with Mazarin, having arrived two days after Pimentel and the cardinal had signed the Paris treaty. In June, he dispatched Dourado to St Jean de Luz with instructions to offer Mazarin one million *cruzados* and the appointment of his nominee to the archbishopric of Evora if the cardinal proved able to secure the inclusion of Portugal in the peace. Haro consistently refused to contemplate such a proposal but Dourado nevertheless remained at the border. Da Costa himself did not travel to St Jean de Luz until the month of October. For additional information, see Prestage 1925: 70–76.

deçir que si Callet ô Lenet, ô ambos, tuuiesen algo que deçirle en este part[r] y yo queria que los oyese, lo haria. Entonçes comenzè â entrar en sospecha de que tenia algun fin particular en querer hablar con ellos y que el disgusto que hauia mostrado el primer dia solo de que huuiese entrado Lenet en mi Barraca hauia sido fingido y con artifiçio para que la permision que me hauia dado el segundo para que le pudiese ver juzgase yo que era solo por querer satisfaçerme y, con esta ocasion, hablar con el, como lo deuia de desear.

Confirmé mas esta sospecha mia por hauer el cardenal, tanto aquel dia como todos los anteçedentes, apretadome mucho a que yo le dixese que Plazas eran las que hauiamos ofreçido al Prin[e] por recompensa, en que yo jamas me hauia querido declarar (como tengo dicho en mis despachos anteçedentes), diçiendole que presupuesto que el excluia de todo punto que se le pudiese recompensar en ningun genero de Plazas a la frontera, me pareçia que era poco neçesario el explicarme sobre este punto. Y juntandose à esta resistençia mia todas las averturas que hauia hecho para verse con Lenet, entrè a sospechar que la razon por que lo deseaua era por sauer (no hauiendolo podido entender de mi) quales eran las Plazas que les hauiamos ofreçido por recompensa. Y temiendo que si Lenet declarase (como era çierto que haria) que vna dellas era Cambray y el Cambresi entrase el car[al] a pretendella para si y ofreçer estableçer por ella al Prinçipe, me pareçio que combenia el procurar apartar este peligro todo quanto se pudiese y que el medio mas encaminado a este fin seria el estorbar yo que Lenet se viese con el. Y assi dandome siempre por entendido de que el hauerse hablandado tanto con la Persona de Lenet era solo por haçerme gusto a mi, perseuerè en deçirle que estimaua la merçed que me haçia pero que de ninguna manera me podia conformar en q̃ Su em[a], por faboreçerme a mi, hiçiese ninguna cosa de que huuiese de reçiuir disgusto, como yo conoçia que le tendria en esto, porque me pareçiò q̃ este seria el mexor camino para impedirlo.

En la conferençia de ayer, estando en lo mas fuerte della, se estrechò vn poco mas este punto, porque boluiendo a proponerme que si Callet ô Lenet tenian algo que deçirle sobre este particular, los oyria con mucho gusto y que no lo haria solo por darmele a mi sino por ver si tenian algo que proponer que pudiese façilitar el tomar algun medio en el negoçio, y viendo que todavia yo no salia â ello, se declarò mas y dixo que el estaua dispuesto â oirle y que el mismo Lenet le hauia embiado a deçir que deseaua verse con el y añadio que hallaua que esto podria tener mucha combeniençia porque, avnque el no hauia de haçer por sus persuasiones mas que por las mias, podria el deçirles la firmeza con que yo defendia los intereses del Prinçipe, porque ellos viesen que de mi parte yo no podia haçer mas, y la obligaçion en que el Prinçipe me quedaua. Aqui reconoçi con mayor evidençia ser çierto todo lo que anteçedentemente yo hauia sospechado, pero juntamente quedé en mayor dificultad de lo que deuia haçer porque hasta entonçes hauia procurado irlo impidiendo con vn pretexto tan deçente y justo como el de no querer que el Car^{al} tomase el disgusto de oyrle por mi. Pero ya hauiendome declarado positiuamente que el mismo Lenet le hauia embiado vn recado, diçiendole que deseaua verle, me pareçio que el impedirlo seria quitar, en çierta forma, la liuertad a Lenet, lo qual no dejò de causarme reparo. Pero con todo, juzgando yo que la intençion del car^{al} en esto se encaminaua solo a sauer si le hauiamos ofreçido a Cambray, para introduçir luego la proposiçion de restableçer al Prinçipe por esta Plaza, y perseuerando yo siempre en este entender que si se pudiesen impedir con algun pretexto aparente estas vistas del Car^{al} con Lenet seria por esta causa muy combeniente el procurarlo, tomé alli sobre el mismo hecho y como el aprieto del negoçio lo pedia la resoluçion y el pretexto que se me ofreçio por mas a proposito para estorbarlo y assi le dixe palabra mas a menos las siguientes: Señor cardenal, VEm^a me ha dado â entender en tres ô quatro conferençias continuas la mortificaçion que por faboreçerme queria VEm^a reçiuir en oyr a Lenet y a Callet sobre los particulares del Prinçipe y yo lo he estimado como debo. Pero VEm^a habrá podido façilmente reconoçer que yo no he salido nunca â ello; y deseando que VEm^a conozca la sinçeridad y confianza con que le hablo en todo, me ha pareçido declararme con VEm^a y deçirle el reparo que se me ofreçe s^{re} esto. Los ofiçios (señor cardenal) que yo hago por el Prinçipe no son por cumplimiento ni por satisfaçer en la apariençia ni a sus criados ni â el, porque creo que ellos y el se hallan en esta parte con toda la satisfaçion que deuen tener; y esta juzgo que no se podrà avmentar avnque VEm^a se sirua de asegurarselo assi, porque ellos lo tienen bien conoçido y si yo les consintiese que fuesen a verse con VEm^a, podria en la apariençia pareçer que yo desamparaua la causa del Prinçipe y que remito ya a sus Agentes que ellos la defiendan por si. Y siendo esto tan contrario a las ordenes que traigo del Rey mi s^r, por ser este el prinçipal negoçio suyo que me ha mandado venir a tratar aqui, VEm^a considere que descargo podria yo dar a Su Mag^d si diese motiuo con esta apariençia para que se pudiese juzgar que le separo de mi y no le trato en aquella conformidad que me lo ha mandado, puesto tambien que si los Agentes del Prinçipe tuuieran algo que proponer, me lo huuieran dicho ya para que llegase por medio mio mas apadrinado a la notiçia de VEM^a. No me pareçio que yo tenia otra puerta por donde poder salir y assi procurê tomar esta.

El cardenal por entonçes me respondio muy mansamente, sin replicar nada; pero creo que el no hauer conseguido en esto lo que hauia deseado deuio de ser lo que le embrabeçio tanto para la disputa que se ençendio despues (que verdaderam^{te} fue terrible), en que al mismo paso que el se yba descomponiendo y haçiendo mayores estremos, yo le yba respondiendo (quando hallaua coyuntura de poder haçerlo) con mayor templanza, pareçiendome que el estado del negoçio (por entonçes) lo pedia assi y por juzgar que, proçediendo todo su furor de verme tan firme sobre este punto y de no hauer podido disponer el verse con Lenet, yo no tenia mas que haçer que dejarle hablar. Seriame imposible referir a VMg^d tantas cosas como dixo y lo que yo le yba respondiendo â ellas, pero por no dejar de deçir a VMag^d alguna de aquellas que puedo juzgar por mas prinçipales, dirè solo que, estando en la mayor fuerza de su discurso y en medio de las demostraçiones de mayor impaçiençia, me dixo lo siguiente:

Segun la forma (señor Don Luis) conque VE sustenta este negoçio, infiero que VE deue de creer que yo no puedo boluerme de aqui sin hacer la Paz. Yo le respondi: Çierto, s^r Car^{al}, que no lo creo assi pero lo que creo es que ni VEm^a ni yo seremos tan malos criados de nuestros amos ni tan enemigos de nosotros mismos que nos hayamos de boluer sin haçer la Paz.

Hasta aqui, s^r, he dicho algo de lo que ha pasado y aora pasare a deçir algo de lo que entiendo. Señor, VMg^d ha considerado siempre por vn punto tan prinçipal deste Tratado la satisfaçion del Prinçipe por ser cossa que pertenece al honor y a la real obligaçion de VMag^d y tan digna y tan propia de los grandes Reyes la proteccion de sus Aliados que, por conseguirlo, se siruio VM^d de resoluer por la vltima consulta del consexo antes de mi partida que yo pudiese dar al Prinçipe â cambray y el cambressi, con algun Territorio mas de ensanche en el Pays de Henao,[112] ô, en su lugar, todo lo que a VMg^d le queda en el Pays de Luzemburg con la villa capital deste nombre; y en esta conformidad he traydo las ordenes de VM^d para ejecutarlo en caso que lo quisiesen consentir assi. Lo que aora puedo deçir a VMg^d es que si VMg^d me permitiera que yo pudiese disponer de la Plaza de cambray a mi aruitrio, segun quanto yo puedo reconoçer quiza me atreuiera â asegurar a VMg^d que el Prinçipe fuera restableçido en todo (que assi van muchas veçes las cosas en este mundo); pero comoquiera que yo debo procurar que no quede esta gran pieza

---

[112] *Henao*: Hainault.

desunida de los Dominios de VMg^d en flandes y mucho mas particularmente en vna negoçiaçion que corre por mi mano (avnque ella, en esta parte del Prinçipe, se me haya entregado en el estado que VMg^d conoçe), quedo trabaxando para ver si, salbando estas cosas mayores, puedo ganar algun paso sobre esta materia, que es en lo que siempre se ha considerado que consiste el haçerse esta Paz con todas çircunstançias de combeniençia y reputaçion; y en orden â este fin, puede VMg^d estar çierto que llegare por todos caminos â aquellas vltimas diligençias y esfuerzos hasta donde yo alcanzare que se puede llegar.

Avnque el carden^l (como dexo referido) me haya dado â entender que Lenet ha mostrado deseo de verse con el, no me atrevo a creer que sea çierto porque el saue muy bien quan poco puede esperar del car^al sino es por medio de mis diligençias (avnque tambien estas juzgue que hayan de ser poco bastantes). Pero con todo, no me ha pareçido deçirselo por no ençender mas fuego entre los dos. Guarde Dios la catholica y real Persona de VMag^d como la christiandad ha menester. De fuenterrauia a 3 de Sept^re 1659.

Dluismendezdeharo

34

Haro to Philip IV: Fuenterrabía, 3 September 1659 [K1623: 73]

Reporting on his interview with Mazarin held on 30 August, Haro informs the king that the Duke of Gramont has been chosen to lead the embassy to Madrid to request the infanta's hand.[113] He will do his best to prevent the duke from leaving for Madrid until all the articles of the peace treaty have been agreed and expects that this will help to speed up negotiations. Even so, Madrid should begin to get ready for the duke's visit.

35

Haro to Philip IV: Fuenterrabía, 6 September 1659 [K1623: 76]

Haro summarises his letter of 3 September (Letter 34) to the king and reports on the ninth interview held on 4 September and lasting six hours. He

---

[113] Priorato (1667: 157–61) records the announcement of Gramont's embassy in his diary entry of 1 September. See also note 84.

reiterates his conviction that Mazarin is completely opposed to a marriage alliance with Spain and describes Pimentel's arrival in Lyons just as Mazarin was about to conclude a marriage agreement with the House of Savoy as 'el mayor golpe que pudo reçiuir el Cardenal' (the greatest blow the Cardinal could receive).[114] He comments on Mazarin's irascible nature, which manifests itself whenever the cardinal fails to get his own way, and explains, in view of this, that his own approach to many of the issues reserved for discussion at the border must of necessity be milder than he would otherwise choose so as to prevent the talks from breaking down altogether. Negotiations have again embraced Condé, La Bassée, Bergues, Juliers and the Conflent but agreement on these matters continues to elude the two plenipotentiaries. All other articles of the treaty, however, have now been more or less agreed. Haro tells the king that when he met with Lenet in order to explain why he had declined Mazarin's offer to meet with Lenet, he discovered, much to his surprise, that the cardinal had already written to Condé's minister to enquire why the latter had not paid him a courtesy visit. Regrettably, Mazarin continues to press for a meeting with Lenet. Haro suspects that he is determined to discover from Lenet what Spain has offered Condé by way of compensation and to learn especially whether or not the offer includes Cambrai. Caracena's envoy has arrived and will advise Haro on the relative values of strongholds in Flanders and Luxembourg.[115]

36

Haro to Philip IV: Fuenterrabía, 9 September 1659 [K1623: 80]

Haro reports on the determination of the French to secure Juliers for the Duke of Neuburg. He notes the recommendation of the Council of State that peace should not be sacrificed over this stronghold; if it must be surrendered, he will do his utmost to get the best possible deal either for Condé or for Spain.[116] He shares the view of the Council of State that, in the event that Juliers is surrendered, precautions will need to be taken to ensure that it does not fall into French hands.

---

[114] See note 75.
[115] In his letter of 10 September to Le Tellier, Mazarin (1693: 103–21) reveals that the name of Caracena's envoy is *Le Sieur d'Aigremont*. In Spanish sources, he appears as the *Conde de Gramont* and is identified as a Burgundian. The Council of State would have preferred a native of Flanders for this mission but there appears to have been nobody suitable available (AGS Estado Francia K1618: 71).
[116] For more information on Juliers, see Letters 26 and 27.

37

Haro to Philip IV: Fuenterrabía, 9 September 1659 [K1623: 81][117]

The conference scheduled for 7 September had to be postponed because of the eve and feast day of Our Lady. Mazarin has again suggested that the negotiations might be undertaken by third persons but Haro has refused and sent word to the cardinal that he will await him on the island at noon.

38

Haro to Philip IV: Fuenterrabía, 9 September 1659 [K1623: 82][118]

Haro responds to the king's letter of 4 September, which stipulates that the ambassador to request the infanta's hand should not set out for Madrid until such time as the treaty has been agreed, signed and ratified and all strongholds which are to be evacuated have been evacuated. Haro understands the reasons for the king's caution but points out that the marriage cannot be delayed until the evacuation of all strongholds has been effected. The French, not unreasonably, will expect the marriage to precede the evacuation of strongholds, and the embassy of the Duke of Gramont to Madrid clearly has to take place before the marriage. Haro requests further instructions on this matter.

39

Haro to Philip IV: Fuenterrabía, 11 September 1659 [K1623: 83a]

Haro rehearses the contents of previous letters with regard to the sequence of events and reports on the visit which he received from Lionne at 4 p.m. on 10 September in order to express French concern over the Spanish

---

[117] Letter 37 arrived in Madrid on 13 September.
[118] Letter 38 was dispatched on 11 September and arrived in Madrid two days later.

decision to postpone the marriage until the spring of the following year.[119] The peace treaty and the marriage agreement will be signed on the same day and the French are understandably unwilling to evacuate strongholds or abandon their allies until such time as they can be certain not only that the marriage will take place but also that it will do so to their satisfaction. Haro refers to the letter of the king dated 6 September which bears on the letters destined for Rome (which were not returned to Haro for reasons to do with the sequence of events leading to the signing of the peace treaty and the evacuation of strongholds) and which reiterates the instructions contained in the royal letter of 4 September. Haro repeats that both documents, namely the peace treaty and the marriage agreement, will be signed the same day. He feels, however, that it is unlikely to be done before the infanta's hand has been formally requested. The French will hardly agree to that.

40

Haro to Philip IV: Fuenterrabía, 12 September 1659 [K1623: 85][120]

A report on the eleventh interview held on 11 September:[121] Mazarin had pushed very hard for the marriage to take place quickly but eventually accepted that the infanta would not be able to travel to the frontier until the spring. However, he had suggested that Gramont at least should undertake his embassy to Madrid without further delay. This suggestion had put Haro in a difficult position: the king had ordered that the embassy should not be undertaken until after completion of the treaty and evacuation of all strongholds, and even though Haro had recommended that it should, still he had not received a reply on this from the king. He had thus responded to Mazarin's proposal by saying that Gramont should not depart until after the treaty had been signed. This reply had not unnaturally infuriated the cardinal, who did not know what to make of it. After all, Haro himself had consistently said that the ceremony of formally requesting the infanta's hand

---

[119] I have not been able to trace Haro's summary of the proceedings of the tenth conference held on 9 September, in which this announcement was made. However, Mazarin (1693: 147–57) alludes to it in his letter of 14 September to Le Tellier.

[120] Letter 40 was dispatched on 13 September and reached Madrid on 16 September.

[121] Priorato (1667: 57) gives 14 September as the date of the eleventh conference.

could not be dispensed with. Accordingly, he asks the king to instruct him on this matter. If the king relents and agrees to sign without a formal public declaration, the French will accept, as this is what they have sought all along. If, on the other hand, the king will not dispense with the ceremony (and Haro believes that he should not), Gramont must be allowed to set off for Madrid as soon as all the articles of the treaty are agreed. France will not sign the peace treaty unless the marriage agreement can be signed at the same time. Following discussion of the marriage and of the safeguards which should cover the handing over of the infanta and evacuation of strongholds, Haro and Mazarin had had a very lively debate over those points still to be agreed.[122] Haro reports that so far as these points are concerned, he has still conceded nothing.

41

Haro to Philip IV: Fuenterrabía, 14 September 1659 [K1619: 37]

Haro has little to report, given that he and Mazarin have not met since his last dispatch and that it is Sunday. Inquisitive observers throng the area around the island on holy days and for this reason he and Mazarin have decided not to meet then. He prepares this dispatch merely so that the king will have frequent news from the frontier. Although he has not met with Mazarin, negotiations have continued through Lionne. Mazarin is apparently keen for negotiations to be conducted by Lionne rather than by himself. Haro has generally resisted this arrangement, only occasionally dealing with Lionne so as not to prolong the negotiations more than is necessary and also to give Mazarin this small satisfaction. The next interview is scheduled for 15 September and Haro expects to discuss the three main items of business outstanding. He will give the king a full report on the outcome in a subse-

---

[122] One of the most tricky aspects of the negotiations was generally agreeing the timing or sequence of events. In his letter of 14 September to Le Tellier, Mazarin (1693: 148–49) reports that a courier from Madrid has brought word that Philip is happy with the two letters intended for the Pope but cannot understand how one can request special dispensation for the marriage before the agreement has been signed and Gramont has been to Madrid. Mazarin agrees and expresses his surprise that Haro should have accepted this sequence of events in the first place. Having thus paved the way, Mazarin then goes on to break the news that the infanta will not after all be able to travel to the border until the spring.

quent dispatch. He closes by telling Philip that he will do everything in his power to ensure that the wedding of the infanta takes place in Burgos, which is where the marriage ceremony of Anne of Austria was celebrated.

Señor

Antes de ayer que se contaron 12 deste,[123] di quenta a VMag^d de lo que hasta entonçes se ofreçia segun lo que me hauia pasado con el cardenal en la conferençia del dia anteçedente. Y avnque aora no tengo cossa muy particular que añadir por no hauernos buelto a juntar oy por ser Domingo y tanta la gente que acude los dias de fiesta del vno y del otro Reyno sobre la vna y otra Ribera, que por asegurar que no sobrevenga algun accidente con el mayor concurso nos hemos combenido el cardenal y yo en escusar las juntas en semejantes dias, Todavia porque a VMg^d no le falten frequentes nueuas de aqui en esta coyuntura y cumplir en esto con mas puntualidad lo que VMg^d me tiene mandado, despacho este correo aora.

Avnque, como dexo dicho, no hemos tenido conferençia en estos dos o tres dias vltimos, no se ha perdido tiempo en los negoçios porque Lione ha estado conmigo diuersas vezes, y, avnque conozco que el cardenal huelga mas de que se traten por su medio que el conferillas inmediatamente conmigo y por esta misma caussa deuiera yo escusar lo primero, Todavia me ha pareçido no reusarlo generalmente, assi por lo que puede conduçir a la mayor breuedad como por dar al car^{al} en lo que se puede esta satisfaçion.[124] Mañana es dia de conferençia y juzgo se boluerà â hablar en los tres puntos prinçipales que estan pendientes, de

---

[123] Letter 40 above.

[124] Haro seems to imply that Mazarin finds him difficult to deal with and would prefer to leave the negotiating to the more robust Lionne. There seems to be some truth in this, although the reason for it is not altogether clear. If we accept French sources, the cardinal was indeed frustrated by constantly having to go over the same ground and, because of his poor health, he was naturally reluctant to make the journey from St Jean de Luz to the island if it was unlikely that progress in the negotiations would be made. So whereas Haro tends to describe as tenacity this unwillingness on his part to let go of a particular issue, Mazarin complains, as we have seen in note 104, that Haro is easily manipulated and that it is, therefore, hard for him to be sure that Haro will not resurrect what has already been discussed and agreed in an earlier interview simply because he has been persuaded to do so back in Fuenterrabía.

que tengo dado [*sic*] quenta a VMg^d estos dias, en que deseare adelantar el seruiçio de VMg^d, como lo pide mi obligaçion, y soliçitar de mi parte, en quanto fuere posible, la breuedad; y de lo que resultare della, dare quenta a VMg^d con otro correo.

Estoy en cuidado de procurar que se remita el desposorio de la s^{ra} Infanta para Burgos, que es donde se çelebrò el de la s^{ra} Infanta Doña Ana; y por mas que me apretaren en lo contrario, no zederè dello hasta hauer dado quenta a VM^d para que se sirua de ordenarme lo q̃ huuiere de executar.[125] Dios g^{de} la cat^{ca} y R^l Persona de VM^d como la christiandad ha m^r. fuenterrauia 14 de s^{re} 1659

Dluismendezdeharo

42

Haro to Philip IV: Fuenterrabía, 14 September 1659 [K1619: 38]

Haro refers to the letter from the king dated 6 September and to his own of 1 September in respect of French claims on the Conflent. The king had enclosed with his letter a copy of the relevant *consulta* (opinion) prepared by the Council of State, adding that the matter of the Conflent had also been referred back to the Council of Aragon. In relation to the Council of State's recommendation that Spain respect the agreement reached with Lionne in Madrid in 1656, Haro, having reviewed his papers, warns that the agreement favours France and that if the Conflent should be found to lie on the French side of the Pyrenees, then Spain must relinquish all claim to it. He notes the king's instruction that he use his best judgement in this matter and he also indicates his agreement with the recommendations of the Council of State. However, since the king has referred the matter back to the Council of Aragon and since Haro wishes to give the king another opportunity to review exactly what was agreed in 1656, he encloses with this dispatch a copy of the agreement, indicating that he will not proceed any further with this aspect

---

[125] This is one of many examples of the contemporary obsession with precedent. In fact, the wedding was eventually celebrated on Thursday, 3 June 1660, in Fuenterrabía, with Haro standing in for Louis XIV. Following the handing over of the infanta to her husband on the Isle of Pheasants on Monday, 7 June, the couple travelled to St Jean de Luz, where their union was blessed before the marriage was consummated. BNM Ms 2387, fols 177–215v.

of the negotiations until he receives further instructions from Madrid. He concludes by outlining the reasons why France is reluctant to refer the matter to commissioners appointed by both sides.

Señor

En carta de los seis deste, se sirue VMag^d de deçirme que, hauiendo visto por lo que yo hauia representado a VMag^d en primero del mismo[126] Los grandes esfuerzos que haçian françeses para quedar con aquel Pedazo de Territorio que se llama el Condado de Conflen, Assi por pretender que es dependiente del condado de Rosellon como por las demas razones que dixe a VMg^d en aquel despacho, se hauia VMag^d seruido de mandarle remitir al Consexo de Estado, El qual hauia representado a VMag^d lo que contenia la consulta (cuya copia se sirue VM^d de remitirme juntamente) y que, si bien hauia VMag^d mandado al de Aragon lo que se deçia en ella sin embargo de que yo tenia acà las consultas y papeles que hauia hecho aquel consexo anteçedentemente sobre esta materia, me mandaua VMg^d que con vista de todo obrase aquello q̃ juzgase por mas combeniente al seruiçio de VMg^d, segun lo que al pie del hecho tuuiese por neçesario.

La consulta del consexo de estado, despues de hauer representado a VMag^d lo que se le ofreçe en quanto a q̃ se podria procurar que esta diferençia quedase remitida a comisarios, Diçe en la vltima parte della q̃ en quanto a lo que se diçe que se trato entre mi y Lione el año de 56 en esa corte, podria VMag^d mandarme remitir este hecho, pues si de acuerdo quedo combenido se diuidiesen estas diferençias con los montes, no hay duda se habra de estar a lo que entonçes de comun acuerdo quedò ajustado, cayendo la Paz que oy se haçe sobre los Tratados que se ajustaron entonçes.

Hauiendo yo reconoçido los apuntamientos que se hiçieron el año de 56 en Madrid de lo que estubo ajustado en aquella Trataçion y aprobado por VMag^d, En quanto a lo que perteneçe a los intereses de cataluña se halla a la letra lo que contiene el capitulo de que remito a VMag^d copia con esta, el qual pareçe que es harto a fabor suyo por la expresion que se haçe de que los Montes huuiesen de quedar por diuision de ambos Dominios, con q̃ si el de conflent està de aquella parte, no creo que

---

[126] Letter 32 above.

habrà razon para poderlo defender;[127] y avnque en este caso le pareçe al consexo, segun lo reconozco por su consulta, que es fuerza combenir con lo que entonçes se huuiese acordado y VM^d se sirue de mandarme remitir la resoluçion a lo que me pareçiere sobre el hecho aqui y yo entiendo lo mismo que el consexo, Todavia, como VMg^d se sirue de deçirme juntamente que se ha remitido al de Aragon por si tiene alguna cossa nueba que alegar y tambien porq̃ VM^d pueda reconoçer si el Articulo de lo que en M^d estubo ajustado (de que va aqui la copia) tiene en su fabor la fuerza que yo supongo, esperarè la respuesta desta carta para executar lo que VMg^d me ordenare, Deuiendo juntamente deçir a VMg^d que de ninguna manera quieren venir en que quede remitido este punto a comisarios porque demas de que juzgan que tienen conoçida justiçia en el, diçen que no conformando los Diputados que fueren nombrados de vna y otra parte, como suele ser ordinario en semejantes occasiones, pueden resultar muchos incombenientes y que para mayor seguridad de la Paz, combiene dejar aora terminadas todas las cosas de manera que no queden ningunas diferençias pendientes que puedan dar motibo a turbarla despues, demas de que siendo ellos dueños oy de aquel Territorio, no conformandose los Diputados, deueran retenerle como poseedores presentes.

De todo lo qual me ha pareçido dar quenta a VM^d para que con vista dello se sirua de ordenarme vltimamente lo que fuere de su real Volunt^d. Dios g^{de} la catholica y real Persona de VMg^d como la christiandad ha menester. De fuenterrauia a 14 de Sept^{re} 1659

Dluismendezdeharo

---

[127] In his letter of 16 September to Le Tellier, Mazarin (1693: 162) claims that the Spanish secretary of state, Pedro Coloma, has confided that Haro is anxious about having ceded the Conflent and the Cerdagne to France because he fears the reaction of the Council of Aragon. Furthermore, we learn that one of the cardinal's advisers in St Jean de Luz named Dr Trobat knows the area well and is persuaded that France has won a great diplomatic victory with these concessions. However, Letter 48 suggests that Haro's understanding of what had been agreed in the earlier interview is very different. He claims there merely to have accepted what had been decided in Madrid in 1656, namely that the Pyrenees should mark the boundary between the two kingdoms. He had assumed that commissioners would be appointed to determine on which side of the mountains the Conflent was located. If this is in fact a genuine case of misunderstanding, it seems unlikely that Haro could have expressed to Coloma the kind of anxiety to which Mazarin refers.

43

Haro to Philip IV: Fuenterrabía, 17 September 1659 [K1623: 89]

Haro refers to his letter (Letter 42) to the king dated 14 September and reports on his twelfth interview with Mazarin held on 15 September. During another heated debate over the articles pending resolution, Mazarin became so worked up that he was forced to leave the conference room for a drink. The catalyst was the discussion over the demolition of La Bassée and restitution of Bergues. Mazarin did, however, eventually calm down and this leads Haro to hope that agreement will shortly be reached on all outstanding articles of the peace treaty without his having to exceed in any way the orders which he has received from the king.[128] The latest news on England is that the king is in Normandy incognito with the Duke of York. Lambert's troops have apparently defeated those who rose at Chester in support of the king, although part of the infantry and all of the cavalry have withdrawn to Chester, which remains loyal to the royalist cause. Haro has also heard that there are movements in support of Charles in Wales and in other parts of the country.

44

Haro to Philip IV: Fuenterrabía, 23 September 1659 [K1619: 43][129]

After an unusually long gap of six days, Haro writes again to Philip. He discusses the marriage agreement; his concern over the ranking of those who will witness the public reading of the document; he fears offending those concerned and requests instructions from Madrid; the French are tussling with the same problem.

---

[128] The diary entry of Priorato (1667: 177–80) for 18 September records that Mazarin has gained three provinces and thirty strongholds without having prejudiced the interests of France's allies. If Priorato's account is accurate, what Haro has to say here about not exceeding his orders must mean that Spain was prepared to make substantial concessions for the sake of peace.

[129] Letter 44 was dispatched with Letters 45, 46, 47 and 48 on 24 September and arrived in Madrid on 27 September. The cost of the dispatch was 734 *reales de plata* because the courier was again given 'medio cauallo mas de ventaxa'; AGS CMC 3551 (2), 27. All four letters deal with important items of business.

Señor

A la otorgaçion de la escritura de capitulaçion matrimonial de la s^{ra} Infante pareçe deuen concurrir todas las Personas de mayor grado y calidad que me asisten y se hallaren entonçes aqui, poniendo sus nombres y grados al prinçipio como se hizo quando se otorgò en Madrid la escritura del casamiento de la s^{ra} Infante Doña Ana (oy Reyna de françia) año de 612. Y deseando yo la satisfaçion de todos en comun y de cada vno en particular por el reparo que podrian haçer en la graduaçion de su nombramiento, me ha pareçido que aseguro el açierto con embiar a VM^d la memoria inclusa de los que oy se hallan aqui y de los que se hallaron en las capitulaçiones de la s^{ra} Reyna Doña Ana, suplicando a VMag^d sea seruido de mandarme embiar orden sobre la graduaçion como huuieren de ponerse en la escritura. Y tengo por tanto mas neçesaria esta declaraçion de VMg^d quanto he entendido que françeses se hallan tambien con este mismo reparo y embarazo. Dios g^{de} la catholica y Real Persona de VM^d como la christiandad ha menester. De fuenterrauia a 23 de septiembre de 1659.

Dluismendezdeharo

45

Haro to Philip IV: Fuenterrabía, 23 September 1659 [K1619: 44][130]

Affairs of England: Mazarin had reported in their last interview that Will Lockhart was reluctant to go to Fuenterrabía for his audience with Haro because he had heard that Haro had been accompanied to the border by numerous Irish troops and because the English king's resident ambassador was also in the town. He had therefore requested an audience on the Isle of Pheasants. Haro rehearses the reasons which he gave for not acceding to Lockhart's request, despite the concern, expressed through the cardinal, over the fate of the English resident ambassador to Madrid some years before. Five or six days after this interview, Lockhart had arrived in Hendaye and requested an appointment with Haro, who agreed to receive him in his residence at 10 a.m. the following day. During their meeting, the English envoy had expressed the good will of the English Republic towards the Spanish Crown and lamented all that the previous Protector had done to sour relations between their two countries. Haro had similarly regretted the

---

[130] Letter 45 was dispatched to Madrid with Letter 44.

damage done to the warm relations which the Spain of Philip IV had always enjoyed with the English crown. Realising that Lockhart was attempting to discover whether or not Spain was ready to open negotiations with England, Haro had emphasised that he had powers only to negotiate a peace treaty and marriage alliance with France. Lockhart's response had suggested to Haro that England was willing to be flexible and to grant Spain very favourable conditions. Even so, Haro had not taken the bait. Since their interview, he has heard no more from Lockhart but has learned from Mazarin that the Englishman returned to St Jean de Luz well satisfied with the reception which he had been given in Fuenterrabía.

With regard to the internal affairs of England, Haro reports the defeat of Booth's army at Chester by Lambert and his parliamentary forces. Lambert is now in control of the port and Booth, who had been taken prisoner whilst trying to escape disguised as a woman, had been sent to the tower of London. It was this setback which forced the English king to remain in Normandy instead of crossing to England as planned. Mazarin has so far had nothing to propose with regard to a joint Spanish–French venture into English affairs, apparently preferring to wait until the remainder of the business of the conference has been completed. Haro is happy to go along with this postponement.

Señor

He dado quenta a VMag^d estos dias del estado de las cosas de Inglaterra y en esta carta, que compreenderà solo este punto, lo haré con mayor parti cularidad p^a que con notiçia de todo pueda VMg^d mandarme dar las ordenes que juzgare por mas combenientes a su real seruiçio.

En vna de las conferençias pasadas me dixo el Car^{al} que hauia respondido a Locart lo que yo le hauia dho en orden a que le daria avdiençia y que el mostraua gran deseo de poder llegar a tomarla; pero que respeto de hauer entendido que en esta Plaça hauia muchos Irlandeses y que entre mi sequito venian algunos ofiçiales desta naçion y que se hallaua aqui el Residente del Rey,[131] le hauia propuesto si, para salbar estos incombenientes, le podria yo oir vno destos dias de conferençia en la Barraca. Respondile que aquel sitio se hauia elijido en el

---

[131] Sir Henry Bennett served as resident of the English king in Spain from 1657. Following the Restoration, he controlled the Privy Purse and later succeeded Sir Edward Nicholas as Secretary of State. Honoured by Charles II with an earldom, he became the first Earl of Arlington. He was known in post-Restoration London for his Catholic and Castilian sympathies.

confin de ambos Reynos en vn lugar Neutro y en la forma que estaua dispuesto solo para ajustar el casamiento y la Paz de corona a corona; y que demas de que no seria justo introduçir otros intereses alli, se deuia considerar tambien q̃ hauiendose por su parte impedido la venida de los embaxadores del Papa y de la Republica de Veneçia y no hauiendose admitido en aquel sitio la concurrençia de los Ministros de los demas Prinçipes que le hauian seguido â el y a mi, pues los vnos y los otros venian a tomar sus Avdiençias y las mias en s.^t Juan de Luz y fuenterrauia y no en aquel lugar que se hauia elijido para tan diferente fin, el admitir en el (haçiendo vna singularidad tan grande) a vn embaxador de vna Republica rebelde y de diferente religion ni yo podia venir en ello ni juzgaua que seria cossa honesta ni para su eminençia ni para mi, ni aprouada en el mundo; y que pues yo me hallaua dispuesto a darle la avdiençia si el tenia orden de su Republica para hablarme, como lo daua â entender, deuia venir a tomarla en el lugar de mi residençia; que el embarazo de los Irlandeses no me tocaua juzgarle a mi, ni en esta Plaza hauia Infanteria desta naçion sino solo dos o tres Maestros de Campo que, entre los demas ofiçiales mayores de Guerra assi españoles como de otras naçiones, me hauian venido siguiendo. A esto me respondio, dando â entender que Locart haçia resistençia por la memoria del accidente suçedido en Madrid al Residente Ascan.[132] Pero comoquiera que yo hauia excluydo totalmente el oirle en la Isla, como juzgué que combenia, y que hauia cumplido bastantemente con hauer ofreçido admitirle a la Avdiençia en esta Plaza siempre que quisiese venir a tomarla y que las dificultades que se interponian eran por hecho suyo y no por el mio, me pareçio dejarme ir corriendo con ellas mientras el no boluiese â hablar; de que tambien se siguia [*sic*] el ir ganando tiempo, que era lo que mas podia combenir.

Cinco ô seis dias despues, se vino Locart vna tarde a dormir a Andaya[133] (que esta debaxo del cañon de esta Plaza, con solo la via en medio) y

---

[132] A reference to the murder of Sir Anthony Ascham, agent of the Commonwealth Parliament to the king of Spain, perpetrated in Madrid on Sunday, 5 June 1650. Ascham had only just arrived in Madrid from Puerto de Santa María, had been taken to 'common lodgings' by his Spanish escorts and had been left there for the night unguarded. During the night he was stabbed to death by a number of his countrymen who broke into his room and accused him of being a traitor. These men, most of whom were soldiers in the service of the Spanish king, subsequently took refuge in a local church. It seems that they were never properly brought to justice. PRO SP94/43, fols 35r–37v.

[133] This is the spelling of *Hendaye* most commonly used in these documents.

embio a pedirme hora para la Avdiençia, la qual le señale para el dia siguiente a las diez.[134] Comenzò su discurso diçiendo que hauiendo sauido su Repp[ca] que venia ha hablarme en este congreso, le hauia mandado que viniese a representarme en su nombre la buena correspondençia y amistad que siempre hauia deseado tener con la corona de VMg[d] y quanto sentimiento tenia de que los Proçedimientos del Protector pasado la huuiesen turbado.[135] A que yo le respondi con palabras Generales cassi en la misma sustançia, diçiendole tambien la buena correspondençia que se hauia conserbado siempre de parte de VMag[d] con aquella corona y hauer VMag[d] reçiuido el mismo sentimiento que ellos mostrauan de que las acciones de Cromuel la huuiesen alterado. A esto respondio reforzando vn poco mas su discurso en la misma sustançia y acabando con deçir que si yo tenia algo que mandarle, daria de su parte los pasos que fuesen neçesarios. Aqui, viendo yo que queria reconoçer si se le daua abertura para tratar, le respondi mostrando de nuebo la buena correspondençia que VM[d] hauia deseado conserbar siempre con aquella corona y q̄ con la misma se hallaua VMag[d] de presente, que es lo que podia deçirle porque VM[d] me hauia embiado â este confin solo a tratar del casamiento y de la Paz con françia y que assi no hauia traydo ordenes ni poderes para tratar otro ningun negoçio y que aora daria quenta a VMg[d] de lo que me deçia. A que respondio luego que el no trataua de darme por la respuesta mas priesa que aquella que yo quisiese tomar porque conoçia que las cosas estauan muy a los prinçipios; que solo hauia querido que yo supiese la buena disposiçion con que se hallaua la Republica y como, siempre que yo lo juzgase por a proposito, daria de su parte todos los pasos que fuesen neçesarios y todos aquellos que fuesen de satisfaçion mia, en que virtualmente, por lo que dixo y en la forma que lo dixo, dio â entender que en quanto a condiçiones se nos daria

---

[134] Priorato (1667: 71–73) has a number of interesting things to say about Lockhart's visit which do not emerge from the Spanish sources I have been able to consult. First, he tells us that Haro was in bed when he received the Englishman 'afin de se degager par là de toute civilité, qui pût estre sujette à contestation, ou tirer à consequence'; second, he confirms that 'par le moyen d'un Interprete, il [Lockhart] confera avec Dom Louis, luy ouvrit les sentiments de sa Republique, tels que nous les avons dits, & en suite ils se separerent avec civilité, & avec des marques reciproques d'honneur & d'estime.'

[135] This is probably a reference, among other things, to the capture of Jamaica by Cromwell. The loss of this island is without doubt what most irritated Philip IV about Cromwell's action on the Spanish main and what prompted Spain to declare war on England in 1655.

toda aquella que pudiesemos desear. Yo le respondi en la misma forma y quedando en los mismos Terminos que lo hauia hecho hasta entonçes pero con palabras de toda cortesia. Y con esto se despidio y se fue a Andaya y despues aca ni me ha embiado a proponer nada, ni el car^{al} me ha buelto a hablar en el mas de lo que me dixo el dia siguiente, que fue de conferençia, diçiendo que Locart hauia estado con el y que hauia buelto con mucha satisfaçion de mi avdiençia.

Las nueuas que se han tenido de dos dias á esta parte de Inglaterra son de que la gente del partido del Rey, que despues de la rota se hauia retirado al Puerto de chester, hauia sido obligada a rendirse á Lambert,[136] que mandaua las Tropas del Parlamento, que, por consequençia, se hauia hecho dueño del Puerto; y que Bot[137] (cabeza de los Presuiterianos y que hauia tomado la boz del Rey) hauia sido preso yendose retirando disfraçado, bestido de muger, y que hauia sido llebado a la Torre de Londres; conque el Rey se hallaua todavia en los Puertos de Normandia, hauiendo dejado de pasar a chester, como estaua determinado, por este siniestro suçeso, que es quanto por aora puedo deçir a VMg^d del estado de aquellas cosas; y que el cardenal no me ha hecho ninguna proposiçion positiua sobre ellas porque siempre ha dado â entender que lo reserba para despues que se hayan acauado de ajustar los Articulos de Paz de corona a corona. Y a mi me ha pareçido esto tan combeniente que de muy buena gana me he dexado correr con ello. Dios g^{de} la catholica y real Persona de VMg^d como la christiandad ha menester. De fuenterrauia a 23 de sept^{re} 1659.

Dluismendezdeharo

---

[136] John Lambert, a Yorkshireman and parliamentary general during the English Civil War, was a principal architect of the Protectorate.

[137] Sir George Booth, although not hitherto a royalist, led the abortive royalist rising at Chester in 1659. The affair was not well planned and Booth's forces were easily put down by Lambert.

46

Haro to Philip IV: Fuenterrabía, 23 September 1659 [K1619: 45][138]

The agent of the Duke of Parma at the peace conference has asked France and Spain to include in the peace treaty a clause in support of the duke's claim before the Pope to have restored to him the Italian estates of Castro and Ronciglione. Haro and Mazarin recommend the inclusion of such a clause in the treaty in order to reduce the risk of further disturbances in Italy. They suggest that the clause should say that both crowns intend to ask the Pope to allow the duke to pay in instalments his debts to the Holy See, together with those connected with the estates of Castro and Ronciglione, and that he should be permitted to dispose of part of the estates in order to raise the necessary capital. Mazarin has also requested a similar clause in support of the Duke of Modena, whose claim on the Valley of Comacchio has encountered all kinds of opposition. Accordingly, Haro requests instructions from Madrid. Mazarin himself recognises that his own motives are not altogether unselfish in this matter since his niece is married to the duke.

Señor

Sobre las instançias que aqui haçe el Agente del Duque de Parma para que en este Tratado se ponga Capitulo çerca de pasar ofiçios vnidamente en nombre de VMag^{d}y del Rey xpt^{mo} con el Papa en orden a la restituçion de sus estados de Castro y Ronçillon.[139] Hemos hablado sobre ello en estas conferençias yo y el cardenal, Y pareçiendo combeniente procurar quitar toda suerte de motibos que puedan ocasionar turbaçiones en Italia, juzgamos serà bien que este capitulo se ponga, diçiendo que se pasaran dichos ofiçios vnidamente como otras veçes se han pasado separados, suplicando a su s^d tenga por bien de conçeder al Duque facultad de satisfaçer en algunos plazos las deudas que tiene con la camara Apostolica y sobre aquellos estados, y que, por empeño ô enagenaçion de alguna parte de ellos, pueda buscar el dinero neçesario para dho efecto.

Con esta ocasion me ha pedido el cardenal que tambien se ponga otro capitulo de ofiçios con su s^d por el Duque de Modena sobre el desembarazo de su pretension a la Valle de Camacho,[140] ora sea por composiçion ô por

---

[138] Letter 46 is another letter dispatched on 24 September and arriving in Madrid on 27 September.
[139] *Ronciglione* and *Castro* are both situated in Latium, close to Viterbo.
[140] *Camacho* is a distortion of Italian *Comacchio*, located southeast of Ferrara.

tela de juiçio. Y avnque aprieta mucho en ello como en negoçio propio por el casami^(to) de su sobrina, no le responderé derechamente hasta que, hauiendo VMg^d entendido la instançia del Cardenal, se sirua de mandarme dar la orden que huuiere de executar;[141] Deuiendo yo juntamente añadir que esta instançia no solo la funda el car^l en la combeniençia publica de procurar acomodar, por esta via de ofiçios, estas diferençias entre los Prinçipes de Italia por lo que puede conduçir a la quietud della, sino que se declara tambien que la haçe por estar el Duque casado con su sobrina. Nro s^r guarde la catholica y real Persona de VM^d como la christiandad ha menester. De fuenterrauia a 23 de sept^re 1659

Dluismendezdeharo

47

Haro to Philip IV: Fuenterrabía, 23 September 1659 [K1619: 46][142]

Haro refers to various letters from the king; a visit from the Duke of Gramont and an interview with Mazarin have prevented him from responding as quickly as he would have liked. The king's dispatch of 16 September, which included a *consulta* prepared by the Council of State on the matter of Juliers, reveals a belief in the council that Haro has not fully understood the recommendations of an earlier *consulta* dated 4 September. Haro emphasises that he shares the view of the council and concedes that the pressures of work probably led him to express himself less clearly in his earlier letter than was his custom. Accordingly, he confirms that Spain should not insist on retaining Juliers if this seems likely to jeopardise the peace process. In fact, Juliers could be exchanged for a stronghold of similar importance or for the satisfaction of Condé. However, Madrid is being over optimistic if it thinks that France will both swap Thionville for Juliers and agree that possession of the latter by the Duke of Neuburg should be subject to the will of the Spanish king. Mazarin's reasoned resistance to this proposal persuades Haro not only that France wants Juliers for herself but also that the terms set by Spain are too high for France to accept. Pimentel and the Count of Gramont, who are familiar with the area, agree with the French assessment

---

[141] Alphonso, fourth Duke of Modena, had married Laura Martinozzi, one of Mazarin's many nieces. He became duke following the death of his father in 1658.

[142] Letter 47 was dispatched with Letters 44, 45 and 46.

of the problem and also argue that control of Juliers will not guarantee the loyalty of the duke, as experience has shown. They maintain that so long as Spanish troops continue to enjoy a right-of-way through the duke's territory, Juliers may be surrendered in exchange for some improvement in the terms on offer to Condé. Haro pledges to get the best deal possible for Spain without breaking the peace.

With regard to the restoration of Bergues and demolition of La Bassée, the recommendation of the council is that Spain could consider surrendering St Omer if France were also to give up Bethune and improve significantly the offer on the table for Condé. Haro acknowledges the additional flexibility which this gives him but, because of the strategic importance of St Omer in Flanders, he will only surrender it as a last resort.

Haro had hoped to make considerable progress in the matters of Bergues, La Bassée and the prince of Condé during his interview with Mazarin of the previous day. Regrettably, however, a violent debate over the Conflent had used up all the conference time. He promises to continue to press for the best deal possible on these issues; he has drafted a separate letter (Letter 48 below) which summarises the state of negotiations with regard to the Conflent.

Señor

He reçiuido diferentes cartas de VMg^d de los 16, 17 y 19 deste en respuesta de las mias de 11, 12 y 14[143]y a todos los puntos dellas satisfaré aora y juntamente daré quenta a VMg^d de todo lo demas que se ofreçe. Pensé poder haçerlo antes de ayer y dejar despachado correo aquella noche pero a las 11 del dia vino a verme el Duque de Agramont para despedirse de mi y siendo ya aquella hora se quedaron a comer conmigo el, el Conde de Tolonjion su hermano, el Marques Gonzaga, el Conde de Quinzè[144] y algunas otras Personas particulares que venian con el. Estubimos a la

---

[143] Letters 39–42 above.
[144] *Conde de Tolonjion*, or Henri de Gramont, Count of Toulongeon and brother of Antoine III de Gramont-Toulongeon, Governor of Soule and lieutenant general in the king's army, member of the embassy of the Duke of Gramont sent to Madrid in order to request the hand of the Infanta María Teresa; *Marques Gonzaga*, a nobleman of the family of the Duke of Mantua; *Conde de Quinzé*, or Joachim, Count of Quincé, who died and was buried in Madrid during Gramont's embassy to the Spanish court. (His funeral costs of 3,500 *reales de vellón* were met by the Spanish treasury; AGS CMC 1818 (1), 1. We may compare this figure with the 20,718 *reales* of a total budget of 50,000 *reales* set aside for the funeral of the young Infante Fernando Tomás, who died around the same time; CMC 1818 (1), 2.)

mesa tres horas, que son cosas inescusables avnque harto molestas y que causan diuersion al tiempo que es neçess^{rio} para los negoçios, y lo restante del dia lo acabó de pasar conmigo, informandose del modo en que se hauia de gouernar en Madrid; y ayer fue dia de conferençia. Refiero lo vno y lo otro para disculpar la dilaçion de no hauer despachado este correo antes de aora.

En carta de los 16 deste, se sirue VMg^d de mandarme remitir copia de la consulta que el Consexo hauia hecho a VMag^d en fecha del mismo dia sobre el particular del Presidio de Juliers y me manda VMag^d que, teniendo presente el discursso y pareçer del consexo en los puntos que contiene, obre yo al pie del hecho lo que tuuiere por mas combeniente, advirtiendome VMg^d que en lo que se deçia sobre Juliers fuese yo con inteligençia de que (como antes VMg^d me lo tiene mandado escribir) es la voluntad de VMag^d que no por esto se deje ni dilate la conclusion de la Paz.

La consulta del Consexo se reduçe en la mayor parte â aclarar lo que hauia consultado a VMg^d en otra anteçedente de los 4 del mismo sobre este particular, juzgando que, segun el contenido de mi carta, yo hauia reçiuido alguna equibocaçion en ello. Y lo que en razon desto se me ofreçe q̃ deçir a VM^d es que seria posible que yo me huuiese declarado menos bien porque la falta de tiempo y carga de negoçios con que siempre me pongo â haçerlo es tan grande que serà bien posible el caer en esta falta algunas veçes; pero que en quanto a la inteligençia, he estado siempre en la misma de lo que el consexo apunta aora que es conforme a lo que propuso a VMag^d en la consss^{ta} çitada de los 4 que, en sustançia, fue aprobar la resistençia que yo hauia hecho sobre este punto y deçir que avnque por el no se deuia romper la Paz, porque la misma neçesidad que hauia obligado a consentir en que se quitase el Presidio de Correjio[145] al Duque de Modena persuadia tambien â esto y que assi podia yo venir en ello, resguardando que la Plaza nunca viniese a caer en manos de françeses y

---

[145] *Correggio* lies just northeast of Reggio Emilia. This principality was given to the Duke of Modena by Philip IV shortly after the duke transferred his allegiance from France to Spain. Unfortunately for Spain, however, the duke soon accepted an invitation to command French troops in Italy and went on to deprive Spain of Valenza and Mortara.

sacando, por quitar el Presidio en esta conformidad, a Tiumbila ô el restableçimiento del Prinçipe.[146]

Siempre lo he tenido presente assi y en esta conformidad (avnque yo no deui de darme â entender bien) he procurado resistirme s^{re} este punto y tenido intençion de no combenir en el sino es sacando dello fruto considerable porque claro estaua (como el Consexo lo representa a VMg^d muy justamente en su vltima consulta de los 16 deste) que no hauiendo de sacarse ninguna vtilidad, era mas ventaxosa seguridad para VMg^d mantener el Presidio que la palabra que se ofreçia y la buena fee del Duque y de sus suçesores. Pero la diferençia que en esto ay es que el presupuesto que se haçia de que françeses pudiesen dar a Tiumbila porque se quitase el Presidio de Juliers, quedando a la deuoçion de VMag^d, no ha salido çierto sino verificadose lo que yo temi y escribi siempre de que la intençion de françeses era de quedarse con esta Plaza; pues luego que yo apurè este punto y di â entender al cardenal que el Duque hauia de quedar obligado a tenerla a deboçion de VMg^d y a no poder benderla, enajenarla ni empeñarla ni reçiuir Presidio de ningun otro Prinçipe, se declaró en que si no es quedando el Duque con entera libertad de su Plaza para disponer della, mal pudiera el dar por esto otra mejor que ella como era Tiumbila. Conque quedò declarado que su intençion era el trocar la vna por la otra y quedarse ellos con Juliers. Y hauiendo yo negado totalmente esto, quedaron perseuerando en que se quitase el Presidio en la forma que yo lo proponia, como lo representè a VMag^d todo mas particularmente en despacho de los 11 deste;[147] a que añado aora que en contemplaçion desto, no daran Plaza mayor ni menor, como lo tienen declarado, ni tampoco en el punto del Prinçipe haran cosa de consideraçion si no es haçiendoles diferentes ofreçimientos porque diçen que Juliers es vna Plaza separada de todas las demas de VMag^d; que todo el Pays es del Duq̄ y el dominio de la Plaza de la misma manera; que no es neçesaria para el pasaxe de Alemania; que tampoco nos da paso sobre el Rin porque està siete leguas del; que VMag^d tiene solo el Presidio y gasta cada año quarenta ô çinquenta mill ducados en sustentarle; y q̄, quedando el Duque obligado a todo lo que yo quiero de tenerla siempre

---

[146] The syntax breaks down from 'avnque por el no se deuia romper la Paz'. However, the meaning is clear. Haro is authorised to surrender Juliers rather than jeopardise the peace process but he must ensure that it does not fall into French hands and must secure in exchange for it either Thionville or satisfaction for Condé.

[147] I have not found a document of this date which deals with this issue.

a la deboçion de VMag^d, dar paso por ella a sus Tropas quando le huuiere menester y a que la françia quede obligada en el mismo Articulo no solo a no ayudar al Duque sino a vnir sus Armas con las de VMag^d para castigarle siempre que faltare a lo que aora ofreçe, quedaua VMg^d tan dueño de la Plaza como lo es oy; y que esto se deuia pretender por cumplir a vn Aliado lo que se le tiene ofreçido por vna capitulaçion expresa pero no dar por ello recompensas, hauiendole de quedar la Plaza cautiba en esta forma. Ellos perseueran en lo mismo y yo en resistirlo si no es que se me de alguna recompensa. Pero Don Antonio Pimentel y el conde de Gramon, que conoçen la Plaza y el Pays, me diçen que no nos da paso sobre el Rin porque està muy apartada, ni nos priba de tenerle de Alemania a flandes, como yo lo juzgaua, ni el Presidio nos sirue avn solo de tener puesto el freno en la boca al Duque para que proçeda como deue, como la experiençia lo mostraua, pues se hauia vnido con la françia y con los demas Prinçipes del Rin contra VM^d sin que esta guarniçion se lo huuiese estorbado; y que como no se repare en el punto del decoro, que es el que a mi me ha causado embarazo siempre de que el Duque salga con esta ventaja hauiendo faltado al seruiçio de VMag^d, por lo demas y quedando el Duque obligado a mantenerla y dar por ella paso a las Tropas de VM^d siempre que le huuieren menester, no juzgan que pueda hauer cossa que importe menos particularmente si se pudiese sacar qualquiera ventaxa, por pequeña que fuese, a fabor del Prin^e. Y yo es çierto que lo procurare en quanto alcanzare avnque por esto, en vltimo casso obedeçiendo lo que VM^d me manda, ni romperè ni retardare la conclusion de la Paz.

En consulta de 16 deste (cuya copia se sirue tambien VMag^d de mandarme remitir) representa a VMg^d el consejo que por la restituçion de Bergas y demoliçion de la Basè se hauia juzgado por tratable el dar a s^n Tomer si ellos se contentasen de añadir â estas Plazas la de Betuna[148] y con calidad que se mejore de manera el Partido del Prinçipe que quede a satisfaçion de VMag^d, con lo demas que se discurre en razon desto; y VMag^d se sirue de mandarme que execute en ello lo que tuuiere por mas combeniente, en cuya conformidad lo que se me ofreçe que deçir a VMg^d es que quedo entendido de la facultad que VM^d se sirue de darme y que harè todo esfuerzo en procurar no llegar a vsar della ni enajenar a s^n Tomer si no fuere en vltimo casso, por ser vno de los prinçipales Valuartes que VM^d tiene en el Pays Vaxo y de cuya importançia habla el conde de

---

[148] Betuna (or *Bethune* in French) was a stronghold in Artois. Today it is part of the department of Pas-de-Calais.

Gramon, segun las ordenes que ha traydo del Marques de Carazena, con mayor encareçimiento.

En la conferençia de ayer, tube esperança que pudiese quedar muy adelantado el punto de la restituçion de Bergas y demoliçion de la Base y avn ganado tambien algun paso en el part^r del Prinçipe; pero hauiendo comenzado â hablar en la diferençia sobre Conflent (de que doy quenta a VMag^d en carta aparte que perteneçe solo a este punto),[149] fue tal la borrasca que se lebantò (como VMg^d lo entenderà mas particularmente por ella) que se consumieron cassi seis horas sin haber lugar para hablar en ninguna otra cossa; y yo he quedado de manera della que demas de lo que contiene esta carta y los otros despachos que lleua este correo, no podre por oy deçir a VMag^d mas de que en quanto a los resguardos del cassamiento, hasta que estè ejecutada la Paz y entregadas las Plaças, fie VMg^d de mi que tomare todos quantos pudieren ser menester para la total seguridad, como quien tambien conoçe aqui sobre el mismo hecho (por muchas razones que dexo de explicar) quan necess^{rio} serà esto; y de la misma manera puede VM^d estar çierto de que sobre la restituçion de Bergas y la Basè y particular del Prinçipe, procuro y procurarè adelantar el seruiçio de VM^d con la menos costa que se pudiere, y gouernarme en todo conforme a las ordenes de VMag^d Cuya Catholica y real Persona g^{de} Dios como la xpt^d ha menester. fuenterrauia 23 de s^{re} 659

Dluismendezdeharo

48

Haro to Philip IV: Fuenterrabía, 23 September 1659 [K1623: 91][150]

This is the separate letter dealing with the Conflent that Haro mentions towards the end of Letter 47. After referring to his letter of 14 September to the king (Letter 42 above), Haro returns to the interview held on 19 September in which Mazarin had become very agitated over the matter of the Conflent and insisted on sticking to what had been agreed in Madrid in 1656. Mazarin had accused Haro of adopting a completely inflexible negotiating stance and of being unwilling to give way on any of the *puntos reservados*, regardless of whether or not reason was on his side. Mortara's reply to Haro's earlier letter suggests that it is possible to argue that the

---

[149] Letter 48 below.
[150] Letter 48 was dispatched with Letters 44, 45, 46 and 47.

Conflent is located on the Spanish side of the mountains and, in light of this, Haro proposes that the question could be referred to commissioners (which is what Spain had always wanted) who would decide where the division should come. Haro had, he says, told Mazarin that he accepted what was agreed in 1656 on the assumption that this meant that the matter would eventually be resolved by commissioners. On this understanding, he had agreed that the article could be referred to Coloma and Lionne for inclusion in the treaty.

In the fourteenth interview held on 22 September, Mazarin had suggested that Coloma and Lionne should be invited into the conference chamber in order to write down what was agreed. When Lionne read aloud the draft version, much to Haro's surprise, the article stated that the Conflent had been ceded to France, no mention being made of the mountains as the determining factor for assigning it either to Spain or to France. Haro had reiterated what he had understood to be the basis of the agreement but Mazarin was unwilling to refer the matter to commissioners, presumably because he recognised the difficulty in deciding exactly where the mountains began. Mazarin said that he feared that commissioners would not be able to reach agreement and that war would break out again. Accordingly, he had insisted that France would not surrender any of the strongholds it held to the south of the Pyrenees nor negotiate any further articles of the treaty until this matter had been settled. Haro has consulted with Marco Genaro,[151] who is familiar with the area and considers the Conflent to be on the French side of the mountains.[152]

---

[151] Marco Genaro is described elsewhere as *Marco Antonio de Genaro, Maestre de Campo*. CMC 3551 (2), 99.
[152] See note 127 for the background to the misunderstanding over what had been agreed in respect of the Conflent. This is a crucial stage in the negotiations for the French. In a letter of 21 September to Lionne, Mazarin (1693: 191–93) expresses the concern of the French king and queen that the negotiations are bogged down. They reproach the cardinal for having misled them into thinking that the peace conference is nearing completion and complain that if the court has to return to Paris without a marriage alliance, this will send the wrong signal across Europe. Similarly, in a letter to Le Tellier dated 24 September, Mazarin (1693: 197ff.) says that Haro will not allow Coloma to do anything without checking with him first. Mazarin had suggested that Coloma and Lionne should join the two plenipotentiaries in the conference chamber precisely so as to speed things up. In this same letter Mazarin confesses to having agreed to refer the matter of the Conflent to commissioners.

49

Haro to Philip IV: Fuenterrabía, 27 September 1659 [K1623: 92]

Haro rehearses the discussion over the Conflent reported in his letter of 23 September (Letter 48 above) and then reports on the interview held on 25 September. Although this had also been largely devoted to the Conflent, Juliers, La Bassée, Bergues and Condé were also discussed, as they are every time the two plenipotentiaries meet. Haro is determined to stand firm on these points, which have yet to be agreed, since neither the peace treaty nor the marriage agreement will be signed until Gramont has been to Madrid and has returned with Philip's permission for the infanta to marry Louis. He will also defend stoutly the interests of the Duke of Lorraine. The roads which the French claim in order to be able to move troops from the Duchy of Bar to Alsace would deprive the duke of the best half of his duchy. It is true that Lorraine's troops are currently in the service of the French king, that the duke has failed to show the kind of loyalty displayed by Condé and that his interests cannot, therefore, be given the same priority as Condé's. However, Lorraine did sign a treaty with Spain whilst in prison and what the French now want to do is unjust.

Haro encloses with this dispatch two letters from Caracena, one of which refers to a meeting with Condé. In that connection, Haro observes that Condé was wrong to suggest that his fate would be sealed if his interests were not secured before the marriage was agreed. He points out that, having agreed the terms of the marriage, he is now in a better position to negotiate with Mazarin on Condé's behalf. Caracena's other letter contains important information on the relative values of various strongholds. England continues to represent one of the most intractable issues of the conference because of the implications for the conquest of Portugal. Haro notes that the cause of the English king does not appear to be prospering at the moment.

50

Haro to Philip IV: Fuenterrabía, 30 September 1659 [K1623: 94]

The articles of the marriage agreement have been prepared in draft form following the model of that of Doña Ana, who is now the French queen. The dowry will be paid in instalments over a period of eighteen months after the pattern of the marriage of Philip II and Isabella. Mazarin has asked that the marriage ceremony take place as soon as possible and that the earliest possible date be agreed for the arrival of the infanta at the frontier. Haro says that he will try to slow things down until full agreement of the peace treaty is in sight. As instructed by the king, he will then spring on Mazarin the news that the marriage ceremony cannot take place until after the infanta has left Madrid.

51

Haro to Philip IV: Fuenterrabía, 2 October 1659 [K1623: 95][153]

This letter deals with the naming of allies in the treaty: whom to include and in what order. Instructions on how to draft this article had been forwarded to Haro by the king on 31 August in response to Haro's letter of 24 August (Letter 24). The whole matter is, nevertheless, still being debated without agreement so that it seems as if all of the allies will have to be named. The only problem with regard to ranking involves the Grand Duke of Florence and the Republic of Genoa. The king has ordered that both should be named but Haro is faced with the difficulty that earlier treaties do not all rank them in the same order. The treaty of Vervins, for example, which was signed during the reign of Philip II, favoured the Grand Duke despite his lack of a relationship with the Spanish royal family. Today, there is a close relationship[154] and, moreover, Genoa has not been so firm in its support of Spain as to merit a reversal of the order in the treaty of Vervins. Haro questions the inclusion of other potentates mentioned in the treaty of Vervins and also their status as allies or enemies.[155]

---

[153] Letters 51, 52 and 53 were dispatched on 3 October and arrived in Madrid on 6 October. The cost of the dispatch was 810 *reales de plata* because the courier was allowed 'vn caballo mas de ventaxa'; AGS CMC 3551 (2), 27. All three are important letters.

[154] The Grand Duke of Tuscany is Ferdinand II (1610–1670), son of Cosme II and Maria Magdalena of Austria. Although the close relationship referred to here is not easy to establish, Haro may have had in mind the fact that Philip's first wife, Isabella of France, was the daughter of Henry IV of France and Maria de Medici, and that Maria was a cousin of Cosme II. I am grateful to Dr Roberto Bruni of the University of Exeter for this information.

[155] When Haro left Madrid for the border, he took with him a large number of documents likely to be of use in his discussions with Mazarin. These included a chancery note on the relative ranking of the Grand Duke of Florence and the Republic of Genoa in earlier treaties. AGS Estado Francia K1623: 96 is a copy of this note.

52

Haro to Philip IV: Fuenterrabía, 2 October 1659 [K1623: 97][156]

Haro summarises developments since 27 September. It has been a stormy time, particularly in the debate over Bergues and La Bassée. He sketches the background to the debate and explains how his unwillingness to give in to Mazarin over compensation for the two strongholds had led eventually to the cardinal's decision to stop Gramont's embassy to Madrid and to abandon the peace conference. Haro was shaken by Mazarin's decision but could not help thinking that it was a ruse to force him to capitulate. He had therefore agreed to meet Mazarin on the island on the morning of Tuesday, 30 September, so that Mazarin might take his leave. However, the meeting had been less strained than anticipated. Mazarin's attitude had softened and Haro, whilst sticking to his guns, had adopted a more conciliatory tone. The two ministers had eventually agreed to meet again the following day. Haro had arrived at this meeting prepared to cede Avesnes, Marienbourg and Philippeville in exchange for Bergues and La Bassée, which would have been entirely in line with what the king had authorised him to do. But the mood of the interview was such that he had felt able to hold out for more, finally securing both Bergues and La Bassée in exchange for only Avesnes and Marienbourg.

Mazarin's persistent attempts in recent interviews to get Juliers for the Duke of Neuburg had persuaded Haro to send an urgent dispatch to Milan in order to seek advice on the strategic importance of this stronghold from the Count of Fuensaldaña. The reply, which had now arrived, stated that Juliers was not so important that it could not be surrendered and that an improved deal for Condé would be cheap at almost any price. Despite this advice, Haro, spurred on by his recent success, has resolved to try to get improved terms for both Condé and the Duke of Lorraine in exchange for only Juliers and Philippeville. His intention is not only not to exceed his instructions but to secure better deals than the king has authorised him to secure.

Finally, Haro reports that half of Gramont's party had left for Madrid that morning. He expects the rest to leave at dawn the next day.

---

[156] Letter 52 was dispatched on 3 October and arrived in Madrid on 6 October.

Señor

A los 27 del passado[157] di quenta a VMag^d de lo que hasta entonçes se ofreçia, y aora la continuare a VMag^d de la borrasca que se ha tenido estos tres o quatro dias vltimos; y para que VMag^d pueda quedar mexor informado de todas sus çircunstançias, me pareçe que debo referir algo de lo anteçedente.

El punto de las recompensas que se hauian de dar por la restituçion de Bergas y demoliçion de la Basè ha sido desde el prinçipio vno de los mas dificultosos deste Tratado y sobre que se ha disputado de parte a parte con mayor fuerza. Estas dos Plazas, como VMag^d saue, les vinieron çedidas por el Tratado de Paris, el qual fue ratificado en Madrid; y el hauer el Cardenal dexado abierta la puerta y remitido a nuestro abocamiento las recompensas que les hauiamos de dar, en caso que quisiesemos quedar con la vna y que se demoliese la otra, fue (segun todo quanto yo he podido alcanzar) solo con intençion de ver si por ser ambas tan considerables y tan internas y no sernos posible a ningun preçio quedar sin Bergas (por las razones que tantas veçes estan consideradas) podia conseguir que esta misma neçesidad y el deseo que se tenia de poder mexorar el particular del Prinçipe me pudiesen obligar a que, juntando ellos â estas dos Plazas la de s^t Venan y alguna otra y ofreçiendome alguna mas ventaxa para el Prinçipe, yo le diese en permuta de todo a Cambray por el deseo grande que ha tenido y muestra siempre della, que es de calidad que no le puede encubrir por mas que le procura. Y hauiendo yo por estas mismas causas respondidole con toda resoluçion que ni por Plazas ni por muchas Plazas ni por alguna menor ni mayor ventaxa en los intereses del Prinçipe ni por nada del mundo yo hauia de çeder a Cambray, Hers ni s^t Tomer por juzgar yo que si no es dandole este total desengaño, jamas podriamos acauar con el negoçio. Y hauiendo el Cardenal visto esto y que le quedaua çerrada la puerta â ello y conoçiendo claramente (como lo sauia) que no podiamos quedar sin Bergas, me pidio por ella y la Basè a s^t Tomer, despues a Duay y a Buchaim,[158] y vltimamente a charlemon;[159] y resistiendome yo a conçederle ninguna dellas, el no deçia mas sino que estas dos Plazas le estauan çedidas a la françia por vn

---

[157] Letter 49 above.

[158] Although *Hers* clearly lies somewhere along the Franco-Belgian border, I have not been able to identify it; *Buchaim* is French *Bouchain* and is located just north of Cambrai.

[159] We learn in Letter 58 that *Charlemont* is situated in the Belgian province of Namur between the rivers Meuse and Sambre.

Tratado hecho y ratificado, que si las recompensas que yo le ofreçiese fuesen de calidad que les estuuiese bien, las açetaria y que si no el no pretendia nada ni queria mas que quedar con ellas, que era lo que en primer lugar deseaua, y que assi no hauia mas que hablar ni que proponer; conque este punto se haçia harto dificultoso de ajustar, no pudiendo yo, segun las ordenes de VMg^d y lo que se me hauia escrito de flandes, quedar sin Bergas por ningun preçio y no queriendo dar tampoco el que se me pedia por ella por ser tan dañoso y tan ageno de toda razon y combenïençia.

VMg^d, conoçiendo esta misma dificult^d y neçesidad de no quedar sin la restituçion de Bergas y sin la demoliçion de la Basè por las razones que tantas veçes estan consideradas, se siruio de deçirme en carta de los 6 del pasado q̄ quando por Auenas y Mariemburg no pudiese yo sacar a Bergas y s^t Venan, las podria çeder por Bergas solo y que si se pudiese conseguir que nos restituyesen a Quenoy juntamente con Bergas, seria muy aventaxada negoçiaçion. A que respondi a VMag^d en 11 del mismo[160] que avnque el car^{al} se mantenia en la misma porfia que hasta entonçes en orden a querer a Buchaim ô a Duay ô quedarse con Bergas y la Basè, procuraria haçer quanto fuese de mi parte en orden â encaminar lo que VMg^d me mandaua, entendiendo que no hauia ni podia hauer otro medio que el mantenerme con toda firmeza y resoluçion hasta el vltimo punto sobre qualquiera destas cosas. Despues en carta de los 16 del pasado con el mismo conoçimiento que a VMag^d le asistia de la dificultad deste punto y de la combenïençia que se siguiria de poder ajustarlo, se siruio VMag^d de deçirme que si sobre Bergas y la Basé se contentasen de añadir â estas dos Plazas la de Betuna y con calidad que se mexorase de manera el partido del Prinçipe de Condé que quedase a satisfaçion de VMg^d, podria yo dar en permuta de todo a s$^{n\,}$Tomer. Y avnque con esta orden de VMag^d me hallaua con facultad para poder acabarlo en esta conformidad, Todavia deseando yo no llegar a çeder esta gran Plaza, por ser vna de las mas prinçipales de todo el Pays baxo y de cuya importançia me ha escrito siempre el Marques de Carazena y hablado el Conde de Gramon aora con gran encareçimiento, me yba procurando mantener con deseo de poder ajustar la restituçion de la vna y la demoliçion de la otra a preçio mas barato.

Sobre estos anteçedentes pasarè a decir a VM^d que hauiendose estado en vna destas vltimas conferençias disputando con gran fuerza de parte

---

[160] This would appear to be the same missing letter referred to in Letter 47 above (see note 147).

a parte sobre este punto y el del Prin^e, Deseando yo que ambos se incluyesen y acauasen vnidos y a vn mismo tiempo y no hauiendo el Cardenal combenido en ello, por cuya caussa se quedo vltimamente debatiendo solo sobre el de la recompensa de Bergas y la Bassè, y estando yo siempre firme en no hauerle de dar ninguna de las Plazas que pretendia Y entrando el quiza en vltima desconfianza de poder conseguir ninguna dellas, comenzo a zeder y, mostrando con grandes demostraçiones de impaçiençia que no tenia ya mas fuerzas para disputar, dixo que quedando ellos con la Bassè (porque se acauase ya con tantas porfias) vendria en dar en su lugar a quenoy; y avnque yo pudiera y deuiera contentarme con esto, siendo lo mismo que VMg^d se hauia seruido de deçirme que tendria por vna aventaxada negoçiaçion, juzgue verdaderamente segun lo que hauia comenzado a zeder (y algunas otras çircunstançias que pude obserbar aquella tarde) que manteniendome mas avn podria sacar mayor ventaxa sobre este punto, a que se añadio el hauerme dicho el Conde de Gramont la noche anteçedente que el puesto de Quenoy no era de gran consideraçion y que combenia increyblemente el procurar la demoliçion de la Basè para dexar en libertad a Lila y a todo su Pays porque de otra manera quedaria con vn gran freno; y que si se pudiese conseguir la restituçion libre desta Plaza como la de Bergas, seria mucho mayor la ventaxa porque no hauiendose podido conseguir que nos permutasen a s^n Venan, seria de gran combeniençia el tener y conserbar a la Basè. Por cuyas causas todas me pareçio no contentarme con la restituçion de Bergas y quenoy sino procurar ganar sobre este punto mayor ventaja y persistir en que se me hauia de dar en lugar de quenoy a la Basè, con que [*MS: conque*] se acabò la conferençia de aquella tarde. Y avnque mostrò disgusto de que yo no me huuiera acauado de contentar con lo que hauia ofreçido, no se despidio con aquellas demostraçiones de destemplanza que le hauia suçedido otras veçes. Pasaron dos dias despues sin hauer tenido mas conferençia por hauer sido dias de fiesta en que desde el prinçipio (por escusar el gran concurso de gente que solia acudir) nos combenimos en no tenerlas y Pedro Coloma y Leone yban ajustando las palabras y los Articulos que ya estauan acordados; y estando las cosas en este estado Lunes que se contaron 29 del passado, embio Leone a pedirme hora para verme aquella tarde y yo se la señale para las quatro sin juzgar que se pudiese ofreçer por entonçes noueded en nada y que venia â ajustar conmigo la hora de la conferençia para el dia siguiente. Pero en entrando, comenzò diçiendo que el car^al le hauia mandado me dixese de su parte que no sauia la forma como se hauia de acabar este negoçio porque en quanto a las recompensas de Bergas y la Base, yo no hauia querido darle ninguna de las que me hauia pedido ni dejarle con estas mismas Plazas que se le hauian zedido por el Tratado que se hallaua ya firmado y ratificado (y que al mismo tiempo pretendia ventajas para el Prin^e) ni tampoco me ajustaua â acabar de ratificar el tratado en todo como venia hecho; que con hauerme mantenido firme en estas demandas hauia tomado la ventaxa de hauer ganado el tiempo de la campaña y hauer evitado los daños que se podian seguir della con que [*MS: conque*] deuia contentarme; que el no podia detenerse mas y que assi me pedia que estuuiese el dia siguiente a las ocho en la Barraca para despedirse de mi y poder partir el siguiente para Burdeos, y que tuuiese entendido que se hauia embiado orden a Irun al Marischal de Agramont para que suspendiese su jornada y boluiese a s^t Juan de Luz como con efecto lo hiçieron, juzgando quiza que me podrian espantar con todo esto junto y obligarme a zeder en los puntos que se estauan disputando.

Yo confieso verdaderamente a VMag^d que avnq̃ tenia hartas razones para creer que el Car^al no podria irse y romper el Tratado con tanta façilidad como lo daua â entender, Todavia comoquiera que no puede hauer total seguridad en lo que se discurre sobre hechos agenos y que en el fin deste negoçio consistia la suma de todos y el reposo de la christiandad, y viendo quan forzado ha entrado el cardenal en el casamiento y en la Paz, no pude dexar de reçiuir algun cuydado con vna nouedad semexante. Pero considerando que despues de hauer oydo aquellas amenazas seria muy contrario a la reputaçion y al bien del mismo negoçio para los puntos que quedauan por ajustar si yo hiçiese qualquiera declinaçion, me pareçio mantenerme con la misma y avn mayor firmeza que hasta entonçes. Y assi sin entrar en discursos con el sobre las recompensas de Bergas y la Basè ni particular del Prin^e, le respondi que me hallaria la mañana siguiente en la Isla a las ocho como el cardenal me lo mandaua y avn mucho mas de mañana si fuese menester; que yo no sauia que tuuiese razones para quererse despedir de mi pero que si perseuerase en ello, yo no le podria detener sino solo quedar por algunos dias en este puesto para que se viese mas a la clara que era el Cardenal el que se yba y yo el que me quedaua, pareçiendome muy justo que tomase esta ventaxa sobre mi. Quiso boluer a entrar (hauiendo oydo esta respuesta mia) en los negocios que se estauan disputando pero yo no se lo admiti y le respondi que yo no tenia mas que deçir que lo que hauia dicho y que me hallaria el dia siguiente por la mañana en la Barraca a ver lo que el car^al me mandaua. Y con esto, se disoluio la platica y la visita.

El dia siguiente Martes, llegue a la Barraca media hora antes de la que se me hauia señalado y el cardenal vn gran rato despues; en sentandose, me comenzò ha hablar en la misma sustançia y forma que Leone pero ya con algunas señales de que hauia comenzado a baxar la creziente con que [*MS: conque*] me pareçio que hauiendo respondido a Leone en la forma que yo lo hauia hecho la tarde anteçedente y viniendo ya el cardenal con notiçia dello y hauiendome comenzado â hablar con menos impetu, deuia yo tambien responderle con terminos mas blandos. Y assi le dixe que ni el ni yo tendriamos razon (y ambos harto en que pensar) para dejar de conformarnos y perpetuar la Guerra en toda la christiandad por la diferençia de los puntos que quedauan pendientes; que yo sentia mucho el causarle disgusto y no hauerme podido conformar desde la primera hora en lo que hauia pretendido sobre ellos por lo que deseaua desembarazalle, conoçiendo el poco gusto con que se detenia y la falta que haçia al seruiçio del Rey xpt^{mo} çerca de su Persona; y que si yo pudiera apartarme de lo que tenia dicho, estuuiese çierto que lo huuiera hecho ya; que le suplicaua que sin pasion considerase las ventajas que hauia tomado en el Tratado de Paris; y que hauiendo venido remitidas aqui las recompensas de Bergas y la Basè, avnque yo conoçia que eran dos Plazas tan considerables y tan importantes por su situaçion (como me deçia), no deuian darse por ellas otras mayores sino antes recompensas que valiesen algo menos, como toda razon lo pedia, pues de otra manera huuiera sido mejor no hauer dejado remitido este punto aqui; que en el particular del Prinçipe, conoçia lo que hauian dicho siempre y lo que le hauian resistido y que hauia venido este Articulo firmado y ratificado pero que le suplicaua que tambien considerase (como se lo hauia representado otras veçes) la forma en que hauia obligado a Don Antonio Pimentel a que lo firmase sin dexarle libertad para despachar vn correo. Conque yo no podia dexar de esperar (como lo hauia esperado siempre) que hauiendonos juntado el y yo en aquella Barraca, hauiamos de boluer con toda amistad a reduçir este punto a lo que fuese de razon, y que el boluer el Prin^e a françia con vn poco de mas satisfaçion lo juzgaua yo tambien por muy conforme al serui^o del Rey xpt^{mo} y a la quietud de su estado. Y con estas y otras razones deste genero dichas muy blandamente, procurè irle mitigando pero continuando siempre en dar â entender que yo no podia çeder en ninguno de aquellos puntos que quedauan pendientes; y el Car^{al} avnque siempre perseuerando en pretender alguna de las Plazas capitales, estubo mucho menos reçio y finalmente se acabo la conferençia en Paz y quedamos aplazados para boluernos a juntar alli el dia siguiente a las diez que fue ayer, cuya conferençia duro seis largas horas en que hubo hartos lançes que fueran dignos de referir. Pero remitiendo la relaçion destos y de otras muchas çircunstançias para quando yo (siendo Dios seruido) tenga la dicha de llegar a los pies de VMg^d, dirè solo a VMg^d aora que avnque yo, quando entrè en la vltima conferençia de ayer, hauia ydo con resoluçion de ofreçer demas de Auenas y de Mariemburg a felipevila[161] (que es vna cosa muy poca) porque en lugar de quenoy me dejasen a la Basè no demolida sino con todas sus fortificaçiones como oy està, y al Conde de Gramont le hauia pareçido que si lo pudiese conseguir en esta forma lo executase luego porque seria vna muy combeniente negoçiaçion, Reconoçiendo despues que entrè en la Barraca (segun el estado en que se fue poniendo el negoçio) que quiza se podria ahorrar a felipeuila, me mantube firme hasta entrar en la sesta hora y finalm^{te} se consiguio que por solo Auenas y Mariemburg se haga la restituçion de Bergas con su jatelania y fuerte real que esta sobre el canal que va a Dunquerque, y, juntamente, la restituçion libre de la Base sin demolerla sino fortificada en la misma forma que oy lo està. Lo qual queda asegurado y acauado y yo con el gusto que se puede juzgar de que se haya podido aventaxar este punto algo mas de aquello con que VM^d me hauia dado â entender que se daria por seruido.

Luego que el cardenal me hizo tan apretada instançia por quitar el Presidio de Juliers y deseando poder gouernarme en ello con mayor luz, despache vn correo yente y viniente al Conde de fuensaldaña, pidiendole me dixese lo que entendia sobre esto (como quien deuia tener tan part^r notiçia desta materia), el qual me ha respondido lo que se contiene en la carta inclusa que remito aqui. Y avnque, segun lo que VMag^d mandarà ver por ella, juzga el Conde que se deue haçer poco reparo en esto por las razones que representa y diçe juntamente que a qualquiera preçio que se pudiere ganar alguna ventaxa sobre el part^r del Prin^e se comprarà muy barato, todavia me quedo manteniendo con deseo de que tampoco para conseguir esto se emplee ninguna Plaza de grande ni mediana consideraçion, pretendiendo yo que con añadir a lo del Presidio de Juliers, en la forma que està dicho, solo a Felipevila, que esta junto a Mariemburg y es vn puesto muy deuil y de poca considerazion, se haya de ajustar en alguna forma que sea bastante assi el punto del Prinçipe como el del Duque de Lorena, el qual tiene tambien mucha neçesidad de mexorarse por todas las razones que tengo dichas a VMg^d por mis anteçedentes, hauiendome pareçido combeniente incluirle ya tambien con el del Prinçipe assi por perteneçer tambien a otro Aliado como porque si se pueden feneçer ambos juntos, vendran a quedar ajustados todos los

---

[161] *Philippeville* is a stronghold in Namur.

articulos de la Paz y ella de todo punto concluyda como tanto se deue desear; y avnque no dudo que el car^(al) viendose ya reduçido â este estado harà todo esfuerzo en procurar sacar por la ventaxa que pretendemos en fabor destos dos Aliados alguna de las Plazas prinçipales, quedo con resoluçion de mantenerme firme dentro destos terminos y no exçeder dellos ni consentir en su demanda con deseo de ajustar este vltimo punto en forma y a preçio que VMag^d se pudiese dar por seruido dello, como lo he procurado en quanto ha sido de mi parte en todo lo demas, como lo pide mi obligaçion.[162]

La mitad de la cassa y de los camaradas del Duq̃ de Agramont ha partido esta mañana de Irun y el partirà sin falta con el resto mañana al amanezer.[163] Dios g^(de) la Catolica y R^l Persona de VMg^d como la christiandad ha menester. De fuenterrauia a 2 de ott^(re) de 1659.

Dluismendezdeharo

---

[162] Gualdo Priorato (1667: 59, 189–93) records that the article relating to Condé was actually signed during the seventeenth conference held on 1 October. Juliers was, apparently, also ceded to the Duke of Neuburg at the same time. Clearly, none of this squares with Haro's record of the proceedings of this conference. If we are to believe Gualdo Priorato, these matters were common knowledge among the French who were at the border; it is therefore difficult to see how Haro could have hoped to conceal them from Madrid.

[163] This fascinating account of why Mazarin decided to stop Gramont's embassy and abandon the peace conference, together with the way in which the whole affair was resolved, bears absolutely no relation to the account which we find in Mazarin's letter of 30 September to Le Tellier. According to Mazarin (1693: 248–57), Haro had insisted on drafting the article relating to Condé and had done so with the assistance of Lenet and supporters of the prince in attendance at the conference. The cardinal was so horrified by the wording of the article that he instructed Gramont not to continue his journey. He also sent Lionne to inform Haro that the article had been referred to the French king and that he would meet Haro on the island the following day. No reason was given to Haro for having interrupted Gramont's embassy. In the meeting of the next day, Mazarin told Haro that he had been ordered to withdraw from the conference if Haro insisted on including the article as drafted in the treaty. Haro was seemingly mortified and begged to be allowed to rewrite the article. He also asked Mazarin for suggestions on how not to deny Condé the correct *tratamiento* (style of address) or make his son out to be a criminal. Mazarin, we are told, finally agreed to see what could be done.

53

Haro to Philip IV: Fuenterrabía, 3 October 1659 [K1623: 98][164]

Haro endorses a request from Mazarin that the Duke of Lorraine should be allowed to leave Madrid and make his way to the border. The articles relating to Lorraine are being agreed quickly and the duke will not now be able to arrive at the conference before they have all been finalised. It seems reasonable, therefore, that he should be permitted to arrive in time for the conclusion of the treaty.

54

Haro to Philip IV: Fuenterrabía, 4 October 1659 [K1623: 99][165]

As the text of the two sets of powers which Haro and Mazarin have each been given will be included respectively in the marriage agreement and in the peace treaty, they have been scrutinised by the two prime ministers. Mazarin has accepted the powers authorising Haro to negotiate the marriage agreement but has objected to those for negotiating the peace treaty. The latter allude to the fact that France started the war and also make reference to which of the two countries initiated peace talks. Mazarin wants both references removed. Accordingly, Haro requests guidance and also encloses translations of the cardinal's powers so that they may be scrutinised in Madrid.

55

Haro to Philip IV: Fuenterrabía, 4 October 1659 [K1623: 100][166]

Mazarin has suggested that galley prisoners, both French and Spanish, should be freed immediately and not have to wait for the publication of the treaty. Assuming that the king finds the cardinal's proposal reasonable, Haro asks him to issue the requisite orders, with appropriate safeguards so that French prisoners are not released before Spanish prisoners.

---

[164] Letter 53 arrived in Madrid on 6 October.
[165] Letter 54 was dispatched on 6 October and arrived in Madrid on 9 October.
[166] Letter 55 was sent with Letter 54.

56

Haro to Philip IV: Fuenterrabía, 5 October 1659 [K1623: 102] [167]

Haro refers to the inclusion, at Mazarin's instigation, of the Dukes of Parma and Modena in the peace treaty and to the orders which he has received from the king on this matter and on that of representing before the Pope the interests of the dukes in respect of the estates of Castro, Ronciglione and the Valley of Comacchio. He declares that it was never his intention, nor Mazarin's, that the ambassadors of Spain and France should attend an audience with the Pope at the same time because this would clearly raise a question of precedence. Their proposal was simply that the two crowns should be united in the way in which they presented the petition to the Pope.[168]

57

Haro to Philip IV: Fuenterrabía, 5 October 1659 [K1623: 103][169]

This letter concerns the Duke of Nájera and whether or not he should be numbered among those who will witness the public reading of the marriage agreement. The king has said that he should not be included because there are legal proceedings pending with regard to his succession to the title. Haro argues, however, that the duke is already in possession of his estates, is receiving revenue and appointing justices. He has also spent vast amounts of money in order to be present at the peace conference. It will look extremely bad if he is not included and the duke himself is likely to feel very aggrieved. In addition, Haro cites the precedent of the Duke of Alcalá, who also faces legal proceedings with regard to his title, and to whom the king himself had referred as 'el Duque de Alcala' in a letter which he wrote to Alcalá's father, the Duke of Medinaceli.

---

[167] Letter 56 was also dispatched on 6 October, arriving in Madrid on 9 October.
[168] For the background to these issues, see Letter 46.
[169] Letter 57 is a fourth letter dispatched on 6 October and arriving in Madrid on 9 October.

58

Haro to Philip IV: Fuenterrabía, 7 October 1659 [K1623: 107][170]

Haro gives a detailed account of how he has managed, against all the odds, to recover Bergues and La Bassée and secure satisfaction for the Prince of Condé and the Duke of Lorraine in exchange for only Avesnes, Marienbourg, Philippeville and Juliers. He summarises what the Paris Treaty had offered Condé and spells out what the final, improved agreement will mean for him and also for Lorraine. He then goes on to list the main obstacles which had been in the way of a favourable outcome of the negotiations in respect of Condé. These include the cardinal's personal antipathy towards the prince, the precedent of Duke Charles of Bourbon, and Haro's own stubborn refusal to give an inch in the matter of the conquest of Portugal. Finally, he refers briefly to the article relating to the Conflent. He pledges to make every effort to ensure that the dispute over this area is resolved in the best way possible and without prolonging the conference more than is necessary. Agreement over the Conflent will conclude the negotiations relating to the peace treaty.

Señor

En carta de los dos deste[171] di quenta a VMg^d de la forma en que quedauan ajustadas las recompensas de Bergas y la Basè y asentada la restituçion destas dos Plazas, quedando la de la Basè fortificada tambien como oy se halla; Y que en quanto al particular del Prinçipe y mexora del del Duque de Lorena me quedaua manteniendo firme con deseo de que tampoco para conseguir esto se emplease ninguna Plaza de grande ni mediana consideraçion y que con añadir a lo del Presidio de Juliers (con todos los resguardos que estan dhos) solo a felipevila (puesto de tam poca [*MS: tampoca*] importançia como VMg^d tiene entendido) se me diese la satisfaçion que fuese bastante sobre ambas cosas. Lo que aora puedo añadir es que aquel vltimo dia de la conferençia venia el cardenal tocado de la gota en la mano izquierda con lo qual, y con hauerle creçido despues algo mas, no la pudimos boluer a tener Jueues, Viernes, Sauado ni Domingo; y en estos quatro dias cumpli con el en toda la mexor forma que juzgue por combeniente, embiando los dos a Don Antonio Pimentel a visitarle de mi parte y los otros dos de la misma manera dos correos yentes y vinientes para q̃ me avisase como hauia pasado la noche.

---

[170] Letter 58 was dispatched on 8 October and arrived in Madrid on 11 October.
[171] Letter 52 above.

Ayer que se contaron seis deste, a las siete de la mañana me avisò que se hallaua en disposiçion de poder venir a la Isla y que entre las nueue y las diez me esperaria en ella, en cuya conformidad hize luego traer las Pinazas y me encaminê alla con deseo de no haçerle esperar, como suçedio, porque llegamos a vn mismo tiempo.

Despues de vnos ligiros [sic] cumplimientos y de hauerle preguntado por su indisposiçion y cumplido con el enteramente en esta parte, se pasò â hablar en los puntos del Prinçipe y del Duque de Lorena (como aquellos que eran solos los que faltauan por ajustar y hauian quedado pendientes por esta causa las conferençias anteçedentes). Persistio en que, por la satisfaçion destos dos Aliados (en que yo tanto hauia insistido), se le hauia de dar, demas del pequeño fuerte de Felipevila (que assi le llamaua), vna de las Plazas prinçipales que hauia pedido y yo, por el contrario, que no hauia de çeder Plaza de semejante consideraçion ni de mucho menos, ni sobre el Presidio de Juliers (quedando la Plaza en la forma que estaua tratada) hauia de dar otra ninguna cosa que a felipevila que, avnque yo le confesaua que no era puesto de consideraçion, todavia, por estar junto a Mariemburg, pareçe que podia desestimarle menos; pero quedando vltimamente perseuerando el en querer, demas de felipevila, a charlemont, diçiendo que esta era vna Plaza entre Sambra y Mossa[172] apartada del çentro de las Prouinçias de flandes y de mucho [sic] menor consideraçion que ninguna de aquellas que hauia pedido hasta entonçes y inferior a muchas que el sauia que se hauian querido dar en recompensa al Prinçipe, y manteniendome yo en resistirlo con deçirle que avnque era çierto que no era de igual calidad ni importançia a Cambray, Hers, s^n Tomer ni Duay, era vna Plaza muy fuerte por naturaleza y por Arte, situada sobre la Mosa, que nos daua paso sobre aquella riuera y nos cubria vnicamente a Namur y todo su Pais, por cuyas causas era imposible que yo pudiese combenir en ello, me dixo que era menester que se aclarase vn poco mas conmigo y debaxo de toda amistad me dixese que el hauer consentido sobre el particular del Prinçipe en que se alterase vna sola letra de lo que hauia sido firmado en Paris y ratificado en Madrid era vna gran falta de reputaçion del Rey xpt^{mo} y de la suya misma, porque se hauia de deçir en todo el mundo (que estaua esperando a ver el fin deste negoçio) que yo hauia tomado esta ventaxa sobre el dentro de aquella Barraca despues de çinquenta horas de disputa (que tenia notado por escrito que se hauian gastado solo sobre este punto), que segun lo que yo adelantaua la reputaçion de VMag^d y el exemplo

---

[172] *Sambra y Mossa*: the rivers Sambre and Meuse.

para otros Aliados, a qualquier preçio me saldria muy barato; y que avnque ellos por esta misma causa no tendrian disculpa de hauerlo hecho avnque se les dieran vna y muchas Plazas, Todavia era menester que se viese que sacauan alguna vtilidad y que para esto era preçisam^te neçesario darles alguna Plaza de importançia y de nombre, porque el quitar el Presidio de Juliers (quedando el Duque obligado a tener aquella Plaza en la forma que se deçia y a dar paso a las tropas de VMg^d por ella y la françia no solo obligada a no poder darle ninguna ayuda si faltase a lo que ofreçia sino a juntar sus fuerzas con las de VMag^d para obligarle al cumplimiento dello) no era cossa que mereçia recompensa, como se hauia conçedido sin ninguna al Duque de Modena en Correjio, porque ni la Plaza nos daua paso sobre el Rin ni nos quitaua el de Alemania ni cubria Pays nuestro por ninguna parte, ni avn nos hauia seruido de freno contra el mismo Duque de Neuburg; y quedando el obligado a tenerla con los grauamenes dichos, quedaua en mucho [*sic*] mexor forma porque VMg^d âhorraua [*MS: â horraua*] çinquenta ô sesenta mill ducados que gastaua cada año en mantener el Presidio sin neçesidad y sin ningun fruto y que esto mismo sauia el muy bien que me habrian dicho el Marques de Carazena y el conde de fuensaldaña si yo se lo huuiese preguntado, como lo suponia con los correos yentes y vinientes que les hauia despachado despues que llegue â esta frontera; y que felipevila era vn fuerte de quatro pequeños baluartes de tierra que en 24 horas de tpo le huuieran ellos tomado veinte veçes que hauian estado con su ex^to en aquel paraxe y que le hauian dexado por no haçer caso del; y que no me contentaua con hauerlos obligado a que vendiesen su reputaçion (dixolo por estas mismas palabras) sino que queria tambien que la bendiesen por nada. Y con estas y otras muchas razones dichas con grandisima vehemençia, perseueró en que se le hauia de dar a charlemont porque de otra manera no se podria combenir. Visto yo esto, el gran disgusto con que estaua y que este tambien se le avmentaua al estar, demas de la inchazon de la mano, tocado tambien ya i[173] con dolor en vna rodilla (de que se quexaua algunas veçes), me pareçio que en todo lo que no fuese çeder en el punto de charlemont, me combenia hablarle con palabras de mucha templanza y ir reconoçiendo muy bien el terreno sobre que yba pisando porque no entrase en mayor alteraçion; y assi le respondi que si lo que yo hauia disputado en todas aquellas horas que el me referia sobre mejorar el part^r del Prinçipe juzgara yo que podia ser contra la reputaçion del Rey

---

[173] The apparent MS reading *i con dolor* gives the sense that 'he was now affected, and painfully, in one of his knees'.

xpt^mo ni contra la suya, no huuiera hablado palabra en ello y que el mismo dia que lleguè â este confin, lo huuiera buelto a firmar; pero que hauia juzgado que antes era muy conforme al seruiçio de su Mag^d y al suyo que el Prinçipe entrase en françia y estuuiese a los pies de su Mg^d con mayor satisfaçion y obligaçion; y a su amistad de la misma manera. Que si esto fuera vna cosa de tanta nota para la reputaçion de ambos como me encareçia, no fuera disculpa el haçerlo por vna ni por muchas Plazas y que mucho mas juzgaua yo que lo podia honestar el aventaxar Su Mg^d xpt^ma al mismo tiempo a otro Aliado suyo conque a interposiçion suya se le quitase el Presidio de Juliers; y que yo entendia que yriamos mexor por este camino que por el de recompensas de Plazas, manteniendome siempre firme en no hauer de çeder a charlemont y persistiendo el todavia en ello y reforzandolo mas con las razones que quedan dichas de que era preçisamente neçesario que se viese que hauian consentido en vna cossa semexante por algo y que era menester que esto fuese Plaza de calidad y de nombre. Le dixe que puesto que su deseo era aquel, se me hauia ofreçido vn medio muy a proposito q̃ era que, presupuesto que teniamos ajustada la restituçion de Bergas y la Base por Auenas y Mariemburg y que yo no podia dar por la satisfaçion del Prin^e y del Duque de Lorena sobre el Presidio de Juliers otro puesto que el de felipevila, podiamos juntarlos todos tres y que por las recompensas de Bergas y la Base quedase Mariemburg y felipevila, Y Avenas se considerase por los intereses del Prin^e. Respondiome que que diferençia hauia en esto pues, en sustançia, venia a ser lo mismo y todavia resistia yo el darle a charlemont. Respondile que era verdad pero que como mostraua desear que en las ventaxas del Prinçipe pareçiese que se hauia consentido de su parte por alguna cosa mas considerable, juzgaua yo que se conseguia este intento con que por la restituçion de Bergas y la Base quedasen consideradas Mariemburg y felipevila y por los intereses del Prinçipe, Avenas. A que me respondio con mucha alteraçion, preguntandome que le dixese si avn desta manera tenia yo a Avenas por lo menos que a charlemont. Respondile que no porque sauia muy bien que era Plaza de mas consideraçion charlemont pero que, presupuesto que yo no podia çeder esta ni hauia de dar mas que Avenas, Mariemburg y Felipevila por Bergas y la Base y la satisfaçion destos dos Aliados en forma combeniente, las repartiese el como fuese seruido, considerando a felipevila y Mariemburg por la restituçion de Bergas y la Basè y a Avenas por los intereses del Prinçipe, pues avnque esta vltima no fuese vna Plaza de todas las calidades de charlemont, no me podia negar que era vn puesto muy diferente que los otros dos y que estuuiese çierto que si yo pudiera çeder desto, lo huuiera hecho ya.

Finalmente, señor, no pudiendo ni siendo façil el referir a VMg^d todo lo que en razon desto pasò en la vltima parte de la conferençia, dirè solo a VMg^d que al cabo vino a quedar el negoçio acabado y concluydo con solo los tres Puestos, quedando Mariemburg y felipevila por recompensa de Bergas y la Base, y Avenas y el Presidio de Juliers en consideraçion de las ventaxas que se haçen al Prinçipe y al Duque de Lorena, las quales quedan ajustadas en la forma siguiente:

Pretendian, como VMag^d saue y yo lo dixe a VM^d mas particularmente en carta de 27 del pasado,[174] quedar en la Lorena con vnos que ellos llamauan caminos en soberania con pretexto de que los hauian menester para pasar con sus Tropas desde el Ducado de Bar a las Alsaçias sin tocar en Dominio ageno; Lo qual, entendida la parte que ellos deçian que hauian menester para esto, venia a ser, en sustançia, dexar despoxado al Duque de mas de la mitad y mejor parte de la Lorena. Conque por vna parte le venian a quitar lo que le dauan por otra. Esto se ha defendido como se deuia y como era razon, porque los caminos quedan negados y el Duque obligado a dar paso al Rey xpt^{mo} y a sus Tropas quando le huuiere menester. Conque queda dueño de toda la Lorena sin que le falte vna Almena y Marsac le queda fortificada y, demas desto, las dependençias de los tres obispados; y a los Dominios de Clermont, Chamez, Estenay y Dura[175] no tenia el Duque ningun derecho por hauerlos çedido al Rey xpt^{mo} por vn Tratado particular que hizo Personalm^{te} en Paris el año de 41 y assi se restituyen aora al Prinçipe de Conde a quien se hauian dado; y hauiendo traydo françeses este Tratado aqui para podermele mostrar y hauiendole visto, lo que puedo deçir a VMag^d es que el que VMg^d ha hecho aora en fabor del Duque, estando el en vna prision en Toledo y sus Tropas siruiendo en françia, es muy ventaxoso para sus intereses al que fue â haçer voluntariamente a Paris, quedando tambien sus tropas siruiendo a la françia. Conque en esta parte creo que se ha satisfecho toda la obligaçion y avn exçedido della si no se huuiera de considerar el hauer sido tan propio de la grandeza de VMag^d y tan

---

[174] Letter 49 above.
[175] *Marsac* seems to be close to Verdun (see Letter 70) but I have not been able to pinpoint its exact position; *Clermont* is likely to be Clermont en Argonne, which lies a little to the southwest of Verdun; *Chamez* is in the same general area but I have not succeeded in identifying it; *Estenay* or Stenay lies to the northwest of Verdun and, like it, is situated on the banks of the river Meuse; *Dura* is again in the same area but scrutiny of a number of historical atlases has not enabled me to locate it.

conforme a todas las consideraçiones de estado el aver procurado aventaxar sus combeniençias hasta el vltimo grado que se haya podido.

En quanto a los intereses del Prinçipe, deuo deçir a VMg^d en primer lugar que en el Tratado de Paris, en que solo le venian conçedidos los vienes Patrimoniales, honores y prerrogatiuas de Prinçipe de la Sangre, venia exceptuada la cassa de Chantilli, diçiendo que esta la reserbaba el Rey para si con calidad de pagarsela.[176] Y hauiendo deseado el Prin^e que se quitase esta exçepcion del Tratado, pues el podria ponerla despues en manos [*MS: malos*] del Rey si gustase della, se ha dispuesto assi y no se habla della. En quanto a todo lo demas que le retenian que eran cargos, ofiçios y Gouiernos de Plazas, Lo que se ha dispuesto es:

Que se dé al Prinçipe el Gouierno del Ducado de Borgoña al qual paso del de la Guiena el Duque de Pernon,[177] que oy le tiene, por quanto el de Borgoña se ha reputado siempre por mas prinçipal y de mucho [*sic*] mayor vtilidad; y por esta causa paso tambien â el desde la Guiena el prinçipe de condè Padre deste.

Assi mismo se da al Prinçipe el Gouierno part^r de la Villa y çiudadela de Dixon y el Gouierno de s^n Juan de Lona q̃ esta sobre la riuera de la Sona,[178] Plazas ambas de toda seguridad para el.

Asse dispuesto tambien que se de al Duque de Enguien[179] el ofiçio de Gran Mre de françia con calidad que si açertare a faltar, buelua a recaer en la Persona del Prinçipe su Padre conque este ofiçio, que estaua antes solo en la vida del vno, viene a quedar aora en la de ambos.

A todos los que han seguido al Prinçipe, se les conçede el perdon, la restituçion de sus vienes y la capaçidad para poder tener cargos y ofiçios; y tomando VMg^d por su quenta el pagarles el valor de los que les retienen para que los buelban a comprar (que pareçe serà vna cant^d moderada), vendran a quedar sin ninguna perdida; y añadiendo VMg^d a esto el dar al Prinçipe vna suma de dinero pagada en algunos años en recompensa de las perdidas que ha hecho de las Plazas que se le han demolido y por quenta de lo que se le està deuiendo por su Tratado, quando no se pueda considerar que queda en alguna parte mejorado (porque solo se le dexa

---

[176] *Chantilly* is sited slightly to the northeast of Paris.
[177] Corruption of the French *Duc d'Epernon*, who became governor of Burgundy in 1651.
[178] *San Juan de Lona* is St Jean de Losne, northwest of Chalon on the banks of the river Saône.
[179] Condé's son, Henri Jules de Bourbon. He was only sixteen years of age in 1659.

de restituir la Plaza de Estenay y en su lugar le queda el ofiçio de mayordomo mayor por dos vidas), por lo menos pareçe que se puede juzgar que el y los que han seguido su partido quedan enteramente restableçidos y VM^d con el Gouierno de flandes libre y con las Plazas que juntamente se le ofreçian en soverania; y al Duque de Pernon y al Prinçipe de Conti que tenian el Gouierno de Borgoña y el ofiçio de Gran Mr͂e, queda por q^{ta} del Rey xpt^{mo} el darles satisfaçion.[180]

Aora es menester ajustar que se quiten del Tratado todas aquellas palabras ofensiuas que se deçian contra la Persona del Duque de Enguien y contra la del Prin^e, pero hauiendose vençido lo prinçipal, espero q͂ suçederà lo mismo en las çircunstançias.

Las dificultades que se han ofreçido en todo el discurso de este negoçio del Prinçipe han sido muchas y grandes y las prinçipales se han reduçido a tres:

La primera el ser vn punto que tanto hauian resistido siempre, el restableçerle en cargos, ofiçios y Gouierno de Plazas, y que ya venia vençido, firmado y ratificado, añadiendose tambien a esto el deseo particular del cardenal de dejar mortificado al Prinçipe.

La segunda que en la Paz del año de 26, hallandose el Rey françisco primero preso dentro de Madrid, no se conçedio al Duque Carlos de Borbon mas q͂ sus vienes, honores y prerrogatiuas de Prinçipe de la sangre pero no los cargos ni ofiçios porque no le restituyeron el de condestable que tenia.[181] Conque siendo solo este el exemplar que hauia en propios

---

[180] The Prince of Conti, Armand de Bourbon, was Condé's younger brother.

[181] This is a reference to the Treaty of Madrid (1526), which provides the precedent relevant to the Peace of the Pyrenees in its prescriptions for a nobleman who has rebelled against his king. Charles Duke of Bourbon (1490–1527) seems to have incurred Francis I's wrath by spurning an offer of marriage from the king's mother, Louise of Savoy. The king deprived him of certain estates and offices and he responded by striking an alliance with Charles V of Austria. When, under the terms of the Treaty of Madrid, Charles was restored to favour, he recovered the honours and prerogatives to which he was entitled as a prince of the blood, but not the offices which he had previously held.

terminos, estaua en fauor suyo y totalmente contrario a lo que de n^{ra} parte se pretendia.[182]

La terçera el no hauer consentido ni podido consentir yo en que se mudase vna sola letra en el Articulo de Portugal al mismo t^{po} que yo pretendia mejorar tanto el del Prinçipe, que es con lo que se me ha hecho toda la mayor resistençia.

El referir a VMag^d los medios de que he vsado y terminos por donde me he conduçido para façilitar y adelantar esta negoçiaçion lo reserbo para su tiempo, porque por escrito seria dificultoso el poder explicarlo a VMg^d por menor y con todas las çircunstançias que el negoçio ha pasado.

En el Articulo de Conflent, quedo procurando que se tome de aqui a mañana todo el mexor expidiente [sic] que se pueda sin que por esto se retarde vn punto la conclusion del Tratado, como VMg^d me lo manda, con que [MS: conque] quedaran enteramente combenidos y ajustados todos los Articulos de la Paz. Y solo deseo verla firmada ya y enteramente concluydo vn negoçio de tan comun interes destos Reynos y de toda la xpt^d, en que no puedo hauer tenido mas merito ni mas parte que la de hauer procurado executar las ordenes de VMag^d, como era mi obligaçion. Dios g^{de} la Catolica y Real Persona de VMag^d como la christiandad ha menester. De fuenterrabia a 7 de ott^{re} 1659.

Dluismendezdeharo

---

[182] Haro emphasises here that precedent (that of the Treaty of Madrid of 1526) was on the side of the French and that it is therefore even more extraordinary that he should have succeeded in recovering for Condé his offices and governments in France. It should be remembered, however, that, according to the settlement, the office of *Grand Maistre de la Maison du Roy* would not be restored to Condé but given to his son, the Duke of Enghien. Only in the event of his son's premature death would Condé recover this important position.

59

Haro to Philip IV: Fuenterrabía, 10 October 1659 [K1623: 109][183]

Haro refers to his letter of 7 October (Letter 58 above), which outlined how he had triumphed over Mazarin in the matter of Condé and also improved the article relating to the Duke of Lorraine. Despite still suffering from gout, Mazarin is apparently no longer in pain and, Haro hopes, will soon be able to return to the conference table. During Mazarin's illness, he has been as courteous as possible. The cardinal responded by sending him a message via the Commandeur de Gault, thanking him for his concern and indicating a desire to resume negotiations at the earliest opportunity. Haro expresses his confidence that Mazarin has no wish to prolong the peace conference unnecessarily since he is less than comfortable in St Jean de Luz, especially now that the usual autumn germs seem to be spreading quickly. Haro expects the English king to arrive at any time, having heard that he is already in Irún. He will govern himself in this matter in accordance with the instructions which he was given before leaving Madrid.

---

[183] Letter 59 was dispatched on 11 October but did not arrive in Madrid until 15 October. This is surprising given that the cost of the dispatch was 810 *reales de plata*, the courier again having been allowed 'vn caballo mas de ventaxa'; AGS CMC 3551 (2), 27. Whilst the content of this letter is not of an urgent nature, one could perhaps suppose a desire on Haro's part to inform the king quickly that he had triumphed over Mazarin in the matter of Condé. On the other hand, Letters 60 and 61, which arrived in Madrid as part of this same dispatch, were clearly urgent in that both required rapid responses from Philip. However, at least one of these did not leave Fuenterrabía at the same time as Letter 59. AGS CMC 3551 (2), 27 informs us that a second courier was dispatched in pursuit of the one bearing Letter 59 ('en alcance del anterior') at an additional cost of 450 *reales de plata*. It seems likely, then, that one of the two letters (either Letter 60 or Letter 61) was sent at the same time as Letter 59. This would certainly explain why the first of the two couriers was allowed an extra horse. The other letter, whichever it might be, would have been entrusted to the courier dispatched later the same day.

60

Haro to Philip IV: Fuenterrabía, 10 October 1659 [K1623: 110][184]

Haro discourses on the difficulties to be faced when he and Mazarin try to reach agreement over the exchange of strongholds by Spain and France and refers specifically to the implications of the timing of the delivery of the Spanish infanta to the frontier for the sequence of withdrawal from these positions. The subject has so far been broached only obliquely and Haro has done his best to avoid the topic because it would have been unwise to reveal to Mazarin, in advance of securing complete and final agreement of the peace treaty, that Spain expected all relevant strongholds to be evacuated not only before the infanta was handed over to the French king but also before the marriage ceremony had taken place. He desperately needs to know the king's mind on this matter and so he proposes to share with him his assessment of the problem so that the king may make an informed decision. Accordingly, he notes that he expects Mazarin to insist that the order of withdrawal should be Italy, Flanders, Spain. He outlines the particular problems associated with the first two theatres of war and stresses the need for suitable hostages to be exchanged so as to ensure that neither side goes back on what is in the end agreed. Finally, he emphasises that the French will not surrender Roses in Catalonia until the infanta is standing on French soil and that he cannot in all conscience advise the king to hand over the infanta before all strongholds, including Roses, have been returned. The solution to this impasse can only be to find a set of safeguards which will satisfy both parties. Again the answer seems to Haro to be an exchange of hostages. He awaits the king's instructions on how to proceed.

Señor

El Tratado de la Paz esta tan adelantado que es neçesario ajustar la forma que se ha de tener en la restituçion y entrega de las Plazas de parte a parte, assi por lo que combiene ejecutarlo con la mayor breuedad que se pueda como por hauerse de expresar en el mismo Tratado. Y deuiendose procurar de nuestra parte que preçeda la execuçion destas restituçiones a la entrega de la Persona de la s^{ra} Infante y no sauiendo yo todavia si ellos se ajustaran â esto ni lo que pretenderan en contrario, Viene a ser vn punto de tal consideraçion que holgara yo harto de poder tener muy frequentes y declaradas ordenes de VMg^d para poder gouernarme con toda puntualidad conforme â ellas sin que quedase nada remitido a mi

---

[184] Letter 60 arrived in Madrid with Letter 59.

adbitrio [*sic*]; pero comoquiera que para ir y venir y boluer resuelto de VMag^d qualquier despacho mio son neçesarios siete, o, ocho dias, y que el cardenal està tan impaçiente y tan de mala gana apartado de la Persona del Rey que se puede creer que darà toda priesa â ajustar estos puntos para boluerse con mayor breuedad, desearia yo hallarme con aquella notiçia de la mente de VM^d que se me pudiere dar por mayor; y para que VMag^d pueda haçerlo con notiçia de lo que a mi se me ofreçe sobre este punto, lo referirè aqui.

El Cardenal me ha tocado estos dias pasados lijeramente esta materia, diçiendo que era menester ajustarla; pero como se estaua disputando tan porfiadamente sobre los puntos del Tratado que faltauan por combenir, no se ha hablado nunca por menor en ella y yo tambien lo yba procurando apartar porque, sauiendo la alteraçion que le ha de causar que yo pretenda la ebaquaçion de todas las Plazas antes de la entrega de la s^{ra} Infante y avn antes que se despose, me pareçia combeniente ir huyendo de entrar en esta platica hasta que se hallasen enteramente ajustados todos los Articulos de la Paz.

Avnque no hemos llegado â hablar sobre este punto positiuamente, segun todo quanto puedo inferir juzgo que el car^{al} querrà que las restituçiones de la parte de españa sean las postreras y que en esta conformidad se hagan primero las de Italia y flandes y que quede para lo vltimo la entrega de Rosas, y que persistirà en esto con gran fuerza por las razones que dirè adelante.

Hauiendose de comenzar por Italia y flandes y combiniendo tanto ganar en esto todo el tiempo que se pueda, juzgo que la ebaquaçion mas façil y mas igual viene a ser la de Italia porque ellos nos han de entregar a Valençia y Mortara y nosotros a Berçeli y el Zencho[185] demolido como se halla, para lo qual juzgaria yo que se deuen embiar las ordenes de VMg^d pero que la disposiçion dello, la forma en que se ha de haçer y las cautelas y resguardos que se huuieren de tomar es fuerza remitirlo al conde de fuensaldaña, suponiendo yo que serà neçesario tomar reenes de vna parte y otra porque avnque se ajuste la entrega de las Plazas en vn

---

[185] *Valençia* is Valenza in the Piedmont, a stronghold to the southwest of Pavia; *Mortara* lies slightly to the north of Valenza and is in Lombardy; *Berçeli* is Vercelli, also situated in the Piedmont and about forty miles west of Milan; *Zencho* seems to be the most probable transcription of the MS reading and may well be a distortion of Italian *Cengio*, which is situated in the province of Savona in modern Liguria. I am grateful to Dr Roberto Bruni of Exeter University for this suggestion.

mismo dia y a vna misma hora, comoquiera que los vnos podrian ejecutarla de buena fee y los otros suspenderla, pareçe que siempre es menester tomar algun resguardo contra este peligro y no pareçe que puede [*sic*] hauer otro que el de los Reenes.

Si VMag^d entendiere que se deue executar assi, se seruirà VMg^d de mandar que se me remitan luego las ordenes para el conde para que, juntandolas con las que se huuieren de embiar del Rey xpt^{mo} para la entrega de Valençia y de Mortara, se pueda despachar correo con las vnas y las otras y remitir con el mismo tambien la orden para que salgan sus Tropas del estado de Milan y pasen los montes.

En flandes juzgaria yo que hauia de comenzar la ebaquaçion de parte a parte por las Plazas mas internas en el Pays de cada vno, como seria: que ellos restituyesen primero a Audenarde y Ipre y nosotros a Hedin y alguna otra Plaza de las tres de Rocroy, Chatelet y Lichans[186] y que, hecho esto, las que quedaren destas dos[187] se permuten al mismo tiempo que ellos nos entreguen a Dixmuda, fornos, Merbila, Menin y demas puestos de la Lisa[188] y los de Borgoña, y Bergas si se pudiese; y que quedase para la [*sic*] vltimo el entregarnos a la Basè que, en fin, avnque Plaza tan importante, està mas afuera que todas las demas que quedan referidas; y nosotros les entregasemos al mismo t^{po} a Auenas, Mariemburg y felipevila.

---

[186] Audenarde is on the banks of the river Scheldt in East Flanders; Ypres lies just inside Belgium in the province of West Flanders; Hesdin is located northeast of Arras and southwest of St Omer; Rocroi is in France just across the border from Namur; and Châtelet is located in the Hainault, close to the point where the river Sambre passes from Namur into the Hainault. Unfortunately, I have not been able to identify the French or Dutch equivalent of what is here transcribed as *Lichans*. However, the text tells us that it is a stronghold situated somewhere in the heart of Flanders.

[187] The text would, I think, be clearer here if it read: 'las dos que quedaren destas'. In other words, the proposal appears to be that one of 'Rocroy, Chatelet y Lichans' should be exchanged, along with 'Hedin', for 'Audenarde y Ipre' and that the remaining two should be added to those strongholds which would figure in the following round of exchanges.

[188] The French equivalents are Dixmude, Furnes, Merville and Menin. Dixmude is on the banks of the Yser in what is today the Belgian province of West Flanders; Furnes is in the same province and lies between the border with France and the river Yser; Merville and Menin are also in West Flanders, along the river Lys.

Pero como estos tres puestos se han permutado por Bergas y la Basè[189] y estas vltimas son Plazas tan importantes y tan internas, temo q̃ las han de querer retener ambas hasta lo vltimo y hasta que se hayan entregado Auenas, felipevila y Mariemburg, pareçiendoles que es mas lo que entregan en las dos que lo que reçiuen en las tres. Y en quanto a la forma, yo no creo que puede [*sic*] hauer otra que la que dexo d^{ho} para lo de Italia que es darse Reenes de toda satisfaçion de parte a parte y que se vayan haçiendo las ebaquaçiones por esta misma regla y saliendo sus tropas de nuestro Pays.

Esto es lo que yo hauia discurrido pero si VMg^d juzgare que se puede disponer en otra forma mexor, ô, que a las Plazas, en quanto a su restituçion, combenga mas darles otro lugar que aquel en que yo las boy graduando, se seruirà VMag^d de mandarmelo deçir, ordenandome lo que en primer lugar debo procurar y aquello en que vltimamente (no pudiendose mas) huuiere de venir.

Resta solo la parte de españa en la q^{al} he reconoçido por muchas señales (avnque el Car^{al} nunca me lo ha d^{ho} claro) que deue de ser su intençion retener a Rosas[190] hasta lo vltimo y no entregarla hasta hauer reçiuido la Persona de la s^{ra} Infanta, sobre q̃ VM^d serà bien que se sirua de ordenarme la forma en que me debo gouernar porque ellos de ninguna manera se conformaran en haçer la entrega de todas las Plazas hallandose todavia S.A. dentro de españa; y, por el contrario, el entregar nosotros a la s^{ra} Infante sin que estuuiesen ejecutadas todas las restituçiones dellas, yo no creo que nadie lo pueda aconsexar y mucho menos quien estuuiese viendo como yo muchas çircunstançias que no pueden verse desde mas lexos. Y assi solo pareçe que resta el ver que resguardos y seguridades reçiprocas se deuen y pueden tomar y dar de parte a parte de calidad que cada vno pueda y deua contentarse con ellas; y al cabo yo no creo que tampoco podrà hallarse otro medio que el de los Reenes.

---

[189] Letter 58 says clearly that Marienbourg and Philippeville were exchanged for Bergues and La Bassée and that Avesnes and Juliers were surrendered in return for improved deals for Condé and Lorraine. The reason for the apparent contradiction between these two letters may amount to no more than what is suggested in Letter 58, namely that the real deal is the one which is recorded in Letter 60 and that what we have in Letter 58 is merely window dressing designed to enable Mazarin to save face in the matter of Condé.

[190] Roses is on the Mediterranean coast in the northernmost part of the Spanish province of Gerona.

Esto es quanto a mi se me ofreçe que deçir y VMg^d se seruirà de ordenarme sobre todo lo que huuiere de executar. Guarde Dios la Catholica y Real Persona de VMag^d como la christiandad ha menester. De fuenterrabia a 10 de ott^{re} de 1659.

Dluismendezdeharo

61

Haro to Philip IV: Fuenterrabía, 10 October 1659 [K1623: 111][191]

Haro summarises the king's letter of 26 September concerning the Conflent. Philip had instructed him to keep to the terms of the Madrid agreement of 1656, which, among other things, stated that France should be given those parts of the Conflent situated on the north side of the Pyrenees. However, if keeping to this agreement proved impossible, Haro should accept whatever proposal Mazarin might make rather than break off the interview and jeopardise the peace process. As an alternative, the matter of the Conflent might profitably be referred to commissioners. If this were to turn out to be the way forward, Haro should do everything in his power to ensure that the work of the commissioners was not used as a reason for delaying the evacuation of strongholds controlled by France in Catalonia. Finally, in the event that he was unable to secure agreement on either of these two points, Haro was instructed not to endanger the peace process but to accept whatever Mazarin proposed.

Haro then reports on the outcome of the most recent negotiations relating to the Conflent. The Madrid agreement has been accepted and commissioners will decide whether or not the Conflent is situated on the French side or the Spanish side of the Pyrenees. A clause has been inserted into the treaty which says that, if the commissioners are unable to reach agreement, the whole question will be referred back to the plenipotentiaries. The purpose of this clause is to reduce the risk of a fresh outbreak of hostilities. The French have already named as their commissioners the Archbishop of Toulouse and the Bishop of Orange. Haro therefore asks the king to appoint commissioners for Spain and notes that he has written to the Marquis of Mortara so as to have someone suitable to propose in case the Council of Aragon is unable to come up with appropriate candidates.

---

[191] Letter 61 arrived in Madrid with Letters 59 and 60.

62

Haro to Philip IV: Fuenterrabía, 12 October 1659 [K1623: 113][192]

Affairs of England: Haro reports that, despite Mazarin's having told Pimentel in Paris that restoration of the English monarchy was one of the most important items to be referred to the peace conference, the Frenchman has thus far made no attempt to discuss ways in which Spain and France might cooperate to that end. He is all the more troubled by Mazarin's reluctance to broach this matter because it is rumoured that the cardinal is scheming to marry his niece to the English king and his nephew to the English king's sister. The departure of the English king from Brussels to join the royalist rising at Chester without requesting any assistance from Spain, together with the Duke of York's recent meeting with Turenne, had increased suspicion that France aimed to restore the English monarchy on its own. Confirmation of French intentions had subsequently come in a recent interview, when Mazarin had carelessly given the game away whilst reading aloud to Haro a letter containing Turenne's account of the unsuccessful royalist rising at Chester.

Haro acknowledges that, although it is only proper to lament the English king's failure in this venture, from the point of view of the conquest of Portugal the royal reverse is good news for Spain. He has instructed Caracena and Cárdenas to maintain good relations with the emissary of the English Parliament in Flanders but not to commit Spain to anything without express instructions from Madrid. This is the policy which he has also adopted with Lockhart. He requests orders on how to respond to overtures from the English Parliament. He reminds Philip that the Resident of the English king is with him at the border and the king himself is expected to arrive at any time. Consequently, it would seem wise for negotiations with the English Republic to be conducted in Flanders if this is the route which Madrid decides to take.

Señor

Las materias de Inglaterra vienen a ser vn negoçio de tal calidad que mereçe muy bien vn despacho aparte; y assi referirè a VMag^d en este

---

[192] Letter 62 was included in a dispatch which reached Madrid on 17 October and cost 810 *reales de plata*, the courier having been allowed 'vn caballo mas de ventaxa'; AGS CMC 3551 (2), 27. The content of the letter is not of a particularly urgent nature. However, Letter 63, which was sent with it, is extremely urgent and would explain Haro's decision to allow the courier an extra horse.

todo lo que se ofreçe sobre ellas para que con esta notiçia pueda VMag^d ordenarme lo que juzgare por mas conforme a su real seruiçio; y para mayor inteligençia de lo que tengo de deçir, me pareçe neçesario tocar algo de lo que anteçedentem^te ha pasado en razon desto.

Juzgo que VMag^d tendrà presente las veçes que Don Antonio Pimentel escriuio desde Paris que el Car^al le hauia dicho que la mayor combeniençia que hallaua en juntarse conmigo en esta frontera no era solo la de haçer la Paz sino el poderse tratar entre nosotros de otras muchas cosas de gran ventaxa para ambas coronas, declarandole que vna de las mas prinçipales era el juntarse ambas a restableçer al rey de Inglaterra assi porque no quedase en el mundo vn exemplo tan escandaloso contra las Monarquias como porque si se dexase estableçer esta nueua Republica, podria ser para lo de adelante de graue peligro para ambos Reyes, en cuya conformi^d fue este vno de los puntos que vinieron remitidos para tratarse entre los dos en este confin.

De la misma manera juzgo que VMg^d tendrá presente que, luego que llegue a San Sebastian, en carta de 6 de Agosto[193] dixe a VMag^d lo que el Marques de Caraçena y Don Alonso de Cardenas me escriuian en razon de la sospecha que se tenia de que por medio de la Reyna de Inglaterra y de los Ministros Ingleses que asisten çerca de la Persona del Rey se trataua de que fuese restableçido por medio de la françia y que para dar mayor apoyo â esto se trataua de que el Rey se casase con vna de las dos sobrinas del Cardenal y su sobrino con hermana del Rey, declarandole por Prinçipe de la sangre de Inglaterra y dandole el Virreynato de Yrlanda por su vida y la renta de aquel Reyno hasta la extinçion entera del gasto hecho por la françia para su restableçimiento; y dixe a VMag^d juntamente que, segun estas notiçias y el creerse esto Generalmente en françia y algunas otras çircunstançias, juzgaua yo que se podia tener esto por muy probable y que la intençion del cardenal fuese que, dandole la françia sola por si Asistençias para su restableçimiento y estrechandose la vnion con los casamientos referidos, quedase el Rey con vna total dependençia de aquella corona y que, hallandose desobligado y ofendido de nosotros, tuuiesemos en el vn enemigo irreconçiliable y que se lo procurarian persuadir para impedirnos por este camino la conquista de Portugal.

Sobre estos anteçedentes pasarè a deçir a VMg^d que en las primeras conferençias, hauiendose ofreçido algunas veçes el leer la memoria de los puntos que venian reserbados a tratarse en esta frontera, siempre que se llegaua a nombrar el de las cosas de Inglaterra deçia el Cardenal

---

[193] Letter 11 above.

que este seria bien dejarle para mas adelante quando estuuiesemos combenidos en los Articulos de la Paz. Y conoçiendo yo que nos combenia mas el anteponer esto y temiendo tambien no me quisiese meter en alguna platica de liga contra Inglaterra que yo no la pudiese admitir por la diuersion que nos haria para la conquista de Portugal, me dejaba lleuar façilmente a la dilaçion de que este punto se fuese remitiendo para adelante, avnque no dejaua de haçer reparo en ello porque reconoçia claramente que el cardenal no tenia gusto de entrar en esta platica.

Despues se comenzò ha hablar en que el Rey pasaba a Inglaterra por el Partido que se hauia lebantado a su fauor en el Puerto de chester y que finalmente hauia partido de Bruselas sin hauer pedido a los Ministros de VMg^d nada para la execuçion dello; y el hauerse sauido juntam^{te} que hauia reçiuido algun dinero de fuera me puso en mayor sospecha de que el cardenal tuuiese alguna inteligençia secreta con el, en la conformidad y debaxo de los presupuestos que se hauia dicho, porque segun el estado de las cosas de Inglaterra era muy dificultoso que se le huuiesen embiado los de su partido de allà ni que huuiesen podido reçiuirle de ninguna otra parte que de la françia.

Fuese avmentando mas esta sospecha mia viendo que, hauiendo dicho el Rey a los Ministros de VMag^d al salir de flandes que yba â embarcarse a los Puertos de Holanda, vino a los de Normandia (donde tenia preuenida la embarcaçion) y que el Duque de Yorc estaua al mismo t^{po} con el Mariscal de Turena en Picardia y que el cardenal se haçia desentendido dello, siendo publico en françia y en todas partes, y esto al mismo tiempo que al Residente de Inglaterra (que vino siguiendome â esta frontera y reside en esta Plaza) no le hauia querido dar avdiençia en s^n Juan de Luz, diçiendo publicamente que estando en Paz la françia con la corona de Inglaterra, deuia mantenerla con qualquiera que tuuiese el Gouierno della y que, estando çerca de su Persona Locart con Titulo de embaxador extraordinario del Parlamento al rey xpt^{mo}, no podia oir al mismo tiempo a vn Ministro de vn enemigo del Parlamento como lo era el Rey; y al residente le embio a deçir al mismo tiempo en secreto por vna Persona particular que escusaua esta apariençia por poder seruir mexor al Rey en la Verdad y que trahia cosas de mucha importançia que tratar conmigo en orden a esto, conque a vn mismo t^{po} procuraua engañar a todos y a Locart el primero avnque es grande amigo suyo.

Estando las cosas en este estado y yo con todas las razones de sospecha que dexo referidas para creer que tenia inteligençia secreta con el Rey por medio de la Reyna su madre y de los Ministros que tiene çerca de su Persona y que deuia de tratar de ver si podia restableçerle por si solo debaxo del Tratado de los casamientos, suçedio vn dia destas conferençias pasadas vna cossa accidentalmente que acabò de confirmar todas mis sospechas anteçedentes como dirè aora.

El cardenal ordinariamente habla mucho y muy apriessa y quando se ençiende en los discursos, se le suelen soltar algunas palabras que, vna vez dichas, no le puede ser façil el boluer a recojerlas de manera que el que estuuiere hablando con el dexe de tomar alguna luz de su intençion. Debaxo deste presupuesto, dirè a VMg^d que en cassi todas las conferençias le yba yo preguntando y el me yba diçiendo las notiçias q̃ tenia del Rey de Inglaterra y del estado y fuerzas que yba tomando el Partido de los solebados en chester; y preguntandole yo que juiçio haçia dellas el Mariscal de Turena (que era el que le embiaua todos los avisos), me respondio que juzgaua bien dellas y que deçia que menores ayudas podrian aprouecharle mas en esta coyuntura que mucho mayores en otra; y boluiendo a preguntarle yo si era verdad que estaua el Rey en los Puertos de Normandia para embarcarse en ellos (pareçiendome esta vna accion muy contraria a la de tener al mismo tiempo vn embax^{or} del Parlamento de Inglaterra çerca de si), me respondio que era verdad pero que se haçian desentendidos dello porque les causaua lastima.

Llegò otro dia de conferençia en tiempo que se estaua esperando por horas la nueua del suçeso que huuiese tenido Lambert con las Tropas del Parlamento contra el Partido de los solebados en chester; y preguntandole yo si hauia tenido alguna nueua, me respondio luego que si y que el caballero Bot (que seguia la boz del Rey) hauia sido roto, que Lambert hauia entrado en chester y que todo quedaua perdido; y lastimandose mucho y sacando la carta del Mariscal de Turena en que le referia todas las çircunstançias del combate y lo mal a proposito que se hauia perdido el Bot, peleando sin neçesidad, fue leyendo la carta de Turena en françes tan aprisa que hauiendo acabado lo que tocaua al suçeso, pasò vn poco mas adelante (sin poderse detener con el impetu que llebaba), leyendo vna clausula que deçia estas palabras: Y por este accidente, no pasaran las Tropas hasta tener otra orden de Vem^a.

Y avnque el cardenal despues, advirtiendo en el hierro que hauia cometido y temiendo el reparo que yo podria hauer hecho, pretendio enmendarlo, diciendome que aquellas tropas en que al fin de su carta hablaua Turena eran vnas que se hauian de embiar de Normandia al Boloñes a refrescar de quarteles, el remedio llegò tarde porque ya estaua tomada toda la señal que era menester; y creo verdaderam^{te} que si, como esperaron a ver el suçeso de chester para embiar aquellas Tropas, se huuieran resuelto â haçerlo de manera que quatro ô çinco mill hombres viejos de aquella calidad Gouernados por Marsin[194] (que estaua con el Rey para este efecto) huuieran llegado a vnirse con los solebados antes que Lambert con las Tropas del Parlamento, se puede probablemente creer que huuiera hecho pie y tomado gran fuerza su Partido porque toda la Prouinçia de Gales estaua ya lebantada y hauia tomado su voz y el General Monc en escoçia no hauia querido obedeçer las ordenes del Parlamento; conque puesto el Rey vna vez en chester con fuerzas y con tan faborables prinçipios, fuera bien posible q̃ se huuieran puesto todas las cosas de aquel Rey^o en vna gran confusion y avn passo a creer que, en este caso, huuiera hecho el car^{al} diligençias con Locart (que es Gou^{or} de Dunquerq̃ y Mardique)[195] para que huuiera puesto aquellas Plazas a deboçion del Rey, y teniendole junto assi para poder persuadirle y gratificarle, juzgo que lo huuiera conseguido sin gran dificultad.

El mal suçeso del Rey se deue sentir por lo q̃ toca a la causa comun de todos los Reyes, pero mirandolo fuera desta generalidad que comprehende a todos y atendiendo solo a los intereses particulares de VMag^d, yo creo verdaderamente que nos ha sido prouechoso porque avnque entiendo que VM^d no ha faltado al Tratado que tiene hecho con el Rey porque el jamas ha tenido Puerto asegurado por si (que es deuaxo de cuya condiçion VMag̃ le hauia ofreçido las ayudas), comoquiera que el se hallaua desobligado de los Ministros de flandes, que hauia sido mal pagado de las pequeñas Asistençias que se le dauan (en que yo no hecho culpa a nadie mas que a la misma dificultad de los Tiempos) y comoquiera que oygo deçir que las Personas que tiene çerca de si son muy opuestas al seruiçio de VMg^d, juzgo que si huuiera sido estableçido en esta occasion con solo las fuerzas de la françia y debaxo del contrato de los casamientos de los sobrinos del Car^{al}, no huuiera podido suçeder para todos los intereses del seruiçio de VM^d y para la conquista de Portugal cossa mas perjudiçial por todas consideraçiones.

Las vltimas nuebas de aquel Reyno son que los Parlamentarios van haçiendo quantas diligençias puedan para preuenirse en adelante contra semejantes solebaçiones y que el Rey venia à este confin pero hasta aora no ha llegado ni se ha tenido mas notiçia del que la que di a VMg^d en

---

[194] *Marsin* is Jean Gaspard Ferdinand, Count of Marchin. This count from Flanders had a varied military career. He fought for France in Catalonia in the 1640s, served with Condé during the Frondes, accepted the position of Captain General in the Spanish army in 1653, and later attached himself to the court of Charles II of England when the latter was in exile in Flanders.

[195] Mardyck is eight miles or so from Dunkirk.

carta de los 10 deste.[196] Y esto es quanto puedo deçir a VMg^d por aora sobre las materias de Inglaterra.

Al Marques de Carazena y a D^n Alonso de car^{as} he ydo escriuiendo siempre que con el embiado del Parlamento que se halla en aquella parte se vayan procurando gouernar de manera que le mantengan en confianza pero sin llegar â haçer empeño hasta tener orden declarada de VMg^d de lo que se huuiere de ejecutar; y estos dias les he buelto a escribir lo mismo con ocasion del mal suçeso que tubo vltimam^{te} el partido del Rey, y yo me he ydo gouernando aqui con Locart en la misma conformidad; y hauiendo yo dado quenta a VMag^d en carta de 23 de sept^{re}[197] de la avdiençia que le di en esta Plaza y de todo lo que pasò en ella y averturas que me hauia dado para el acomodamiento, diçiendo que daria quantos pasos fuesen neçesarios para el y todos quantos fuesen de satisfaçion mia, solo lo que se me ofreçe añadir es que el otro dia en la Isla vn secretario suyo buscò a otro mio y le dixo de parte de su amo que estaua esperando a ver si yo le mandaua algo sobre las proposiçiones que me hauia hecho; y vltimamente me ha escrito el mismo Locart la carta que remito a VMg^d inclusa aqui y avnque las palabras parezcan solo de cumplimiento, Virtualmente se puede juzgar que se ençierra en ellas lo que su secretario explicò mas claram^{te} en voz en quanto al deseo con que estaua de tratar conmigo. Yo le he respondido a lo primero por medio de su mismo secretario en voz en la misma conformidad que hasta aqui, manteniendole en confianza y sin haçer ningun empeño, diçiendole que espero las ordenes de VMag^d s^{re} esta materia. Y aora suplico a VMg^d se sirua de mandar deçirme si tengo de responder a su carta por escrito ô no y la sustançia en que lo he de hacer y si deuo continuar el escribir a Don Alonso de cardenas y al Marques de Carazena que se gouiernen en la misma forma allà para que yo pueda gouernarme en todo conforme a la intençion de VMag^d; y avnque no debo entrar a deçir mi pareçer sobre esta materia particularmente estando tan llena de dificultades y de consideraçiones diuersas por todas partes, Todavia no puedo dexar de deçir a VMag^d que en casso que se resoluiese el comenzar a tratar con la Republica y oyr sus proposiçiones, no creo que seria honesto ni combeniente que esto fuese por medio mio por muchas consideraçiones, siendo vna dellas el hallarse al mismo tiempo vn Residente del Rey çerca de mi y siendo tambien posible que concurriese el mismo Rey y que

---

[196] Letter 59 above.
[197] Letter 45 above.

juzgo seria lo mas a proposito el remitir el Tratado a flandes para q̃ los oygan el Marq^s de carazena y D Alonso de car^{as}, pues creo que tienen poder de VMag^d para este efecto; y si Locart buelue a su Gouierno de Dunquerque, como se diçe, estaria en sitio muy a proposito para ello. Juzgo que mereçen alguna reflexion las palabras de la carta de Locart, en que me diçe que anteve que sus superiores le han de mandar retirar de françia dentro de pocos dias, porque, si han llegado â entender ô a sospechar lo que el Cardenal ha intentado en fabor del partido del Rey, yo no dudo que se lo mandaran assi porque la naçion es muy soberuia y lo habrà quedado mas con este vltimo suçeso; y el Locart, avnque a mi me hablò con gran modestia y sumision, no creo que deue de ser mas humilde. Guarde Dios la Catolica y real Persona de VM^d como la xpt^d ha menester. De fuenterrabia a 12 de ott^{re} 1659

Dluismendezdeharo

63

Haro to Philip IV: Fuenterrabía, 12 October 1659 [K1623: 114][198]

More on the naming and ranking of allies in the treaty: the king has decided to give precedence to the Grand Duke of Tuscany over Genoa. Haro points out that once it is known that the allies are ranked according to precedence, the ranking of the Dukes of Mantua, Parma, Modena, of the Republic of Venice and of certain other powers becomes extremely problematical. Moreover, Lionne has suggested that the French may give the emperor (Leopold I) only the title of King of Hungary on the grounds that they were not informed of his elevation to the imperial throne. Haro is sure that the French will create as many problems as possible for Spain in this matter; he is becoming more and more persuaded of the wisdom of the proposal made by the Count of Brienne.[199] If it were adopted, the emperor and certain other important allies could be presented with a fancy document which confirmed their status as allies of Spain without their having to resort to requesting it. Haro stresses that the whole question of ranking is of such importance that it must be resolved by the king himself. Accordingly he requests further instructions.

---

[198] Letter 63 arrived in Madrid with Letter 62.
[199] For details of the count's proposal, see Letter 24.

64

Haro to Philip IV: Fuenterrabía, 17 October 1659 [K1623: 118][200]

In early October, Mazarin had suffered an attack of gout so severe that the negotiations had to be interrupted. Consequently, the nineteenth interview, initially scheduled for 6 October, had not taken place until 16 October. The interview had been devoted mainly to improving the form and wording of the peace treaty. Coloma and Lionne had joined the two prime ministers for the second half of the proceedings in order to write down the revised articles. Haro is delighted to report that everything is now almost complete. Articles have been added, revised and removed so as to take account of the latest negotiations over Condé, Lorraine, Bergues and La Bassée. All of the changes have been to Spain's advantage, as the king will realise when he compares the final agreement with the Paris treaty. The next conference will look at the implementation of the peace, especially the evacuation of strongholds. Haro expects the French to push very hard in that meeting for the marriage to take place as soon as possible but he assures the king that he understands what he must do in this regard. Finally, article twenty-three of the Paris treaty has been almost entirely rewritten. He encloses both versions of the article, which relates to the marriage of the Infanta María Teresa and the French king.

65

Haro to Philip IV: Fuenterrabía, 19 October 1659 [K1619: 60][201]

Continues the series of letters on precedence. Haro is concerned about the order in which to present the names of those who are to witness the marriage agreement. He is not persuaded by the response which he has had from the king on this matter and discusses the precedent set on the occasion of the marriage of Anne of Austria. Joseph Gonzalez and Francisco Ramos have already offered representations based on current practice in Madrid. Haro requests specific instructions from the king to ensure that what he does is in harmony with the royal will.

---

[200] Letter 64 was dispatched on 18 October.
[201] Letter 65 was dispatched on 19 October and arrived in Madrid on 23 October.

Señor

Sobre la forma de nombrar las Personas que han de concurrir a la capitulaçion matrimonial de la s^{ra} Infante escribi a VMag^d en 13 de sept^{re} [202] el reparo que se me ofreçia, a que VMg^d se siruio mandarme responder en 28 del mismo, remitiendome VMg^d este punto, juntamente con vna memoria de los que VMag^d juzgaua que podrian concurrir, para que yo le disponga como me pareçiere mas conueniente. Sobre lo qual me hallo obligado a representar a VM^d que, llegando el acto practico, se ofreçen muchas dificultades en quanto a la graduaçion, porque (hauiendolas hallado tambien el Car^{al} por los que han de concurrir de la parte de françia) el punto se ha dibulgado, conque muchos estan atentos a ver la forma en que se graduan. Y avnque VMag^d se sirue de deçirme en el despacho çitado que en las capitulaçiones de la señora Infante Doña Ana pareçe que no hubo graduaçion, mirando aquel Instrumento y las Personas que interuinieron por testigos (de que buelbo â embiar a VMg^d la memoria inclusa), debo representar a VMg^d que no pareçe que la dejò de hauer porque todos los nombrados fueron grandes, entre los quales nunca se considera graduaçion porq̃ se reputan todos por vn mismo cuerpo; y despues dellos vienen nombrados dos consexeros de estado por sus antiguedades y, al cabo, vn consejero de castilla.

Demas desto, hauiendo hecho buscar el Instrumento de las renunçiaçiones que hizo la señora Infante Doña Ana en Burgos antes de su desposorio, he hallado que fueron nombrados los que se contienen en la memoria que tambien remito a VMag^d aqui, por donde se reconoçe que todos los Testigos fueron grandes, pues el Arzobispo de Burgos tambien se cubre delante de VMg^d, y los demas Ministros por la graduaçion de sus consexos; y el Limosnero mayor y el Maestro de VMg^d (siendo Prinçipe) fueron nombrados despues del consexero de Castilla; y juzgo que se deua [sic] reparar mucho en que, siendo fuerza que en ambos actos hayan concurrido muchos Gentiles hombres de la camara y Mayordomos señores de casas tan prinçipales como lo suelen de ordinario ser todos los que llegan a mereçer este honor de VM^d, en ninguno de ambos Ynstrumentos està nombrado ninguno, lo qual no pareçe que pueda dexar de hauerse fundado en algo; y es bien probable que haya sido por la misma dificultad que se topa aora.

Joseph Gonzalez y Don fran^{co} Ramos me han hablado ya esta tarde en la materia, diçiendome el primero que goza las preheminençias de

---

[202] This seems to be the date in the MS. However, the content clearly matches a letter written by Haro on 23 September. See Letter 44 above.

Presidente de Haz^da, Los quales concurren con igualdad con los Consejeros de Estado y con los grandes en las juntas en M^d, y el segundo que, por ordenes y declaraçiones de VMg^d, preçede vn consexero de Castilla a todos los Titulos en qualquiera concurrençia donde se halla, ô en el consexo ô fuera del; y al consejero de Guerra creo que le suçede lo mismo porque ellos y los de Castilla se preçeden igualmente segun la antiguedad de cada vno.

El nombrar a los vnos y otros Consexeros (que tambien de Guerra se hallan dos aqui) primero que a Don Manuel Henrriquez y al Conde de s^n Tisteuan y a otros hombres semexantes, yo no se si podrà ser grato â estos vltimos; y el anteponerlos, pribando a los primeros de aquel grado y antelaçion que VMag^d les tiene dada y que se obserba en su misma corte, tampoco puedo atreuerme â ejecutarlo ni seria razon que lo hiçiese sin tener vna expresa orden de VMg^d para ello; y no permitiendome estas consideraçiones el poder tomar resoluçion sobre esta mat^ria sin dar quenta a VMg^d della, Sup^co a VM^d tenga por bien de mandarme embiar orden preçisa y clara de lo que es su real Volunt^d que se haga para que yo la execute como debo; y entretanto se yran poniendo los Ynstrumentos en forma, dejando para lo vltimo la nominaçion de los Asistentes ô Testigos, como se ejecuto en el de las renunçiaçiones, de manera que, en llegandome la orden de VMag^d, no se difiera la otorgaçion por defecto de no estar corriente la escritura. Dios guarde la catholica y R^l Persona de VM^d como la xpt^d ha menester, fuenterrauia a 19 de ott^re 1659.

Dluismendezdeharo

66

Haro to Philip IV: Fuenterrabía, 20 October 1659 [K1623: 122][203]

Mazarin has conveyed to Haro the protestations of the Electors of Mainz and Cologne over the billeting of Spanish troops in the Liège. Apparently, the troops have not been withdrawn despite attempts by the Elector of

---

[203] Letters 66, 67, 68 and 69 were all dispatched on 22 October, arriving in Madrid on 25 October. The cost of the dispatch was 650 *reales de plata*; AGS CMC 3551 (2), 27. Given the seriousness of the situation affecting the Liège described in Letter 66, it is perhaps surprising that Haro does not allow the courier an extra horse on this occasion.

Cologne to persuade the Marquis of Caracena to observe the treaty of Tirlemont in so far as it refers to this issue. The electors have consequently issued three demands: (1) immediate withdrawal of troops; (2) the inclusion of an article in the treaty of the Pyrenees to the effect that neither the Spanish king nor his allies will henceforth billet troops in the estates of the elector; (3) compensation for damage according to the terms of the treaty of Tillemont.[204] Haro encloses a copy of the letter which he has written to Caracena, ordering immediate withdrawal of troops from the Liège. He has refused to accept the elector's second demand but agreed to refer the third demand to the king. Accordingly, he requests instructions. He notes in closing that, under the terms of the cessation of hostilities negotiated by Pimentel in Paris, there is very little room in Flanders for the billeting of Spanish troops and he therefore understands Caracena's dilemma. He hopes for a speedy conclusion of the treaty so that the situation in Flanders may be eased.

67

Haro to Philip IV: Fuenterrabía, 20 October 1659 [K1623: 123][205]

Madame de Lionne has been making a nuisance of herself, visiting the Spanish apartments in the conference centre and also San Sebastian. She has decided to visit Madrid. Pimentel failed to persuade either her husband or Mazarin to stop her, and she left for the Spanish court with two of her young children the previous week, her planned itinerary to include Burgos, Valladolid, Salamanca, Avila and Toledo. By the time she has visited all these places, Haro expects to be back in Madrid. If he is not, she will go to Seville instead of proceeding directly to the capital. Haro notes, however, that she may yet change her mind and go to Madrid early. Lionne has asked

---

[204] The treaty of Tillemont between Spain and Cologne was signed on 17 March 1654 by Leopold William, Archduke of Austria and Governor General of the Spanish Netherlands, and by Maximilian Henry, Elector of Cologne. This treaty of neutrality included a clause which prohibited the billeting of Spanish troops in the Liège. Tillemont is situated in the Brabant about twelve miles southeast of Louvain.

[205] Letter 67 was dispatched on 22 October and arrived in Madrid on 25 October.

that she be allowed to stay there with Damian's wife.²⁰⁶ Haro is happy to agree.

68

*Haro to Philip IV: Fuenterrabía, 21 October 1659 [K1623: 124]*²⁰⁷

Haro reports the arrival of the English king in Saragossa and remits a note which he has received from him via O'Neil.²⁰⁸ He expects the king to arrive in Fuenterrabía on 22 October. He acknowledges receipt of Philip's letter of 17 October informing him of the Duke of Lorraine's departure from Madrid and discusses the arrangements which he needs to make for the accommodation of these two illustrious guests. For the moment, Haro is occupying the best rooms in Fuenterrabía but he will cede these to Charles when he arrives.²⁰⁹ If necessary, he is also prepared to give up the alternative rooms which he has reserved for himself during the English king's visit so that the duke may have them. He intends to send Don Jerónimo de Quiñones²¹⁰ to meet the duke at Tolosa and to see whether he is in fact prepared to come to Fuenterrabía, given that Charles will also be housed there. Haro expects the duke to be reluctant to lodge in a *plaza cerrada* (walled town) after his imprisonment in Toledo, and he therefore intends to arrange additional alternative accommodation for him in Irún.

Haro confirms that he will do his best to prevent Charles from visiting Madrid. He requests 30,000–40,000 *escudos* to give to the king when he leaves Spain. Since Spain cannot help Charles regain his kingdom, it must at least comply with its promise to pay him a pension of 3,000 *escudos* a month.²¹¹ The English king is currently owed more than twelve payments

---

²⁰⁶ In his letter of 24 September to Le Tellier, Mazarin (1693: 215) informs us that Damian is the 'premier valet de chambre de Dom Louis en qui il a grande confiance, & à qui il a fait donner une de ses litieres pour s'en aller à Bordeaux'. Lionne himself had stayed with Damian when he was in Madrid for peace talks in 1656. Although the Council of State recommended that Damian return to Madrid to attend personally to Madame de Lionne, this assignment was eventually given to another. AGS Estado Francia K1618: 99.
²⁰⁷ Letter 68 was dispatched with Letter 67.
²⁰⁸ Daniel O'Neil was at this time the king's Groom of the Bedchamber.
²⁰⁹ See Letter 7 for more on Haro's accommodation in Fuenterrabía.
²¹⁰ D. Jerónimo de Quiñones is identified elsewhere as *Maestre de Campo*. CMC 3551 (2), 27.
²¹¹ For Spain's commitments to the English king, see note 42.

and there are good reasons for honouring the debt. For example, the situation in England remains uncertain and it is therefore crucial that the king should not feel entirely without obligation to Spain. Finally, Haro reports that the Earl of Bristol and the Marquis of Ormond are travelling with the king.

69

Haro to Philip IV: Fuenterrabía, 21 October 1659 [K1623: 125][212]

Mazarin is unwell and has been bled and purged. The French say that he is melancholy. Lionne is making frequent visits to Fuenterrabía in order to finalise the wording of the articles already agreed. Although disagreement over the final text is not substantial, there is nevertheless some dispute over the most appropriate form of words. Haro complains that what the French agree to today, they renegue on tomorrow. He is desperate to sign the treaty and see the end of it all.

70

Haro to Philip IV: Fuenterrabía, 26 October 1659 [K1623: 127]

Watteville was sent to Irún on the night of 23 October to meet the Duke of Lorraine and escort him to his rooms, where servants were awaiting his arrival. The duke had elected to stay in Irún rather than in Fuenterrabía. Watteville had then reported to Haro at 11 p.m. that night and Haro had paid a courtesy call on the duke at 10 a.m. the following morning. The visit had lasted two and a half hours and Haro had been surprised to find that the duke appeared totally unaware of the outcome of the negotiations in so far as they related to him. Haro had informed him that he would retain the whole of old Lorraine together with the dependencies of the three dioceses of Metz, Toul and Verdun and the fortified town of Marsac.[213] He went on to explain that the deal represented a substantial improvement on what the duke had personally negotiated for himself in Paris. The duke had requested

---

[212] Letter 69 was dispatched with Letters 67 and 68.
[213] Metz is in the French department of Moselle; Toul is in the department of Meurthe-et-Moselle just west of Nancy; Verdun lies on the river Meuse and is in the department of Meuse. For information on the general location of Marsac, see note 175.

compensation for the jewels and tapestries confiscated at the time that he was taken prisoner in Flanders and Haro had explained that these had been entrusted to his brother François. In response to the duke's expressed desire to recover the Duchy of Bar, Haro had insisted that he had secured the best possible deal for him but that he was free to approach Mazarin for himself. On 25 October, the duke had visited Haro in Fuenterrabía and announced that he intended to make his way to St Jean de Luz in order to see Mazarin. He had asked Haro on that occasion to try to persuade Mazarin to restore to him the Duchy of Bar. Haro had agreed but held out little hope of success. He repeats to the king that he has secured a better deal for the duke than anyone could have anticipated.

71

Haro to Philip IV: Fuenterrabía, 26 October 1659 [K1623: 128][214]

Haro has received the king's despatch of 20 October, which includes a copy of the *consulta* issued by the Council of State on the best way of dealing with the English question. He stresses his complete agreement with the council that it is essential to maintain good relations with the English king without antagonizing the English Parliament and without making a commitment to either side. He further agrees that Spain should meanwhile make the most of the fact that England is currently not in a position to assist Portugal, in order to prosecute its recovery as speedily as possible. Accordingly, he promises to respond to Lockhart's[215] note in general terms, as instructed by the king. The English king is expected to arrive that afternoon and he is rumoured to be virtually destitute. Apparently, he had been forced to send to Toulouse for a new suit of clothes for his arrival in Fuenterrabía. In view of this, Haro again recommends payment of the monies owed to Charles. Otherwise, the king may decide to request payment in Madrid.

---

[214] Letter 71 arrived in Madrid on 30 October.
[215] See the final paragraph of Letter 62 above.

72

Haro to Philip IV: Fuenterrabía, 26 October 1659 [K1623: 129][216]

Haro acknowledges receipt of the king's dispatch of 20 October, which reports both Gramont's embassy to Madrid and the king's positive response to the request made on behalf of the French king and queen for the hand of the infanta in marriage. He acknowledges too the king's instruction that he may now sign the peace treaty and the marriage agreement as soon as they are ready. He then summarises the progress made in his twentieth interview with Mazarin held on 23 October. Agreement has been reached on virtually every item of business and the treaty is at last more or less in its final form in both languages. All that remains is for the two plenipotentiaries to agree the manner of the implementation of the peace and of the evacuation of strongholds and the date of the royal wedding. He and Mazarin have determined to address these issues in their next interview, which is scheduled for 27 October.

73

Haro to Philip IV: Fuenterrabía, 28 October 1659 [K1623: 132][217]

The twenty-first interview held on 27 October had been devoted exclusively to a discussion of the evacuation of strongholds and the wedding of the infanta. Mazarin had pressed extremely hard for the papal dispensation to be requested immediately and for the wedding to be celebrated as soon as possible after the dispensation had been given. It had finally been agreed that evacuation of strongholds should occur twenty days after the ratification of the treaty; that the marriage ceremony should be celebrated in Burgos, following the pattern of that of Doña Ana; that the French should retain one key stronghold until such time as the infanta had been delivered to the frontier and that Spain should, in accordance with customary practice, receive from France hostages of Spain's choosing to ensure that the French complied with this part of the agreement; lastly, that all other strongholds should be handed over before the wedding. Before he concludes, Haro notes that the English king will arrive in Fuenterrabía that evening.

---

[216] Letter 72 also arrived in Madrid on 30 October.
[217] Letter 73 arrived in Madrid on 31 October.

74

Haro to Philip IV: Fuenterrabía, 31 October 1659 [K1623: 133][218]

The English king had arrived on the very stormy evening of 28 October. Watteville and a company of guards had been sent to Rentería[219] to receive him and Haro had waited for them at the end of the sea wall. Haro and the king had then travelled together by coach to Fuenterrabía and had held a meeting the following day. Haro suspects that Mazarin had tried to prevent the king from making his way to the conference because he knew that Spain would discover that Turenne had been waiting with 3,000–4,000 men to accompany the Duke of York to assist Booth at Chester. A reliable source in England has informed Haro that Lambert aspires to become protector and that the whole country is completely divided. Now that they have made peace, Spain and France do not need their troops and Haro observes that the political situation in England is such that 4,000 infantry and 500 cavalry would be enough to swing things Charles's way. He then discourses over likely French designs in the matter of England, noting that Mazarin has not yet married his niece and nephew to the English king and his sister. The cardinal, he notes yet again, had insisted to Pimentel that he wanted to discuss with Haro the possibility of restoring the English monarchy, but now that the opportunity to do so has presented itself, he will not seize it. Instead he merely laments having to dispatch an army under Turenne to Germany in order to support Sweden. All of this persuades Haro that the French intend to restore Charles without Spanish assistance so that he becomes entirely dependent on France and hostile towards Spain. Finally, Haro reports that his twenty-second interview with Mazarin had been held that day.

75

Haro to Philip IV: Fuenterrabía, 1 November 1659 [K1623: 134][220]

Haro briefly rehearses the content of his letter to the king of 28 October (Letter 73 above) and then summarises his interview of 31 October with

---

[218] Letter 74 was dispatched with Letters 75 and 76 on 1 November and arrived in Madrid on 4 November.

[219] Rentería lies a short way inland from the port of Pasajes, slightly to the southeast of San Sebastian. The English king had travelled to Rentería from Saragossa.

[220] Letter 75 was dispatched with Letters 74 and 76.

Mazarin. The cardinal had urged that the letters requesting papal dispensation for the royal marriage be dispatched immediately and the wedding be celebrated as soon as Haro was back in Madrid. Haro reminds the king that discussion of the royal wedding had been concluded in an earlier session (that of 27 October) and complains that one of the most tiresome features of the negotiations is the absence of certainty that points which have been debated and agreed will not be reintroduced for further discussion in subsequent interviews. Mazarin had also proposed that the evacuation of strongholds should not begin until the infanta had reached the frontier. This would mean either that the infanta would be kept waiting at the frontier for days or that she would be handed over to the French before the exchange of strongholds was complete, with the result that Spain would lose the security which the infanta represented and Spanish territories would have to endure the burden of the enemy's presence rather longer than anticipated. Finally, however, it was agreed that the wedding should take place at the border and that France, whilst retaining as security Roses and Cadaqués in Catalonia, should grant appropriate hostages to Spain so as to guarantee the subsequent return of these two strongholds. Strongholds in Italy and Flanders, on the other hand, would be restored as soon as the treaty and marriage agreement were ratified. The exact procedure for evacuating strongholds was still under discussion, the Count of Gramont having suggested that the larger territories should be evacuated first so as to provide more room for the billeting of troops. Haro hopes that agreement on the evacuation procedure will be reached that afternoon. Instructions will eventually have to be given to military commanders on how to conduct the evacuation and these will include details of the order in which strongholds should be returned and the safeguards which will be required. Finally, Haro emphasises that it is not reasonable to suppose that the French will restore all strongholds before the wedding has been celebrated and the infanta has been delivered to her husband.

76

Haro to Philip IV: Fuenterrabía, 1 November 1659 [K1623: 135][221]

Haro acknowledges receipt of two slightly variant sets of revised powers with alternative rephrasings of those parts which refer to the outbreak of

---

[221] Letter 76 was dispatched with Letters 74 and 75, arriving in Madrid on 4 November.

war between Spain and France and to the overtures for peace. Haro notes that it is hoped in Madrid that one of the two will meet with Mazarin's approval. Since it will take four or five days to produce a clean copy of the whole treaty and check the Spanish and French versions against each other for accuracy, Haro notes that the delay will allow time for him to consult the king further over the exact wording of the powers. Although Mazarin does not wish the powers to imply that it was France that had made overtures for peace, he has never said that the text should suggest that they came from Spain. It is important to remember that the treaty is to be printed and published and the wording should therefore be less precise. Haro is himself unhappy with it as it stands: not only does the wording not need to be so specific but France does not require it. Consequently, Haro returns the powers to Madrid in the hope that the king will agree to their being emended along these lines.

77

Haro to Philip IV: Fuenterrabía, 7 November 1659 [K1623: 138][222]

Haro announces that the peace treaty and the marriage agreement have at last been signed and praises the king for the willingness which he has displayed throughout the negotiations to subordinate his own interests to those of the cause of universal peace. Now that all is signed and sealed, Haro feels free to reveal to the king just how difficult the final stages of the peace conference have been. He refers specifically to the recent tragedy in the Spanish court and to its implications for the negotiations. News of the tragedy had caused the French to rethink their position and to consider withdrawing from the talks. Furthermore, Lockhart and the Portuguese ambassador had seized the opportunity to put additional pressure on Mazarin not to sign either the treaty or the marriage agreement. Fortunately, however, God had seen fit to prosper the cause of peace and Haro had finally managed to settle with Mazarin, to the satisfaction of Spain, the timing of both the marriage and the evacuation of strongholds.

---

[222] Letter 77 was dispatched on Saturday, 8 November, and arrived in Madrid on Tuesday, 11 November.

77: 7 Nov] *Letters from the Pyrenees* 133

Señor

Las Capitulaçiones y la Paz quedan firmadas; y el justo y santo çelo con que VMag^d ha procurado (Sacrificando tantos intereses propios) dar este vnibersal reposo a sus Reynos y a toda la christiandad espero en Dios se ha de seruir de premiarle, conçediendo a VMag^d y al Prinçipe n^{ro} s^r muy larga vida y dilatada suçesion, como todos sus criados y Vassallos se lo deuemos pedir y lo hemos menester.[223]

Estos dias vltimos hauia ydo dando quenta â VMag^d de las dificultades que se ofreçian y nouedades que se intentauan sobre algunos de los puntos en que ya estauamos de acuerdo, pero sin explicarme por menor en ellas ni en sus causas por no acreçentar a VMg^d Cuydado ni renobarle memorias ni çircunstançias de sentimiento; pero ya que Dios se ha seruido de que todo se haya vençido y de que la Paz quede firmada, no puedo dexar de deçir a VMg^d que el accidente suçedido estos dias (con tanto Sentimiento de todos) en essa corte, sobrevino en la peor coyuntura de quantas pudiera suçeder por hauer sido al mismo tiempo que se estaua disputando aqui sobre el plazo del Desposorio de la Señora Ynfante y de la evaquaçion de las Plazas.[224] Lo qual causò grauisimo perjuiçio y les obligò a intentar salirse afuera de lo que ya teniamos cassi ajustado en razon de ambas cosas, pareçiendoles que, siendo posible en la inçertidumbre de las cosas desta vida el sobrevenir otro accidente semexante, les combenia no restituir sus Plazas hasta que la señora Ynfante se hallase despossada por no quedar en aquel caso aventurados a que, despues de hecha la restituçion dellas, nos hallasemos obligados a retener la Persona de S.A.

---

[223] On 7 November, Coloma read aloud the marriage agreement in the company of the witnesses representing both crowns. Out of deference to the infanta, the document was read in Spanish only and Mazarin even crossed the floor into the Spanish half of the conference room in order to sign it where it lay on Haro's desk. On no other occasion did either of the plenipotentiaries leave his half of the room. For details, see Gualdo Priorato 1667: 215–16.

[224] The tragedy referred to is the death of the younger of the two Spanish princes. Fernando Tomás de Austria was born in December 1658, and died in October 1659 during Gramont's embassy to Madrid (see BNM Ms 2387, fols 152–63; Gualdo Priorato 1667: 211–12). He was survived briefly by his elder brother, Felipe Próspero, born in November 1657. The impact of the death of Fernando Tomás on the negotiations was apparently immediate, since the French feared that if a similar fate were to befall the surviving prince, Spain would renegue on the marriage agreement and also keep those strongholds which were to be returned in advance of the *entrega* of the Infanta.

y a no poder continuar en la resoluçion de su cassamiento; a que tambien se añadio el hauer en estos vltimos lançes el embaxador Locart hecho grandisimos esfuerzos para impedir la Paz, ofreçiendo grandes partidos a la françia contra nosotros y no menores Don Juan de Acosta, embaxador de Portugal, que hauia venido estos vltimos dias a san Juan de Luz para este efecto, representando ambos vnidos y separados a françeses este mismo peligro de que despues de entregadas las Plazas y haçiendose la ebaquaçion dellas antes del Desposorio de S.A., les retuuiesemos su Persona; y los ofreçimientos de Portugal creo que hayan llegado hasta terminos de ofreçer entregarles dos o tres Puertos prinçipales de aquel Reyno.

Todas estas dificultades juntas, sobrevenidas en el vltimo termino desta negoçiaçion, me han tenido en el intimo cuydado que VMag^d juzgarà façilmente; pero hauiendome procurado oponer â ellas por todos quantos caminos y medios he juzgado que podia combenir, finalmente ha sido Dios seruido de que la Paz quede firmada, el desposorio de la señora Infante remitido para quando llegare â esta frontera y ajustada la restituçion de las Plazas en forma y en termino tan breue que deuo esperar que VMag^d se darà por seruido dello, de que darè mas distinta quenta a VMag^d con otro correo,[225] no deteniendome ha haçerlo aora por no dilatar a VM^d esta nueba.

En toda esta negoçiaçion he deseado encaminar el mayor seruiçio de VMag^d como deuia. Si VMag^d se diere por seruido dello, serà solo efecto de su grandeza y el mayor premio que yo puedo tener ni desear. Dios guarde la Catolica y Real Persona de VM^d como la christiandad ha menester. De fuenterrauia a 7 de Nouiembre 1659.

Dluismendezdeharo

---

[225] In Letter 79 Haro apologises for still not providing this report; it is finally sent in Letter 81.

78

Haro to Philip IV: Fuenterrabía, 10 November 1659 [K1623: 139][226]

About the release of French and Spanish galley slaves: the French have sent orders to Marseilles and Toulon[227] for the release of Spanish prisoners and for French representatives to visit the Spanish squadrons in Genoa, Naples and Sicily for the purpose of overseeing the release of their prisoners. Spain has already ordered the release of French prisoners but France wants the orders repeated. France also wants Spain to issue an additional order to cover the release of all Catalan galley slaves who are serving at the oars as prisoners of war, since they too are included in the treaty.

79

Haro to Philip IV: Fuenterrabía, 11 November 1659 [K1623: 140][228]

Haro excuses himself for not having provided the king with a detailed report on the procedures which will govern the evacuation of strongholds. He has been extremely busy preparing orders for Flanders and Italy in connection with the evacuation process and the English king and the Duke of Lorraine have also taken up a good deal of his time. He promises that he will write to Philip in detail on this matter as soon as possible. For the moment, he encloses dispatches from Caracena in respect of changes to be introduced in the government of Flanders which will greatly improve the regulation of affairs in this province. He tells the king that he has just come from his last interview with Mazarin, who is scheduled to leave the border area on 13 November. He himself intends to wait until Lorraine and the English king depart before making his way back to Madrid. Finally, he notes that news has arrived that army officers have dissolved the English parliament.

---

[226] Letters 78 and 79 were dispatched on 12 November and arrived in Madrid on 15 November. The cost of the dispatch was 810 *reales de plata*, the courier having been allowed an extra horse; AGS CMC 3551 (2), 27. The orders relating to the release of French prisoners and Catalan galley slaves requested by France (Letter 78) would explain the urgency of this dispatch.

[227] A French seaport about 30 miles east of Marseilles.

[228] Letter 79 was dispatched with Letter 78.

80

Haro to Philip IV: Fuenterrabía, 12 November 1659 [K1623: 141][229]

A brief note in which Haro informs the king that he has decided to send Pedro Coloma back to Madrid ahead of his own party so that he may avoid having to confront the worst rigours of winter during his journey. Coloma has served well at the conference, as one would have expected. He carries with him the peace treaty and the marriage agreement.

81

Haro to Philip IV: Fuenterrabía, 16 November 1659 [K1623: 143][230]

The last letter written from the Pyrenees consists of detailed reports on the procedures which will govern the exchange of the French and Spanish versions of the peace treaty and marriage agreement (following their ratification) and the evacuation of strongholds. Right up to the end Mazarin had pressed for the restitution of strongholds to be delayed until the infanta had been delivered to the frontier but this obstacle had eventually been successfully overcome. It was thus finally agreed that thirty days should be allowed for the ratification process and that the documents should be exchanged at the border. A delay of a further twenty days would be necessary before the evacuation of strongholds could occur, because the requisite orders would be dispatched to the responsible military commanders only after the ratified documents had been exchanged and had reached their respective destinations, and before the process could be initiated there was also a great deal for generals to do on the ground, such as securing the appropriate safeguards. Haro has, however, been able to negotiate an early date for the restitution of strongholds in Milan. Accordingly, he has written to the Count of Fuensaldaña informing him that this will happen on 30 November, and he has enclosed a letter from the king instructing the count to follow Haro's orders in this matter. Vercelli and also Châtelet in Flanders will likewise be evacuated on 30 November; Haro confirms that he has already sent the necessary orders to Caracena and has written separately to Condé, who is in command of Châtelet.

---

[229] Letter 80 was dispatched on 14 November.
[230] Letter 81 was dispatched on 16 November and arrived in Madrid on 20 November.

The plenipotentiaries expect that the ratified treaties will be exchanged on 7 December and that the evacuation of positions in the heart of Flanders (Audenarde, Merville, Menin and Commines[231] by France; Rocroi and Lichans by Spain) will occur on 27 December. Eight days later, France will surrender Ypres, Bergues, La Bassée and all emplacements in Catalonia except Roses and Cadaqués. Also on 4 January, Spain will hand over Hesdin, Philippeville and Marienbourg. The whole process is expected to be concluded four months before the royal wedding, although Roses and Cadaqués will be retained by France as security until the infanta reaches the border. Avesnes and Juliers will be surrendered only after: (1) the Duke of Neuburg has lodged with Caracena a signed document confirming his acceptance of the conditions which will govern his tenure of Juliers; (2) Condé has returned to France; and (3) the Duke of Longueville has in his possession all of the letters patent relating to the offices, charges and governments to be given to the Duke of Enghien. Condé will advise Caracena when this has been done. This is also the moment when France will surrender emplacements in Burgundy. Strongholds are to retain only those troops necessary for their defence, the remainder being recalled according to the terms of the treaty.

Haro discusses Condé, the Duke of Lorraine and the English king. He announces that he has managed to improve the deal on the table for Condé's followers. They will have lost nothing and should be fully satisfied with the outcome of the conference. The Duke of Lorraine had returned from his audience with Mazarin extremely angry with Spain and had to be persuaded by Haro that Spain had in fact been more generous in his case than had France. The English king intended to depart for Flanders on 17 November and had obtained a passport to travel via Paris, where he would visit his mother. England, Haro observes, continues to be in turmoil and he will have several things to tell the king about Mazarin's designs with regard to England, Portugal and Germany (which he had been instructed to try to discern) when he gets back to Madrid. If the English king does indeed depart on 17 November, Haro will begin his return journey to Madrid that afternoon or early on 18 November. He closes this last dispatch, noting that it has been snowing heavily and expressing his fear that the mountain passes will be blocked.

---

[231] Commines is situated just inside the Belgian province of West Flanders, where the river Lys crosses into France.

Bibliography

Archival sources in manuscript

1. Archivo General de Simancas, Valladolid (AGS)
   a. *Contaduría Mayor de Cuentas:* Legs 2233, 2766, 2772, 2985, 3523, 3551.
   b. *Sección de Estado*
      Alemania, Hamburgo, Polonia, Prusia y Sajonia: Legs 2370, 2372, 2374–2376.
      España: Legs 8334, 8339, 8340–8343.
      Estados pequeños de Italia: Legs 3680, 3851.
      Flandes: Legs 2050–2053, 2055, 2059, 2064, 2066, 2068–2075, 2078–2079, 2081, 2082, 2088, 2085, 2089, 2091, 2093, 2094, 2096, 2097–2099, 2100, 2250, 2944.
      Francia: Legs K1385, K1386, K1417, K1419, K1424, K1425, K1614A, K1614B, K1616–K1625, K1643–K1645, K1670, K1686.
      Génova: Legs 3608–3610.
      Inglaterra: Legs 2521, 2524, 2530, 2532.
      Milán: Legs 3374, 3378.
      Nápoles: Legs 3273, 3284.
      Roma: Legs 3030, 3033.
      Venecia: Legs 3554, 3556, 3558.
   c. *Escribanía de Rentas*
      Quitaciones de Corte: Legs 7–11, 14, 16–18, 20–25, 27, 28, 31, 33–35, 37, 40.
   d. *Guerra Antigua:* Legs 585, 768, 828, 1235, 1362, 3222, 3402, 3472, 3483.

2. Biblioteca Nacional, Madrid (BNM)
   Colección Osuna: Legs 2384, 2387, 1100.

3. British Library, London (BL)
   a. *Additional MSS:* 14000, 14001, 20722, 28472, 34329.
   b. *Egerton MSS:* 347, 2542.
   c. *King's MSS:* 139.

4. Public Record Office, London (PRO)
   State Papers, Spanish: Series SP 78, vols 113–116; SP 94, vols 37–49.

5. Bibliothèque Nationale de France Richelieu, Paris (BNP)
   Manuscrits Français: 529, 4214, 4240, 5884, 10653, 11191, 13969, 15865, 18254, 20789, 21721.

6. Bibliothèque de l'Arsenal, Paris (BAP)
   Manuscrits Français: 4231, 4232, 5420, 5421, 6821, 7458.

Printed contemporary sources

Braybrooke, Lord Richard, ed., 1929. *Diary and Correspondence of Samuel Pepys, F. R. S., Secretary to the Admiralty in the Reigns of Charles II and James II*, London: Allen & Unwin

Brienne, Comte de, 1824. *Mémoires*. In M. Petitot, ed., *Collection des Mémoires* [see below], XXXVI, 1–281

Castillo, Leonardo del, 1667. *Viage del Rey Nuestro Señor Don Felipe Quarto el Grande a la Frontera de Francia. Funciones reales, del desposorio, y entrega de la Serenissima señora Infante de España Doña Maria Teresa de Austria. Vistas de sus Magestades catolica y Christianissima, Señora Reyna Christianissima, y Señor Duque de Anjou. Solemne juramento de la Paz, y sucesos de ida, u buelta de la jornada*, Madrid: Imprenta Real

Dobson, Austin, ed., 1906. *The Diary of John Evelyn*, II, London: Macmillan

González Dávila, Gil, 1623. *Teatro de las grandezas de la villa de Madrid*, Madrid: Tomás Junta

Gourville, J. H., 1826. *Mémoires*. In A. Petitot et Monmerqué, ed., *Collection des Mémoires* [see below], LII, 181–537

Gramont, le Maréchal de, 1826–1827. *Mémoires*. In A. Petitot et Monmerqué, ed., *Collection des Mémoires* [see below], LVI, 245–480, and LVII, 1–118

Gualdo Priorato, Galeazzo, 1667. *Histoire de la Paix conclüe sur la Frontière de France et d'Espagne entre les deux Couronnes*, Cologne: Pierre de la Place

Mazarin, Jules, 1690. *Lettres du Cardinal Mazarin où l'on voit le secret de la Négotiation de la Paix des Pirenées; et la relation des conférences qu'il a eües pour ce sujet avec D. Louis de Haro, Ministre d'Espagne. Avec d'autres lettres tres curieuses écrites au Roi et la Reine, par le même Cardinal, pendant son voyage*, I, Amsterdam: André Pierrot

——1693. *Lettres du Cardinal Mazarin où l'on voit le secret de la Négotiation de la Paix des Pirenées*, II, Amsterdam: Henri Wetstein

Montglat, Marquis de, 1826. *Mémoires*. In A. Petitot et Monmerqué, ed., *Collection des Mémoires* [see below], LI, 1–161

Montpensier, Mademoiselle de, 1825. *Mémoires*. In M. Petitot, ed., *Collection des Mémoires* [see below], XLII

Motteville, Madame de, 1824. *Mémoires*. In M. Petitot, ed., *Collection des Mémoires* [see below], XL, 1–315

Petitot, M., ed., *Collection des Mémoires relatifs à la France, depuis l'avénement de Henri IV jusqu'à la Paix de Paris conclue en 1763*, XXXVI (1824), XL (1824), XLII (1825), Paris: Foucault

Petitot et Monmerqué, A., ed., *Collection des Mémoires relatifs à la France, depuis l'avénement de Henri IV jusqu'à la Paix de Paris conclue en 1763*, L (1826), LII (1826), LVI (1826), LVII (1827), Paris: Foucault

Modern secondary sources

Barrios, Feliciano, 1984. *El Consejo de Estado de la monarquía española 1521–1812*, Madrid: Consejo de Estado
——1988. *Los Reales Consejos. El gobierno central de la Monarquía en los escritores sobre Madrid del siglo XVII*, Madrid: Universidad Complutense
Bluche, François, and others, 1990. *Dictionnaire du Grand Siècle*, Paris: Arthème Fayard
Deleito y Piñuelo, José, 1942. *Sólo Madrid es corte. La capital de dos mundos bajo Felipe IV*, Madrid: Espasa Calpe
Domínguez Ortiz, Antonio, 1973. 'España ante la Paz de los Pirineos', in *Crisis y decadencia en la España de los Austrias*, Barcelona: Ariel, 155–93
Elliott, J. H., 1963. *The Revolt of the Catalans. A Study in the Decline of Spain 1598–1640*, Cambridge: CUP
——1984. *Richelieu and Olivares*, Cambridge: CUP
Elliot, J. H., and others, eds, 1991. *1640: la monarquía hispánica en crisis*, Barcelona: Editorial Crítica
Devèze, Michel, 1970. *L'Espagne de Philippe IV (1621–1665)*, I, Paris: Société d'Edition d'Enseignement Supérieur
——1971. *L'Espagne de Philippe IV (1621-1665)*, II, Paris: Société d'Edition d'Enseignement Supérieur
Escudero, José Antonio, 1969. *Los secretarios de estado y del despacho*, Madrid: Instituto de Estudios Administrativos
Feiling, Keith, 1930. *British Foreign Policy*, London: Macmillan
Fraser, Antonia, 1979. *King Charles II*, London: Weidenfeld and Nicolson
Guth, Paul, 1972. *Mazarin*, Paris: Flammarion
Hume, Martin, 1907. *The Court of Philip IV. Spain in Decadence*, London: Eveleigh Nash
Jusserand, J. J., 1892. *A French Ambassador at the Court of Charles II. Le Comte de Cominges from his unpublished correspondence*, London: Fisher Unwin
Lasso de la Vega, Miguel (Marqués del Saltillo), 1941. 'Don Antonio Pimentel de Prado, embajador a Cristina de Suecia 1652–1656', *Hispania*, 3: 47–107
——1949. 'Don Antonio Pimentel de Prado y la Paz de los Pirineos', *Hispania*, 7: 24–124
Levin, Michael, 1999. 'Sixteenth-Century Spanish Diplomacy: a Bibliography', *Bulletin of the Society for Spanish and Portuguese Studies*, 24. 1: 6–16

López Oliván, J., 1944. *Repertorio diplomático español. Indice de los tratados ajustados por España (1125–1935) y de otros documentos internacionales*, Madrid: Artes Gráficas

Montáñez Matilla, María, 1953. *El correo en la España de los Austria*, Madrid: CSIC

Palacio Atard, Vicente, 1960. 'El tratado de los Pirineos', *Revista Enseñanza Media*, 162: 3–16

Prestage, Edgar, 1925. *The Diplomatic Relations of Portugal with France, England and Holland from 1640 to 1668*, Watford: Voss & Michael

Regla Campistol, Juan, 1951. 'El tratado de los Pirineos de 1659. Negociaciones subsiguientes acerca de la delimitación fronteriza', *Hispania*, 11: 101–66

Routledge, F. J., 1953. *England and the Treaty of the Pyrenees*, Liverpool: Liverpool University Press

Sahlins, Peter, 1989. *Boundaries: the Making of France and Spain in the Pyrenees*, Berkeley: University of California Press

Sanabre, Josep, 1981. *El tractat dels Pirineus i la mutilació de Catalunya*, Barcelona: Barcino

Saint-Aulaire, Comte de, 1946. *Mazarin*, Paris: Flammarion

Stradling, R. A., 1988. *Philip IV and the Government of Spain 1621–1665*, Cambridge: CUP

Tomás y Valiente, Francisco, 1963. *Los validos en la monarquía española del siglo XVII. Estudio institucional*, Madrid: Instituto de Estudios Políticos

Torroja Menéndez, Carmen, and Concepción Menéndez Vives, 1991. *Tratados internacionales suscritos por España y convenios entre los reinos peninsulares (siglos XII al XVII)*, Madrid: Ministerio de Cultura

Trewinnard, Richard Giles, 1991. 'The Household of the Spanish Monarch: Structure, Cost and Personnel 1606–65', unpublished doctoral thesis, University of Wales, Cardiff

Valladares Ramírez, Rafael Jesús, 1989. 'El tratado de paz de los Pirineos: una revisión historiográfica (1888–1988)', *Espacio, Tiempo y Forma*, serie IV, *Historia Moderna*, II, 125–38

Valfrey, Jules Joseph, 1877. *Hugues de Lionne: ses ambassades en Italie 1642–56. D'après sa correspondance conservée aux Archives du Ministère des Affaires Etrangères*, Paris: Didier

——1881. *Hugues de Lionne. Ses ambassades en Espagne et en Allemagne. La Paix des Pyrénées d'après sa correspondance conservée aux Archives du Ministère des Affaires Etrangères*, Paris: Didier

Zanger, Abby E., 1997. *Scenes from the Marriage of Louis XIV: Nuptial Fictions and the Making of Absolutist Power*, Stanford: Stanford University Press

Index

References are to letters, not page numbers

Acosta (Costa), Juan de (João da), Portuguese ambassador, 77
Agramont = Gramont
Alcalá, Duke of, 57
Alsace, 49, 58
Andaya = Hendaye
Anjou (Anxù), Duke of, 20
Anne of Austria, 5, 6, 8, 22, 25, 26, 27, 29, 41, 44, 50, 65, 72, 73
Antonio, Cardinal (Antoine Barberini), 31
Aragon, Council of, 32, 42, 61
Ascham (Ascan), Sir Anthony, 45
Audenarde, 60, 81
Avesnes (Avenas), 30, 33, 52, 58, 60, 81
Avila, 67

Bar, Duchy of, 49, 58, 70
Bassée, La, 2, 22, 30, 33, 35, 43, 47, 49, 52, 58, 60, 64, 81
Bateuila = Watteville
Bayonne, 3, 27
Bayonne, Bishop of, 14
Bennet, Sir Henry, English Resident in Madrid, 45, 62
Berceli = Vercelli
Berdun = Verdun)
Bergues (Bergas), 2, 22, 28, 30, 33, 35, 43, 47, 49, 52, 58, 60, 64, 81
Bethune (Betuna), 47, 52
Bidache, 3, 5
Billeting *See* Troops, billeting of
Booth (Bot), Sir George, 45, 62, 74
Bordeaux (Burdeos), 8, 20, 25, 29, 52
Borgoña = Burgundy

Bouchain (Buchaim), 52
Bourbon, Duke Charles of, 58
Brienne, Count of, 24, 63
Bristol, Earl of, 68
Brussels, 2, 62
Buchaim = Bouchain
Burgos, 41, 65, 67, 73
Burgos, Archbishop of, 65
Burgundy (Borgoña), Duchy of, 58, 60, 81

Cadaqués, 75, 81
Caillet (Callet), Pierre, 10, 29, 33
Calais, 20
Camacho = Comacchio
Cambrai, 10, 33, 35, 52, 58
Caracena, Marquis of, 2, 5, 8, 11, 12, 20, 22, 28, 30, 33, 35, 47, 49, 52, 58, 62, 66, 79, 81
Cárdenas, D. Alonso de, 5, 11, 62
Carignano, Princess of, 23
Castro, 46, 56
Catalonia, 9, 15, 42, 61, 75, 81
Cengio (Zencho, el), 60
Cessation of hostilities, 12, 15, 66
Chamez, 58
Chantilly, 58
Charlemont, 52, 58
Charles II, King of England, 7, 8, 9, 11, 18, 20, 43, 49, 59, 62, 68, 71, 73, 74, 79, 81
Charles of Bourbon, Duke, 58
Châtelet, 60, 81
Chaussée (Sose), Baron de la, 20
Chester, 43, 45, 62, 74
Clermont, 58

Cologne, Elector of, 66
Coloma, Pedro, 21, 27, 48, 52, 64, 80
Comacchio (Camacho), Valley of, 46, 56
Commines, 81
Condé, Louis de Bourbon, Prince of, 1, 10, 25, 26, 27, 29, 33, 35, 36, 47, 49, 52, 58, 59, 64, 81
Conference venue and Centre (Barraca), 3, 4, 5, 8, 9, 13, 14, 16, 19, 20, 33, 45, 67 *See also* Pheasants, Isle of
Conflent, 32, 35, 42, 47, 48, 49, 58, 61
Conti, Armand de Bourbon, Prince of, 58
Contreras, Fernando de Fonseca Ruiz de, 22
Correggio, 47, 58
Costa = Acosta
Council of Aragon *See* Aragon, Council of
Council of State *See* State, Council of
Cromwell, Oliver, 11, 20, 45
Cromwell, Richard, 20

Damian, 67
D'Este (Deste), Cardinal, 31
Dijon (Dixon), 58
Dixmude, 60
Douai (Duay), 33, 52, 58
Dunkirk (Dunquerque), 12, 33, 52, 62
Dura, 58

Emperor Leopold I, 24, 63
Enghien, Duke of, 58, 81
England, 5, 9, 11, 12, 18, 43, 45, 49, 62, 68, 71, 74, 81 *See also* Charles II
English Commonwealth, 9, 11, 12, 20, 45, 62, 71, 79
Enríquez *See* Henríquez
Epernon (Pernon), Duke of, 58
Estenay = Stenay
Evacuation of strongholds, 38, 39, 40, 60, 61, 64, 72, 73, 75, 77, 79, 81

Faria de Sousa, Jorge 1, 9
Felipevila = Philippeville
Fernando Tomás, infante, 77
Flanders, 2, 5, 6, 7, 9, 10, 11, 12, 14, 18, 26, 28, 29, 30, 33, 35, 47, 52, 58, 60, 62, 66, 70, 75, 79, 81
Florence, 20, 24, 51
Fornos = Furnes
François I, 58
François, brother of the Duke of Lorraine, 20, 70
Fuensaldaña, Count of, 12, 52, 58, 60, 81
Fuenterrabía, 5, 8, 9, 14, 33, 45, 68, 69, 70, 71, 73, 74
Furnes (Fornos), 60

Galley slaves, 55, 78
Gault (Goo), Commandeur de, 3, 5, 14, 59
Genaro, Marco, 48
Genoa, 20, 24, 51, 63, 78
Germany, 26, 47, 58, 74, 81
González, D. Joseph, 27, 65
Gonzague, Marquis of, 47
Goo = Gault
Gramont, Count of, 47, 52, 75
Gramont (Agramont, Gramon), Duke of, 3, 34, 38, 40, 47, 49, 52, 72
Gravelines (Grauelingas), 33
Guipúzcoa, 28
Guise, François de, 20, 70
Guise, Henry of Lorraine, Duke of, 6
Guyenne, Duchy of, 58

Hainault (Henao), 33
Hendaye (Andaya), 45
Henrietta Maria, mother of Charles II, 11, 62, 81
Henríquez, D. Manuel, 65
Hers, 52, 58
Hesdin (Hedin), 60, 81
Holland, 62
Hostages, 60, 73

Index   145

Idiáquez, D. Cristóbal, 7
Indies, 20
Ipre = Ypres
Ireland, 11, 62
Irish troops, 45
Irún, 5, 14, 52, 59, 68, 70
Isabella of France, 5, 6, 8, 27, 50
Italy, 9, 46, 60, 75, 79

Juliers (Jülich), 25, 26, 27, 28, 33, 35, 36, 47, 49, 52, 58, 81
Junta de Estado, 9

Lambert, John, 43, 45, 62, 74
Lenet, Pierre, 33, 35
Leopold I, Emperor, 24, 63
Lerma, Duke of, 6
Lichans, 60, 81
Liège, 66
Lille (Lila), 52
Lionne (Leone, Lione), Hugues de, 5, 7, 8, 13, 14, 16, 20, 21, 25, 27, 29, 32, 39, 41, 42, 48, 52, 63, 64, 67, 69
Lionne, Madame de, 67
Lisa = Lys
Lockhart, Sir William, 9, 11, 20, 45, 62, 71, 77
London, 45
Longueville, Duke of, 81
Lorraine (Lorena), 49, 58, 70
Lorraine (Lorena), Charles, Duke of, 1, 8, 9, 20, 27, 49, 52, 53, 58, 59, 64, 68, 70, 79, 81
Louis XIII, 6, 27
Louis XIV (*selected references*), 14, 20, 22, 25, 26, 28, 29, 33, 58, 60, 64, 72
Luxembourg, 10, 33, 35
Lyons, 26, 35
Lyons, Archbishop of, 21
Lys (Lisa), River, 60

Madrid (*selected references*), 28, 38, 40, 42, 47, 49, 50, 52, 53, 58, 67, 71, 72, 75, 81

Madrid Agreement of 1656, 32, 42, 48, 61
Madrid, Treaty of 1526, 58
Mainz, Elector of, 66
Mantua, 20, 63
Marchin (Marsin), Count of, 62
Mardyck (Mardique), 62
Mariana of Austria, Queen of Spain, 20
Marienbourg (Mariembourg), 30, 33, 52, 58, 60, 81
Marriage, of Emperor and daughter of Duke of Orleans, 7
Marriage, of Infanta Doña María Teresa de Austria, 6, 22, 23, 25, 26, 27, 28, 31, 34, 35, 38, 39, 40, 41, 44, 45, 47, 49, 50, 52, 54, 57, 60, 64, 65, 72, 73, 75, 77, 80, 81
Marriage rumours, Mazarin's niece and nephew to wed English king and his sister, 5, 11, 62, 74
Marsac, 58, 70
Marseilles, 78
Marsin = Marchin
Martinozzi, Laura, niece of Mazarin, 46
Mayenne (Vmena), Duke of, 28
Medinaceli, Duke of, 57
Menin, 60, 81
Merville (Merbila), 60, 81
Metz, diocese of, 70
Meuse (Mossa), River, 58
Milan, 12, 52, 60, 81
Modena, Duke of, 46, 47, 56, 58, 63
Monk, General George, Duke of Albermarle, 18, 62
Mortara, 60
Mortara, Marquis of, 12, 15, 48, 61
Münster, 21

Nájera, Duke of, 57
Namur, 58
Naples, 10, 78
Neuburg, Duke of, 25, 26, 27, 33, 36,

47, 52, 58, 81
Normandy, 43, 45, 62

O'Neil, Daniel, 68
Olivares, Count Duke of, 23
Orange, Bishop of, 61
Orleans, Duchess of, 20
Orleans, Duke of, 7
Ormond, Marquis of, 68
Ortunia, 13

Papal dispensation, 28, 31, 73, 75
Papal representatives, 20, 45
Pamplona, Bishop of, 14
Paris, 11, 29, 58, 62, 70, 81
Paris treaty, 1, 2, 7, 10, 12, 29, 32, 52, 58, 64, 66
Parma, 20, 46, 56, 63
Pastrana, Duke of, 28
Pernon = Epernon
Perpignan, 32
Pheasants, Isle of, 5, 8, 9, 13, 14, 41, 45, 58, 62
Philip IV (*selected references*), 6, 10, 23, 27, 31, 33, 40, 42, 45, 47, 49, 55, 68, 77
Philippeville (Felipevila), 52, 58, 60, 81
Picardy, 62
Pimentel, D. Antonio, 1, 3, 5, 6, 7, 8, 9, 10, 11, 12, 13, 14, 15, 16, 18, 20, 23, 26, 29, 33, 35, 47, 52, 58, 62, 66, 67, 74
Ponce de León, D. Luis, 31
Pope, Alexander VII, 20, 21, 24, 28, 31, 45, 46, 56
Portugal, 11, 33, 49, 58, 62, 71, 77, 81
Powers, 6, 9, 16, 45, 54, 62, 76
Precedence, 4, 5, 8, 9, 13, 20, 23, 24, 44, 51, 56, 63, 65

Quesnoy, Le, 2, 33, 52
Quincé, Count of, 47
Quiñones, D. Jerónimo de, 68

Ramos, D. Francisco, 27, 65
Rentería, 74
Renunciation of rights by infantas, 25, 26, 65
Retz, Cardinal of, 2, 12
Rhine (Rin), 47, 58
Rocroi, 60, 81
Rome, 21, 31, 39
Ronciglione (Ronçillon), 46, 56
Roses, 60, 75, 81
Roussillon, 32, 42

Sacchetti, Cardinal, 21
Salamanca, 67
Sambre, River, 58
Santistebán, Count of, 65
Saône (Sona), River, 58
St Jean de Losne (San Juan de la Lona), 58
St Jean de Luz, 3, 4, 5, 8, 11, 13, 14, 15, 28, 45, 59, 62, 70, 77
St Omer (St Tomer), 33, 47, 52, 58
St Venant, 2, 33, 52
San Sebastian, 1, 7, 14, 29, 62, 67
San Telmo, 7
Saragossa, 68
Sardinia, 10
Savoy, 20, 22, 35
Scotland, 18, 62
Seville, 67
Sicily, 10, 78
Sobremonte, D. Gaspar de, 31
Soissons (Suason), Count of, 23, 28
Sona = Saône
Sose = Chaussée
State, Council of, 17, 20, 33, 36, 42, 47, 65, 71
Stenay (Estenay), 58
Sweden, 74

Tapestries, 16
Thionville (Tiumbila), 33, 47
Tillemont, Treaty of, 66
Toledo, 58, 67, 68

Tolosa, 68
Toul (Tul), diocese of, 70
Toulon, 78
Toulongeon (Tolonjion), Count of, 47
Toulouse, 71
Toulouse, Archbishop of, 21, 61
Troops, billeting of, 5, 9, 66, 75
Tul = Toul
Turenne (Turena), Viscount of, 62, 74
Tuscany, Grand Duke of, 63

Valenza (Valençia), 60
Valladolid, 67
Vateuila = Watteville
Venetian representatives, 20
Venice, 45, 63

Vercelli (Berceli), 60, 81
Verdun (Berdun), diocese of, 70
Vervins, Treaty of, 51
Vicariate General of Italy, 10, 29
Vidache = Bidache
Villeroy, Maréchal de, 14
Vmena = Mayenne

Wales, 43, 62
Watteville (Bateuila, Vateuila), Baron of, 1, 5, 7, 13, 16, 70, 74

York, Duke of, 43, 62, 74,
Ypres (Ipre), 60, 81

Zencho = Cengio?

TABLE OF CONTENTS

Introduction …………………………………… v

Text and editorial criteria ……………………… xxv

Acknowledgements ……………………………… xxviii

Letters …………………………………………… 1

Bibliography …………………………………… 139

Index …………………………………………… 143